Leasing

By the same author

Currency Fluctuation – The Accounting and Taxation Implications

Leasing – The Accounting and Taxation Implications

Accounts for Managing The Smaller Business

Waterlow books on finance and business

A Director's Guide: Duties, Liabilities and Company Law
by Colin McArthur and Ian Barnard

How the City of London Works: An Introduction to its Financial Markets
by William M Clarke

Finance For Your Business *by Peter M Walker*

The Law of Corporate Insolvency *by Ian Snaith*

Consumer Credit Agreements: A Working Handbook to Truth in Lending
by J Karpinski and S Fielding

The Franchise Option: A Legal Guide *by Mark Abell*

The International Franchise Option *by Mark Abell*

Leasing

David Wainman

First edition 1991

© SAWD PUBLICATIONS 1991

Waterlow Publishers
50 Fetter Lane
London EC4A 1AA
A division of Pergamon Press plc

ISBN 0 08 040865 6

British Library Cataloguing in Publication Data

Wainman, David
    Leasing.
    1. Great Britain. Industrial equipment. Leasing
    I. Title
    658.15242

Printed in Great Britain by
Media Print, Sittingbourne, Kent.

Contents

Author's Preface

Equipment leasing had a somewhat mixed reputation in the late 1970s and early 1980s. The variety of accounting procedures in use not only often made impenetrable many lessees' figures, but also raised doubts over whether a number of lessors themselves understood where they stood. Too much of the business was driven by the tax reliefs rather than the straightforward commercial advantages it provides.

That is history. Tax is no longer of such overwhelming significance and accounting has been 'standardised'. But if this has turned down the probably unwelcome spotlight under which the leasing industry has operated for so long, it has not been accompanied by any noticeably greater understanding of what leasing is, and how it works.

It is at that gap that this book is aimed. My primary aim has been to produce a work which can be read from beginning to end by, for instance, someone entering the industry, or assuming responsibility for his company's capital spending. But if the resulting volume also helps those who seek a reference book into which to dip for answers to specific questions, I will be well satisfied.

David Wainman
February, 1991.

To Susannah

CHAPTER 1

Introduction

Elements of the transaction

1.01   The legal description of leasing is 'a contract of bailment'. Which leaves most people far less confident that they understand what it is all about than they were before they were given this priceless information. It seems more sensible to avoid the legal terminology for the time being, and instead to try to make sure we understand the concepts, described in simple language. If Mr Smith 'owns' a yacht, we need to view that 'ownership' as consisting of a bundle of rights:

- he has, for instance, the right to go on board at any time, and, subject to any rules made to protect his own or any other mariners' safety, to sail it hither and yon;

- he has the right to dispose of the yacht at any time, and the right to do whatever he likes with the proceeds;

- he has the right to charter his yacht to someone else that is to say to give that other person possession and use of it for a specified time;

- if he does charter it out in that way, the principal rights remaining in the bundle which then constitutes his 'ownership' consist of the right to receive a charter-hire during the time concerned, and at the end of it to have the yacht returned to his own possession and use;

- At a more abstruse level, he would almost certainly retain during the period of the charter (as well as before and after it) the 'insurable interest' in the yacht. This is a legal concept, that only someone who suffers loss as a result of the happening of any of the perils insured, can require the insurer to compensate him. A wife can insure her husband's life, because the law assumes that she would lose his support and earning power if he were to die; but she cannot insure the life of her next door neighbour, because a neighbour's death does not, normally, give rise to monetary, or otherwise quantifiable, loss.

- If the terms of the charter are such that the yacht's owner does have the insurable interest, and does insure the vessel, the charter will probably stipulate what rights the charterer has to demand that the original vessel be replaced or repaired after any mishap, and what rights he has to demand the use of a substitute yacht until such replacement or repair can be achieved. In this area the owner's 'rights', to receive the insurance moneys, are clearly matched by 'obligations', how he must use those moneys.

These examples of rights and obligations which, bundled together, make up 'ownership' are only a few among the many that can be seen to exist. We could therefore say that ownership of any asset can not only be thought of as a bundle, but that on the analogy of the yacht's charter, it is possible for some of those rights to be unbundled. Leasing is just that, the separation by the owner, and his transfer to another party, of his own rights to possession and use of his asset. The owner who does this is called a lessor, and the person thereafter enjoying possession and use is the lessee. The agreement between them is of course the lease, and the period for which the lessor gives the lessee possession and use of the asset is the lease term. The numbers of ways in which it is possible to structure this transaction is almost infinite, as we will see through subsequent chapters of this book, but at this point it is worth looking from our prospective lessor's point of view at two particular aspects of the arrangements.

Financing and the risks financiers face

1.02 Although this is not universally the case, companies acting as lessors are usually financially orientated. In that 'usual' situation:

- the lessor derives the greater part of his profit from the difference in values between the immediate capital sum he lays out to provide the leased asset, and the stream of rents he receives from the lessee through the term of the lease. It is often suggested that from the lessor's point of view the transaction is analogous to his lending money to the lessee, repayable by a stream of equal payments each comprising principal and interest. On that basis a financially based lessor could describe his profits as the 'interest' element built into the calculation of the rentals;

- that analogy, if followed through, leaves the lessor carrying the two risks that financiers might normally face: that the lessee could default on his rental obligations, leaving the lessor to recover what he could by selling the asset and at the same time taking any action available against the lessee for the balance owing; and secondly that interest rate changes at some point during the lease term may increase the lessor's costs without his being able to compensate for this by correspondingly altering the levels of rentals payable. These are referred to as the credit risk and the interest rate risk.

But it is entirely possible to make the arrangements differently. For instance, the lessor does not himself need the financial wherewithal to acquire and carry the asset (until the lessee pays him off) if another financier can be found to stand behind the lessor to provide that finance. The interest rate risk would automatically shift from the lessor to that second financier, if the latter does not insist on having the right to change the rates charged to the lessor during the loan's life (itself matching the lease term). It is also possible that the risk related to the lessee's credit can be channelled directly through to that second financier. For instance one can construct a deal under which that financier's entitlement to continued interest and repayments of principal from the lessor cease if and when the lessee defaults on his payments to the lessor; the second financier is said in these circumstances to be providing 'non-recourse finance' in that he has abandoned his right of recourse against the lessor for unpaid interest and principal.

Putting a price on financial risks

1.03 In the straightforward lessor and lessee arrangements envisaged at the beginning of the previous paragraph it seems inherent that the level of the rentals will be determined by market forces; which is another way of saying that in any deal between two independent parties, the profit the lessor can achieve, and the cost to the lessee of his possession and use of the asset are primarily fixed by supply, demand and competition in the leasing market. But when one moves into the less standard arrangements, and particularly when three parties are involved, one immediately multiplies by at least ten the complexity of any pricing rules one tries to identify. For instance:

• We analogised a straightforward financial lease to a loan repayable by equal instalments of principal and interest through the lease term. Since we envisaged the rentals being fixed from the start we should perhaps have specified that we had in mind a loan with an interest rate fixed from the start, thus leaving the lessor carrying the interest rate risk, should his own cost of finance alter. But we can shift that interest rate risk to the lessee if the lease specifies that the rentals will alter in sympathy with changes in interest rates. The analogy is then a variable rate loan rather than one with a fixed rate of interest. And the effect on the deal's 'pricing' of this shift of the interest rate risk from lessor to lessee should be capable of being deduced from other similar, risk-shifting deals.

• But if both the credit and interest rate risks are shouldered by a second financier as we envisaged, one who stands behind the lessor but himself borrows variable rate funds from the market, and if that financier and the lessee are associated companies, then it is clear that the lessor has had both risks removed from him, and that the associates are effectively borrowing variable rate funds. But the credit risk has quite different characteristics from the interest rate risk. It is seldom right to assume that a group of companies would allow one of its number (the lessee) to default, whilst ensuring that another (the second financier) stood by its obligations. Thus moving the credit risk away from the lessor does not necessarily place it onto the shoulders the documentation might suggest, those of the second financier. It must almost certainly be the case that this credit risk now lies with the general body of the creditors of the lessee's and second financier's group – and that what the special arrangements have achieved is, for this particular debt only, to remove the lessor from among those general creditors, leaving all the others more exposed.

This last conclusion, if correct, shows that 'open market prices' might be able to indicate the amount by which the lessor's rewards should decrease when the credit risk is removed from him; but that if the second financier alone manages to take the equivalent increase in reward he does so only because the general body of his group's creditors are unaware that it is they who now bear the credit risk. Throughout this book we shall be analysing risks and attempting the far from straightforward task of showing whether, and if so how, those who do actually bear those risks derive an adequate level of reward for doing so. There is no more important aspect of pricing for those offering to write leases, or of lease evaluation for potential lessees trying to decide whether the deal offered to them is fair and reasonable.

The residual risk

1.04   Still looking at our financially orientated lessor, we can see that there is a different area of risk intrinsic to his leasing activity. Again there are ways in which this can be shifted from the lessor to some other party, but that does not cause it totally to cease to exist. We identify 'residual risk' by recognising that the lessor has only parted with possession and use for a time, (the lease term), and asking ourselves what happens thereafter:

- if a vehicle distributor offers three year leases of cars and vans to its business customers, it might fix the rentals it charges them on the assumption that the value it will be able to realise three years later from its leasing of a particular vehicle would be more than wiped out, if in fact the sale produced only half the expected figure;

• in the case of second hand cars and vans, one might expect the single largest factor affecting prices would be supply and demand, the latter itself affected not only by availability and cost of new vehicles but by any changes in motoring costs, (for instance road fund duty, 'congestion' taxes, taxes on fuel, and also costs of insurance and repairs). It is perhaps less likely that cars and vans would lose their value as a result of technical obsolescence in three years – but in the medium term increasing pressures for environmental protection must adversely affect the utility, and value, of older vehicles. Obsolescence is a very much more significant part of the residual risk for certain other classes of assets such as computers.

• If we considered the self-drive car hire market, we would find lessors needing to estimate the sums they would realise from selling used cars at twelve months old, rather than at three years. But in this case the other aspect of residual risk is clear; the lessor's profit is dependent on his constantly being able to re-lease his vehicle immediately each individual hirer returns it to him throughout the twelve months he has it available for customers' use.

1.05 Residual risk is therefore the phrase which identifies the lessor's vulnerability to being unable to sell his asset at the price he expected when it comes free from the lease; or alternatively his being unable to re-lease it to another lessee at that point. It is, as already indicated, entirely possible for the lessor to push this risk onto the lessee's shoulders. Under the 'full payout lease' (which might be the deal normally offered for instance for small items of office furniture and equipment), the rentals are calculated to reimburse the lessor the entire cost of the items, plus 'interest' on that amount: or to put it another way, the rentals are calculated assuming that when the lessee hands the assets back at the end of the lease term, the lessor needs to realise nothing to provide him his target profit. If they can in fact be sold, the lease agreement will often provide that a substantial proportion of the proceeds should go to the lessee as a rebate of rentals. It is therefore the lessee who bears the whole of the risk that the assets will fail to realise whatever price he expected when he signed the lease that they should be capable of producing at its end. A less usual method of achieving the same effect is as follows. The rentals are calculated on the footing that the asset will realise (say) twenty percent of its original cost when sold at the end of the term, so that although the lessor is still financing the whole of the asset's cost, he assumes that eighty percent of that principal will be repaid by the lessee, and twenty percent by the asset's sale, (the lessee of course also paying the whole 'interest' element). Then, if the asset realises more than the target sum, the lessee participates only in the excess. But correspondingly, if it realises less, the lessee is liable to pay an extra 'rental' to make good what would otherwise have been the lessor's residual loss. Any such final rental, but particularly one whose size cannot be calculated until the asset has been sold, is referred to as a 'balloon rental'.

Security

1.06 Probably one of the reasons why such end-of-term, indeterminate, balloon rentals are less standard than the 'full payout' route is that the lessor is in a less strong position when demanding payment of any such final rental from the lessee than he is at any earlier point during the lease term. Then his threat to repossess his asset might be more effective because it could be expected to disrupt the lessee's business activity, in addition to the worries caused to the lessee by the lessor's taking action for any balance of monies owing. 'Security' used in the borrower's and lender's sense is the counterbalance to risk – and as might be expected it will be a recurring subject for our consideration throughout this book.

Assignment by the lessee

1.07 There is a further legal concept which it is appropriate for us to examine at this point, still using as far as possible simple language rather than legal terminology. The lessee, during the term of the lease, has:

- the right to possession and use of the asset;

- the obligation to pay rentals to the lessor;

- the obligation to return the asset to the lessor at the end of the term;

- almost certainly a number of further rights and obligations flowing from the above but which we can ignore for simplicity's sake.

In principle, a lessee could transfer these rights and obligations to another person. One would normally expect that he would at the least need the lessor's permission for any such transfer (for reasons explained below): many leases are worded so as totally to exclude such a transaction, but the lessor may be persuaded to permit it to take place. Why one's reaction is correct, that the lessor's permission would be necessary, is one of those relatively straightforward ideas which is more difficult to put into words than it is to believe intuitively. The absolute owner of any asset should be able to sell or transfer it to another party without needing anyone's permission, and that is as true of the kind of asset we have characterised as one of the lessee's 'rights' as it is of any other. But the equivalent transaction under which the lessee seeks to transfer to that other party the obligations he owes to the lessor must also be looked at from the lessor's point of view. The obligation owed to him by the lessee is itself an asset of that lessor. Moreover, the nature of that asset is a 'right' to demand rentals, and the final return of the leased asset, from the specific person with whom the lessor made the original contract, and not from any substituted lessee. One could thus say that a lessee's transferring his obligations onto the shoulders of another party affects the lessor not because the latter's asset ('right') ceases to belong to him, but that it ceases to be the same asset that it was before. That is why the lessor will usually want to be able to control the substitution by one lessee of another in his place, or may make it a condition of the lease that no such change may be made at all. In passing, it is worth noting that this transaction, one party transferring his obligations to another, is sometimes described as 'subrogation', but that strictly that word means something rather different in law. However, assuming that the lessor's consent is given, and that the lessee did transfer to another the 'bundle of rights and obligations' which he held under the lease, it would be legally correct to call that transfer an 'assignment'. We will use that word wherever we need to remind ourselves that obligations as well as rights are being transferred.

Carving out smaller interests

1.08 As an alternative to the lessee's transfer as in the preceding paragraph of the entirety of his rights and obligations, it may be possible for him to transfer something less than the whole. This perhaps hardly needs spelling out, because we must all be familiar with the real property transaction under which a lessee, holding land and buildings for instance under a headlease from the freeholder, can sublet all or part of them, for any term shorter than his own lease, and to one or more subtenants. But the possibilities do not stop there: one can endlessly multiply variations on these themes. To take just three examples:

- A lessee could transfer the entirety of his rights and obligations under a lease to another, whilst retaining the right to have the recipient re-transfer it to him at some later point in the lease term. Or, instead of the re-transfer being an absolute requirement, it could be made optional – one or other party being given the entitlement to call for it to be effected.

- Lessees can, and in the case of long leases of residential property very frequently do, charge their 'bundles of rights and obligations' under the lease as security to a mortgagee, against a loan made to enable them (the lessees/mortgagors) to acquire the leasehold. This applies whether the relevant acquisition is by means of an assignment from a previous leaseholder, or a grant of a new lease from the landlord.

- Where a lessee's interest under a lease does have a considerable value, (and once again the most common example must be leases of real property granted many years ago at rentals which are now well below the market rate), it may be possible to extract cash by means of the transaction known as lease and lease-back. The leaseholder assigns his whole interest for a lump sum to another party on condition that that other will 'carve out' and grant back to him a subtenancy, probably for a shorter term than the original lease, and probably also at a higher rent. Clearly, what the assignee gets is the entirety of the leasehold interest, including possession once the subtenancy comes to an end, and in the meanwhile a stream of income in excess of his outgoings. It is for those benefits that he may be prepared to pay a lump sum.

The second and third of those examples may appear more relevant to the leasing of real property than to other items, but there is no principle which prevents the same type of arrangements for any type of lease. Obviously the law relating to the ownership of real property and the requirements for documentation of its transfer are different from those for other assets. Also, since one view of the overall effect could be that the lessee is 'buying' a lump sum of cash for a stream of (tax deductible) increased rental payments, there are anti-avoidance provisions in the tax law to prevent purely artificial transactions. The first point affects the way in which the transactions can be done, and the second may affect the levels of rentals, but neither should of themselves prevent the transactions being done at all.

The lessor's assignments

1.09   In the previous two paragraphs we have been focusing on ways in which the lessee may transfer all or part of his rights and obligations to some other. We need also to consider what the lessor may want to do. His rights and obligations can be thought of as the mirror images of those of the lessee:

- the right to receive rentals during the lease term;

- the right to the asset's 'reversion', that is to say to receive it back at the end of the term;

- the obligation to give the lessee possession and use of the asset — which may often involve ensuring that the asset is repaired and maintained so that it remains serviceable, and is insured, and replaced if it should be destroyed or lost in any other way.

Once again there will be further rights and obligations flowing from the foregoing and from the particular terms of the lease. And in particular we must not forget that what we have set out above as three very straightforward points may in reality be much less easy to 'deal with', because when closely examined the points concerned may be rather less straightforward than indicated above. For instance, in the full payout lease mentioned briefly in paragraph 1.04, we envisaged the lessor charging a rental during, say, a five year term which reimbursed him in full for his original purchase of the equipment, interest on his funds thus tied up, the administrative costs he incurred, and with a margin for his profit. If the asset were then returned to him at the end of that lease term, and he were able to sell it, we envisaged the greater part of the proceeds being passed back to the lessee as a rebate of rentals. The lessor had after all achieved his aimed at profit by setting the rentals where he did; and the sale proceeds of the asset probably owed something to the lessee's care in using the asset. (But the true rationalisation of the lessor's being prepared to grant a rebate of rentals is that his competitors do so, and he would write less business if he did not). The same goes for another condition one would expect to find in a full payout lease, namely that the lessee has the option to extend the primary term into a 'secondary term' during which the rentals fall to a relatively nominal figure, (often one percent per annum of the asset's original cost), but entitling the lessee to retain possession and use during that secondary term. Correspondingly the lessee delays the point at which he may get a rebate of rentals from an eventual sale of the asset, and he may also decrease the amount of any such rebate if, as one might expect, the older and more used asset realised less when it was finally sold.

1.10	But if the lessor is trying to assign his rights and obligations, he and his assignee need to bear in mind the facts that:

- the lessor's right to rentals does not necessarily come to an end after five years — the lessee may exercise his option to continue paying, albeit lesser amounts, for an indeterminate period thereafter;

- the lessor has the right to the asset's reversion, but just when this will occur is again a matter within the lessee's control rather than his own.

Other rights and obligations may be similarly impossible for the lessor to fix with certainty — even if he can say that the levels of incomings and outgoings which may or may not continue, will be small in relation to those which he and the lessee did originally agree for the 'primary' five years. Against that background, the lessor can 'assign' all or some of his rights and obligations under the lease. (It is not appropriate to attempt a full explanation here of the legal methods open to the lessor for achieving such a transfer. He must appreciate that his obligations can be split, like those of a lender under a normal loan agreement, into existing obligations and future commitments – continuing to charge the same interest rate on funds already advanced would fall into the first category, whereas the commitment to advance more funds when requested would fall into the second. The legal routes available to a lender trying to make such a transfer are novation, statutory or equitable assignment, and sub-participation, but each has its different effects). The position is basically the mirror image of that of a lessee attempting to assign his rights and obligations, but made more complex by the possibility that many of these rights and obligations may be somewhat open-ended. And also made complex by the fact that there are tax questions and uncertainties over the lessor's resulting position. This is not the place to try to resolve every tax problem, but it is entirely appropriate that we mention how some at least of them arise, because this is integral to the concepts of leasing.

The consideration for the lessor's assignment

1.11 Some of those problems surrounding the lessor's assignments are as follows. Let us suppose the lessor assigns for an immediate lump sum his right to the rental stream, but retains all his other rights and obligations under the lease. This would appear to be a simple way of setting up the 'non-recourse finance' route described at the end of paragraph 1.02 above, under which our lessor looks to another financier standing behind him to provide through this lump sum the funds needed for the purchase of the asset; thus leaving on the shoulders of that other financier the credit risk that the lessee may be unable to keep up the rental payments, because if this should happen the only remedy the financier has is against the lessee, not against our lessor as well. We have had to assume that the fact that the other financier's uncertainty, (what precisely the rental stream may turn out to be), does not mean that he is unwilling to buy. (Or perhaps that our lessor sold him only the rentals for the five year primary term, retaining the right to any rentals which might be receivable in any secondary term). But the tax position of someone who sells a stream of future income for a lump sum is that that lump sum is itself immediately taxable as income. The lessor would therefore appear to have set himself up with a very high level of income, and a correspondingly large outflow of tax to the Revenue Authorities, at the beginning of the lease term, with tax depreciation allowances on the asset and administrative expenses of later years in danger of not being capable of deduction against any income in those years. We will see throughout subsequent chapters of this book that sensible management of tax liabilities, (timing income and allowances so as to defer payment as far as it can be deferred), is an essential element in the making of profits from leasing. So one would almost certainly need to find a route by which the lessor and the non-recourse financier could achieve their objective without the tax disadvantages outlined above.

1.12 Now let us look at a different area of uncertainties, this time surrounding the total assignment of all rights and obligations. If we were to suppose, as an alternative, that the lessor assigned not just the rental stream, but the whole of his rights and obligations, and that he did so, for instance, two years into the primary term of the lease, then one might expect the consideration for such an assignment to need to be somewhere in excess of 'the net cash invested in the lease'. This, as we will see in the next chapter (the figures are shown at paragraph 2.24, and their explanation set out at paragraph 2.26), is a phrase describing the concept that a lessor starts by borrowing, (mainly, although he may use some of his own funds as well), to invest the total lump sum in the purchase of the asset, and thereafter is able to reduce his commitment to the lender by some part of each rental he receives. The lessor needs to use part of those rentals to meet his own interest payable, to meet expenses, and for his own profit, but the balance goes towards 'paying out' the lease, (or to go back to the borrowing analogy used earlier, to repay the principal originally regarded as lent to the lessee). In most (not necessarily all) cases, that consideration might be expected to be greater than the market value of the asset – so if one needed to analyse what the recipient thought he was getting by paying it, one would come back to our basic concepts of leasing:

• he would be buying the right to a rental stream for the remainder of the lease term;

• he would be buying the right to the reversion of the asset, not the asset itself: and if the actual form of that reversion was that, although he received the asset from the lessee at the end of year 5, he was required at the lessee's option to sell it and pass (say) ninety eight percent of the proceeds to the lessee, one can see that the real value of the 'reversion' itself may not be a very valuable asset;

• against those two 'rights', the purchaser would be taking on at least some 'obligations', for which he would want to make a deduction in arriving at the net figure to be paid to our lessor.

It is fairly easy to see that that analysis, if it were correct, would force us to the same conclusion as we arrived at on the different assumptions in the example with which we started the previous paragraph – that the real asset, which the lessor is assigning for real money, is his entitlement to the future rental stream.

What are the lessor's rights and obligations?

1.13   There is a different view. One can see it most clearly by splitting into much smaller components what we have so far described as the lessor's rights and obligations. On this more detailed analysis, the lessor is regarded as transferring:

- a free and unfettered asset;

- an obligation to give the lessee possession and use of that asset for another three years. This obligation is a 'personal' obligation of the lessor, and will become a personal obligation of his successor in title. It does not affect the value of the asset itself; one could say that an analogy is the indisputable fact that the amount borrowed on a mortgage does not affect the value of the house charged as security for that mortgage – all it does is to put the mortgagor under a personal obligation to use an appropriate part of any sale proceeds of the house to repay the mortgage, (if he does not use other funds to do so);

- an obligation to give the lessee ninety eight percent of sale proceeds of the asset in three years time. Once again it is clear that the obligation to make a payment of cash cannot have any effect on the asset's value. Further it seems unlikely that the lessor could be forced to sell the asset: if he failed to pay and the lessee took him to court, any damages the court might award would simply be a cash sum, rather than an order that the cash concerned must be derived from the sale of the particular asset;

- a right to receive three further rental payments.

If that is the correct view, and if it is accepted that the rights and obligations acquired by the purchaser are mirror-imaged in the consideration paid by him to the lessor, then:

- the disposal proceeds for the leased asset would be at least its full market value, disregarding the fact that the lessor does not at present have possession and use, and disregarding also the fact that he will have no right to retain ninety eight percent of its eventual sale proceeds;

- the purchaser does admittedly obtain the entitlement to a stream of rentals into the future, but he also assumes a counterbalancing stream of financial and non-financial obligations over the same future period and the net amount he might be prepared to pay for all of this could not be large.

Therefore on this line of argument one concludes that the entire consideration can rationally be attributed to the asset, because even if it is the case that the figure marginally exceeds the asset's value, the Revenue Authorities could have such difficulties challenging the value the lessor put on that asset that they would not take up the argument in the first place.

Rights in rem and rights in personam

1.14   We thus have two diametrically opposite ways of looking at the same transaction:

- the leased asset has little or no value, goes the argument at the end of paragraph 1.12, because one must have regard to the fact that it is wrapped around with obligations which effectively reduce its worth to the lessor to zero;

- not so, is the contrary line set out in paragraph 1.13; the asset's value is not affected by the fact that the owner has taken on himself certain financial and other obligations.

It must be said that the analogy of the mortgage borrowing not reducing the house's value is not an entirely fair one. Borrowing against an asset, including charging the asset as security, creates only contingent obligations – that the borrower deal with the asset in a particular way, those contingencies crystallising if and only if there is a breach of the original terms of the loan. There is nothing contingent about the lessor's obligations under the lease. It seems however that the view set out in paragraph 1.13 (that the asset should be fully valued, without regard to its wrapping) will generally be the correct one. The explanation for this is as follows, (but it must be stressed that both that statement and this explanation are prefaced by the word 'generally'). Generally, the lessee's remedy for any breach by the lessor of any obligation under the lease would be an action *in personam*. So also would be the remedy available to the assignee, if the lessor failed to fulfil the contract he had made to assign to the latter all his interests under the lease. Professor David Walker, in *The Oxford Companion to Law*, defines this action by contrasting it with its opposite:

> "The term (personal action) is now frequently given to an action *in personam*, where the judgment of the court is a personal one, normally for payment of money, as contrasted with an action *in rem*, where the plaintiff seeks to make good a claim to or against certain property in respect of which, or in respect of damage done by which, he alleges that he has an actionable demand."

Professor Walker gives an example of an action *in rem* in the case of maritime liens, which

"are enforced by proceedings *in rem* whereby the court will seize, and if necessary sell, the ship or cargo to satisfy the (lien) holder's claim."

If it were to be the case that a lessee's action against a lessor who failed to perform his obligations under the lease was an 'action *in rem*', claiming that the damage he had suffered should be made good out of the asset's sale, then it would follow that the assignee's remedy against a defaulting assignor/lessor was also to ask the courts to order the sale of the leased asset. One would then have to assume that a large part of the proceeds of the asset's sale would in each case have to go to the lessee, to compensate him for his loss of possession and use for the ensuing three years, and for his loss also of the prospective ninety eight percent of a later sale's proceeds. Thus one would arrive at the conclusion in paragraph 1.12 that only a small part of the value the purchaser sought to obtain from taking an assignment of the lessor's interest could be attributed to the interest he was acquiring in the leased asset itself.

1.15   It has been suggested, however, (and this does not derive in any way from the quotation from Professor Walker), that ships are the only form of asset whose chartering can give rise to an action *in rem*. In all other cases, both real property which is subject to a lease and items of plant or machinery, the rights acquired by parties to a leasing deal would be remedied by actions *in personam*. And from this would follow the conclusion in paragraph 1.13, that the leased asset should be looked at, in effect, with its lease unwrapped from around it: and for all practical purposes it becomes true that the consideration for an assignment of the lessor's interest can be attributed wholly to that asset, and does not need to be attributed to such other 'rights' as the stream of future income. But the author did say 'generally'. There are almost certainly ways of achieving the opposite result. And one of these appears to be the transaction outlined at the beginning of paragraph 1.11. There, the lessor assigned only the rental stream; it would be hard to gainsay the price he was able to achieve in the open market for this part of his 'bundle of rights and obligations'. If he subsequently and separately assigned the remainder of the bundle to a second purchaser, it would be equally hard to challenge the fact that the composite price for that second assignment would be next to nothing. Then, if the second of those purchasers were to buy the income stream from the first, one has further evidence (it would seem) that it was not the leased asset that could be regarded as valuable. This is heavy, technical, stuff; not what one might hope to find in an introduction, claimed to introduce leasing concepts, and to explain them in simple language. But it is an indication that one needs a clear eye, and a head for heights, when one starts to deal with lessors, lessees, their financiers, and the complexities in which they can and frequently do enmesh themselves. No apologies are offered for this early shock treatment of the reader.

Tenants' improvements and rights

1.16   Since we have referred to some extent in the last few paragraphs to assignments of leasehold interests in land as well as of other forms of lease, it is appropriate to explain a different leasing concept – but one also particularly relevant to land. This can most clearly be illustrated in relation to the letting of shop units constructed at street level under new office blocks. These are frequently let as 'bare shells', that is to say as no more than three concrete walls, open to the street at the front, and without wall-linings or flooring in a finished state. The lease gives the tenant the right to fit out the premises to his own design (subject to his complying with planning consents) and it would be unusual for the landlord to want either to compel the tenant to do that fitting out in a particular way, or to prevent him from doing it in another way. Any equipment or furnishing the tenant moves into the shop remains his own property, but any building work which he carries out becomes an integral part of the 'structure' and therefore becomes 'owned' by the landlord. This follows from the principle of English law, that buildings are not separate, nor capable of being separated, from the land on which they stand. But we do have to be clear what implications follow from this. The fundamental is that the shop-keeper's lease gives him the right to occupy and use the premises for the term of that lease. Only at its end does he need to surrender it up to the landlord. We can therefore see that, although the landlord may be the freeholder, his right is to the 'reversion'; he gets back his original bare shell together with the tenant's improvements in (say) twenty years' time. Meanwhile the tenant has his possession and use of that bare shell and of his own 'leasehold improvements'. If the landlord rather than the tenant had paid for the 'improvements' he would obviously need to charge a higher rent. The jargon is that the lessor 'rentalises' the additional capital expenditure that the lessee requests him to undertake. If on the other hand the responsibility for the fitting out expenditure is left on the tenant's shoulders, that tenant is saved the increase in annual outflows.

1.17   It is untrue in two separate senses to say that the tenant is simply giving money away to the landlord when he makes his leasehold improvements:

- What the tenant is adding to the landlord's wealth is the present value to the landlord of the (almost certainly marginal) increase in the value of the premises at their reversion in twenty years' time. What the tenant is not giving away is the value of possession and use of those leasehold improvements during the next twenty years.

- The landlord originally fixed the rent of the bare shell on the basis that that was all it was: he did not charge the higher rent he could have obtained for a fully fitted shop. Further, it is clearly established in law that in any subsequent rent reviews during the twenty year lease term, the landlord will be able to increase his rent only in relation to what he put into the creation of the shop, and what the tenant added by way of leasehold improvements will be left out of account in the calculation of the revised rent.

In certain cases, (tenancies of agricultural land are one class), an outgoing tenant has a right under statute to be paid by the landlord for the 'unexpired value' of major improvements the tenant may have made, for instance barns and other agricultural buildings erected on the farm at the tenant's expense.

Why lease?

1.18 At this point it is relevant to pause to ask why an intending lessee might consider leasing a better way of obtaining possession and use of his asset than outright purchase, with any borrowing that the latter might entail. A number of possible reasons come to mind, some that have already been hinted at, and others that we have yet to examine. It is certainly not true that the arguments in favour of leasing outweigh those against (or vice versa). In every case the particular circumstances have to be looked at afresh, and that means in particular that we have to have a clear picture of the terms on which a lease deal could be agreed, as opposed to the terms on which the asset could be acquired outright (and necessary borrowings agreed). Lease evaluation techniques are something we will come to in chapter 5. But we can list the main potential advantages, grouped under two heads, as follows. The paragraph references shown are those in which the concepts are first explained in some depth, but in the nature of this book, many of them are also re-examined elsewhere from different points of view:

'Quasi borrowing'

- leasing can provide fixed rate finance, (if the agreement does not allow the lessor to adjust rentals when his finance costs alter), or can provide floating rate finance, paragraph 1.02;

- generally, the leased asset itself will be the lessor's security, so that the additional 'borrowing' which is achieved by a lessee does not require any review of security given to existing lenders over other assets, paragraph 1.06;

- the finance charges in a lease, which are the analogue for interest on a borrowing, may be at a highly competitive rate. This arises partly from the tax advantages that lessors are perceived as obtaining, paragraph 2.19 et seq, and partly from the competitive nature of the market which they see themselves operating in, and which they take into account in the way in which they price deals, paragraph 2.27;

- although some leased assets, and associated 'borrowing' must be shown on the balance sheet of the lessee, some need not. This is sometimes seen as valuable to the lessee who might otherwise appear over-borrowed, and under-capitalised, paragraph 3.09;

'Commercial'

- there may, in many cases, be little or no disadvantage in the lessee's not having the absolute ownership of the asset, if his possession and use of it for its useful life is assured, paragraphs 2.07 and 2.08;

- he can effectively dispose of the asset, in many cases, even though he does not have the absolute ownership by means of assignment of his lease or by the carving out of lesser interests, paragraph 1.08;

- he may ensure that the lessor rather than he bears the residual risk, paragraph 1.04;

- but that previous point is very much wider than it may seem when expressed only in those terms. A truer way of describing the picture could be to say that the lessee may bear, in the calculations of the rentals charged to him, only the lessor's holding costs for the asset for the term of the lease, plus what the lessor expects to be its fall in value during that period. If one asks what a lessor might charge for the availability for twelve months of a five year old jumbo jet, the answer could be dramatically different from the amount a potential purchaser would need to find to buy such a plane outright (its expected total life being perhaps 20 years), paragraphs 3.05 and 3.06;

- the lessee may have the right to a replacement asset during periods when the leased asset is 'off the road' (to use a phrase appropriate to one type of asset for which this facility is often provided), paragraph 1.01;

- the lessee may be offered attractive arrangements when he wishes to trade-in the original leased equipment, if he wants to lease a newer generation of the same equipment in its place, paragraph 3.08;

- but the author has his doubts whether lessees should be seduced by the claim that if they are not in a tax paying position, whilst the lessor is, then leasing has inbuilt advantages over purchase, paragraph 5.06.

Leasing, and other types of transactions

1.19   It is convenient to end this introduction by listing a number of ways in which it is possible to acquire an asset, either involving acquiring absolute ownership, or acquiring merely possession and use for a period. In this listing process we can clearly indicate the differences between the methods; and we can also identify those that we will, and those we will not, be examining further in this book.

Purchase for deferred consideration
The vendor transfers full title (ownership) to the purchaser at the same time as he delivers over the asset. But by agreement with that vendor, the purchaser spreads the payment for the asset over a period, starting at that delivery, but extending over weeks, months or even years. This is not a transaction we will be looking at further.

Purchase where the vendor reserves title (Romalpa clause)
The vendor physically transfers the asset, but does so under a legal contract which delays the passing of ownership until such time as the price has been fully paid. The courts have accepted the validity of such clauses, although it is obvious that they may give rise to many practical and other difficulties. Perhaps the most obvious of those difficulties, and one which was fundamental to the Romalpa decision itself, is that referred to in the case as 'mixed goods'. It is thus interesting to note that this had been long since anticipated in the civil law systems, for instance Scots law, in the principle of 'specificatio'. If a person uses materials which are the property of another to create a new object, he acquires no title to the object (or its materials) so long as the latter can be restored to their former state. Thus the silversmith who uses someone else's silver to make a coffee pot would find the law requiring him to melt it down to return the silver. But the restaurateur who used someone else's coffee beans to make coffee could keep the spent grounds, and would be required by law to compensate the beans' former owner. However, reservation of title is not a subject we shall be looking at.

Hire purchase
The legal form of this transaction is that the asset's owner transfers possession and use to a hirer (lessee), but gives him in addition an option to acquire the title to the asset at the end of the period provided that all of the conditions of the hiring have been fulfilled. Because the whole price of the asset (together with interest) is paid over in the form of hire over a relatively short period, usually between one and three years, and the 'option' requires the payment only of a nominal sum, the general public

have always regarded hire purchase as being no more than a method of spreading out the payments on an asset which, throughout was in all but name the hirer's own. Therefore government, responding to the public's concern over certain vendors' sharp practices, has built a number of protections for the hirer into the structure of the law – but has done so only for contracts below a certain size; above that level, the parties are deemed capable of looking after themselves. These protections come in two groups. First those protecting the hirer from having overly onerous conditions imposed on him, and in particular preventing the asset's owner from re-possessing it after a specified number of instalments have been paid. Secondly, over the years there have been many different forms of control imposed on the making available of credit to the public – so that for substantial periods the law prescribed minimum levels of initial deposit required to be paid under hire purchase, and the maximum period the contract could last. At the time of writing, these credit controls have been abolished, but hire purchase is one of the forms of contract subject to the Consumer Credit legislation, giving the hirer the benefits, for instance, of a 'cooling off period' after the contract's original signature, before it becomes binding. We will look in some detail at hire purchase in Chapter 6.

Finance leases and operating leases
We have already glanced at finance leases, in what might be regarded as their 'purest' form, namely the full payout lease. The difference between them and operating leases is that in the latter the lessor needs to have regard to, (and is dependent upon for his profit), the residual value of the asset at the end of the term, including the prospective re-leasing of that asset. Leases of land, for example, would almost always be operating leases, one possible exception being the case of some mineral leases where the only value in the land consists of the leaseholder's rights to extract those minerals. However as we will see in Chapters 2 and 3, when we examine finance and operating leases, the dividing line has to be drawn between shades of grey, rather than black and white. One of the important effects flowing from the division is the accounting one: lessees which are limited companies, and which must thus comply with accounting standards promulgated by the accounting bodies, are compelled to show a value, as a fixed asset, for all items held on finance leases, and correspondingly to show also a 'borrowing' in respect of future rentals. For operating leases, the item is dealt with 'off balance sheet', that is to say the only accounting entry is the charge to profit and loss account of each period's rentals.

Purchase options
Although for tax reasons it is unusual for the lessee to be given any option to purchase the leased asset, there are some leases in which this option

is given. More often options for an eventual repurchase may be held by another party, for instance the original supplier of the asset. All that we need to note at this stage is that such options can take one of two forms: the 'bargain purchase option' permits its holder to acquire the asset for a purely nominal sum, well below what might be expected to be its open market value at the point at which the option may be exercised. The 'fair value purchase option' is the antithesis, as its name clearly indicates.

CHAPTER 2

Finance leases

The analogy with borrowing

2.01 We have already noticed in paragraph 1.02 that leasing is often analogised to a loan by the lessor to the lessee. It is from the lessee's end, and using this particular viewpoint, that it is convenient to start our examination of an example of a finance lease. The data are:

Cost of asset	£10,000
Lease term	Five years
Rentals	£672 per quarter payable in advance
Asset's residual value assumed by lessor	Nil

That last item gives the key to the simplicity, perhaps over-simplicity, of this illustrative transaction. The lessor is to be regarded as lending £10,000 to the lessee, and the whole of that sum is to be repaid by the lessee in cash, in the form of lease rentals: no part of the original loan is expected to be repaid out of any proceeds of sale of the asset at the end of the term. (This is in contrast to the example given at the end of paragraph 1.04, in which the lessor expected that the sale would realise 20 percent of the asset's original cost; that these proceeds could be used to repay a part of the loan; and that therefore the rentals could be reduced so as only to repay the remaining 80 percent of the loan). The lessee's repayment is to be achieved by equal instalments, each of which will include both some repayment of the loan's principal, and an interest element calculated on the then outstanding principal. The next paragraph sets all of this out in the form of a cashflow statement.

Cashflow – lease treated as a borrowing by the lessee

2.02 The conventional way of looking at what is deemed to be a borrowing by the lessee is to set it out in the form of a cashflow as in Table 1. The format is explained in the next paragraph, and the significance of the figures then commented on in those that follow.

	Borrowing at start of period	Rental paid	Borrowing after rental	Interest payable	Borrowing at end of period
Yr 1 Qtr 1	10,000	672	9,328	313	9,641
Qtr 2	9,641	672	8,969	301	9,270
Qtr 3	9,270	672	8,598	289	8,887
Qtr 4	8,887	672	8,215	276	8,491
				1,179	
Yr 2 Qtr 1	8,491	672	7,819	262	8,081
Qtr 2	8,081	672	7,409	249	7,658
Qtr 3	7,658	672	6,986	234	7,220
Qtr 4	7,220	672	6,548	220	6,768
				965	
Yr 3 Qtr 1	6,768	672	6,096	205	6,301
Qtr 2	6,301	672	5,629	189	5,818
Qtr 3	5,818	672	5,146	173	5,319
Qtr 4	5,319	672	4,647	156	4,803
				723	
Yr 4 Qtr 1	4,803	672	4,131	139	4,270
Qtr 2	4,270	672	3,598	121	3,719
Qtr 3	3,719	672	3,047	102	3,149
Qtr 4	3,149	672	2,477	83	2,560
				445	
Yr 5 Qtr 1	2,560	672	1,888	63	1,951
Qtr 2	1,951	672	1,279	43	1,322
Qtr 3	1,322	672	650	22	672
Qtr 4	672	672	–	–	–
				128	
		13,440		3,440	

Table 1

Lessee's cashflow, five year full pay-out lease, rentals £672 quarterly in advance, no rebate assumed, implicit rate 3.357 percent per quarter.

2.03 The total over the five years of the lessee's rental payments comes to £13,440. Of that, £10,000 is regarded as equivalent to the repayment of the principal of the loan; and the balance of £3,440 is interest on the outstanding balances during the period. As an alternative to the way the foregoing cashflow sets out the transactions, it is possible to think of them in the following way, but it is immediately clear that the answer is the same. It is in fact customary to set out the calculations as shown in the previous paragraph, with a horizontal line for each quarter, the rental paid at the beginning of that quarter being shown as a deduction, and the interest

Borrowing at start		£10,000
Less first rental wholly a repayment of principal		672
Borrowing throughout first three months		9,328
Second rental	672	
of which, interest for the first three months which end		
with that second rental payment	313	
balance, being repayment of principal	359	359
Borrowing throughout second three months		8,969
Third rental	672	
of which, interest for the second three months		
which end with that third rental payment	301	
balance, being repayment of principal	371	371
Borrowing throughout third three months		8,598

'payable' as an addition. It is precisely because that interest is not separately paid during the quarter concerned, but is in effect met out of the rental on the day following the quarter's end, that it is rational to describe the figures on each quarter's line, in the final column of our cashflow statement, as 'borrowing at end of period'. It should come as no surprise, if the reader has a basic understanding of repayment mortgages, that in the first year a relatively large part (£1,179) of the year's rentals (£2,688) is the interest component, giving relatively low principal repayments (£1,509). By the last year, the interest component is substantially down (£128), and the principal repayment up (£2,560). Each of those principal repayment figures can be read straight out of the final column of our cashflow – £1,509 being the difference between the £10,000 starting figure and the end of the first year balance of £8,491, with £2,560 being the balance still to be repaid before the final year commences.

The implicit rate

2.04   The one calculation we have not yet explained is the interest. A quick calculation would show that it is at the rate of 3.357 percent per quarter. The borrowing outstanding throughout the first three months (after the lessee had paid the first rental) was £9,328. 3.357 percent of that is £313, which is the interest figure shown in the tables in each of the last two paragraphs. The equivalent rates for quarterly rentals of £662 and £682 would be:

Rental	Quarterly interest rate implicit	Annual equivalent interest rate implicit
£662	3.175 percent	13.318 percent
£672	3.357 percent	14.119 percent
£682	3.540 percent	14.930 percent

If the rate of 3.357 percent per quarter is 'compounded' into an annual rate, it is 14.119 percent per annum. That rate is described as the 'rate implicit in the lease'. If the rental level is known, the implicit rate can be calculated. Obviously, with twenty rentals over the five year lease term, the 'interest' element of the rentals would be £3,240, £3,440 and £3,640 for the three levels of rental – but what we need is a basic grasp of the fact that the shift from the higher to the lower rental levels represents over 1.6 percent per annum on the implicit rate of interest.

Calculating the implicit rate

2.05 The calculations of the implicit rates in the previous paragraph can

Rental	£662	£672	£682
Quarterly interest rate	3.175	3.357	3.540
Year 1 Qtr 1	662	672	682
Qtr 2	366	359	352
Qtr 3	377	371	365
Qtr 4	389	383	377
	1,794	1,785	1,776
Year 2 Qtr 1	402	396	391
Qtr 2	414	410	405
Qtr 3	428	423	419
Qtr 4	441	438	434
	1,685	1,667	1,649
Year 3 Qtr 1	455	452	449
Qtr 2	469	467	465
Qtr 3	484	483	482
Qtr 4	500	499	499
	1,908	1,901	1,895
Year 4 Qtr 1	515	516	516
Qtr 2	532	533	535
Qtr 3	549	551	553
Qtr 4	566	570	573
	2,162	2,170	2,177
Year 5 Qtr 1	584	589	593
Qtr 2	603	609	615
Qtr 3	622	629	636
Qtr 4	642	650	659
	2,451	2,477	2,503
Total	10,000	10,000	10,000

Table 2
Calculations of implicit rates for full pay-out leases of five years, rentals quarterly in advance £662, £672 and £682, no rebates assumed.

quite easily be done (by trial and error) on a pocket calculator, even if this is a slightly tedious exercise. Table 2 sets out the calculations.

If we start at the line for "Year 5 qtr 4" the figures are the three rental levels, £662, £672 and £682, divided respectively by 1.03175, 1.03357 and 1.03540. Those three divisors are themselves

$$\frac{100 \ + \ i}{100}$$

where "i" is the rate of interest − but of course it is these rates of interest which our trial and error was aimed at evolving. The figures in the line above, "Year 5 qtr 3", are those first figures divided a second time by the same 1.03175, 1.03357 and 1.03540. The figures in the line above that are the second figures divided a third time by those same divisors; and so on up the columns until we get to the top figure in each column which is the rental itself. But if we look at the top three figures in the middle column, (Year 1 qtrs 1-3), the figures are £672, £359 and £371. And we might recognise those as being the 'principal' (as opposed to interest) elements of the first three rental payments, as shown in paragraph 2.03. The whole of the first rental went towards repayment of the original 'loan', and of the second and third rentals, £313 and £301 respectively were 'interest', leaving £359 and £371 as the repayments of principal. That is why the columns add to £10,000 in each case; what we have arrived at is the overall pattern of principal repayments. And as indicated, the way we have done this, using only pocket calculators, is by a process of trial and error − to find the rate of interest which, divided repeatedly into the rental figure, produces the precise level of repayment needed for the lease which we have analogised to a 'loan'. In the real world, lessors would not use quite such primitive implements to work out their lessees' implicit rates. But in our own trial and error process we rapidly come to appreciate that changing the interest level up or down by the same number of percentage points will alter the 'repayment' by different numbers of £s − or to put it another way, compound interest calculations produce answers on a curve, not a straight line. However, very small changes in the interest rate give rise to answers which are so nearly on a straight line that it is perfectly easy to interpolate − and so to arrive at the exact rate we seek. For reasons that we will come to in dealing with the lessee's accounting for an asset obtained on a finance lease, the lessor should always let the lessee know what implicit rate is built into the lease rentals he is asking for. But if he does not do so, the lessee can work it out for himself, even if the trial and error calculations are slightly time consuming; no lessee has to acquire a computer on a second lease for this purpose, in addition to the asset which it was his first objective to lease.

The lessee's accounting

2.06 If the lessee had actually borrowed, and if he had actually acquired an asset, he would have reflected both asset and liability on his balance sheet. Each would have started at £10,000 at the commencement of the lease, and each would have declined thereafter. If we assume that he might have chosen a 20 percent straightline depreciation rate, the figures would be as set out in Table 3.

Liability		Asset
£10,000	At commencement	£10,000
	2,688 paid to lender in year 1	
1,509	1,179 of which represents interest	
	depreciation for year 1	2,000
8,491	End of year 1	8,000
	2,688 paid to lender in year 2	
1,723	965 of which represents interest	
	depreciation for year 2	2,000
6,768	End of year 2	6,000
	2,688 paid to lender in year 3	
1,965	723 of which represents interest	
	depreciation for year 3	2,000
4,803	End of year 3	4,000
	2,688 paid to lender in year 4	
2,243	445 of which represents interest	
	depreciation for year 4	2,000
2,560	End of year 4	2,000
	2,688 paid to lender in year 5	
2,560	128 of which represents interest	
	depreciation for year 5	2,000

Table 3

Lessee's repayment in equal instalments of £672 per quarter over five years (principal and interest at 3.357 percent per quarter), and provision of depreciation at 20 percent straightline, on asset treated as acquired by borrowing.

The outstanding liabilities at the intervening year ends can of course be read straight out of the cashflow in paragraph 2.02. What is equally apparent is that the lessee's notional borrowing is shown as declining more slowly in the lease's opening years than the carrying value of the asset. This follows inevitably from

- the 'compound interest' effect, that principal repayments start at a low level, but increase as the lease progresses

- whilst 'straightline' depreciation is reflected in level decreases in the asset's carrying value through those same years.

The reverse of the same coin is that of the profit and loss account charges would decrease through the lease term:

Year 1	Interest	£1,179	
	Depreciation	2,000	3,179
Year 2	Interest	965	
	Depreciation	2,000	2,965
Year 3	Interest	723	
	Depreciation	2,000	2,723
Year 4	Interest	445	
	Depreciation	2,000	2,445
Year 5	Interest	128	
	Depreciation	2,000	2,128
			13,440

The whole of this paragraph has been expressed in the subjunctive – what a lessee's accounts would reflect, were he to account as if he had borrowed, and as if he had acquired absolute title to the leased asset. Bu that is in fact how he must deal with the transaction in his accounts, for the reasons more fully explained in the next paragraph.

2.07 In the preceding paragraph, our description of the lessee's asset and liability as "notional" is factually and legally correct. Possession and use of the asset lies with the lessee, but ownership does not; and correspondingly the lessee has not borrowed to acquire that asset. However there are a number of interlocking arguments whose thrust is in the opposite direction:

- as we have constantly noted, possession and use, rather than legal ownership, is the factor which enables the lessee to employ the asset in his earning of profits in his business;

- if his accounts reflect those earnings, but fail to reflect the asset's existence, a wholly wrong impression is given of the business's return on assets, (or on capital employed);

- reflecting the asset's existence, and the profits generated from its possession and use, implies making a charge against those profits for its depreciation;

- the business is committed, from the date it first signs the lease, to make all five years' rental payments; the commitment is not separately or repeatedly undertaken in respect of one year's obligations at a time;

- the aggregate cash commitment exceeds the asset's cost, and exceeds the principal sum that would need to be borrowed if the asset were to be acquired. The excess is the compensation required by the lessor for expenditure he incurs at the 'front end', but which is only reimbursed to him through the term of the lease. The analogy with interest income for the lessor has already been made, and the same arguments are relevant in relation to the lessee's reflecting an interest charge in his profit and loss account as have already been rehearsed above in relation to his reflecting a depreciation charge on the asset.

'Standard accounting practice' for the lessee

2.08 The Accounting Bodies issued in August 1984 a Statement of Standard Accounting Practice in which the thrust of those arguments is summarised as being:

> "The lessee has substantially all the risks and rewards associated with the ownership of an asset, other than the legal title..."

Elaborating on this conclusion, the Statement also explains that

> "The effect of a lease is to create a set of rights and obligations related to the use and enjoyment by the lessee of a leased asset for the term of the lease. Such rights constitute the rewards of ownership transferred under the lease to the lessee, whilst the obligations, including in particular the obligation to continue paying rent for the period specified in the lease, constitute the risks of ownership so transferred..."

It is obvious that not all leases transfer to the lessee a sufficiently comprehensive 'bundle' of rights and obligations for this to be an appropriate conclusion, but

> "...where the rights and obligations of the lessee are such that his corresponding rewards and risks are, despite the absence of an ability to obtain legal title, substantially similar to those of an outright purchaser of the asset in question..."

then the Statement requires that the lessee should

> "capitalise...the purchase of rights to the use and enjoyment of the asset, with simultaneous recognition of the obligation to make future payments"

Thus it is not necessary to argue that the 'substance' of a lease is a borrowing and an asset purchase. We know that that is not its form, and despite the analogies we have drawn, neither is it its substance. But it is possible to argue that the lessee's accounts would be worse distorted, (and thus less useful), if they showed only form and substance than if they showed our analogy – in the circumstances that:

• the lessee's rights and obligations are no less real, even if they are legally distinguishable from those of a borrower and purchaser;

• those rights and obligations are sufficiently comprehensive to be capable of being described, as we have described them, as analogous to the borrower/purchaser position.

That is why finance leases are 'capitalised' by the lessee, as 'best' accounting practice, (compulsorily in all cases in which the lessee's accounts must comply with Statements of Standard Accounting Practice). Finally, the Companies Acts require that a company's accounts disclose separately amounts due to creditors within 12 months of the balance sheet date, and amounts due later. The total lease creditor figure in the lessee's accounts is the whole of the future rentals payable, less the amounts included therein in respect of future finance charges. SSAP 21 requires that the disclosure splits this into "less than 12 months", "2 – 5 years", and "over 5 years". The figures can be read straight out of the cashflow in paragraph 2.02 – for instance at the end of year 1, they are:

Within 12 months (8,491 – 6,768)	£1,723
Between 2 & 5 years	6,768
Over five years	nil
Aggregate lease creditor	8,491

It may seem too obvious to need explanation why the correct figure is net of future finance charges, but to the extent such an explanation is needed, it fits into paragraph 2.59 more conveniently than here.

Depreciation in the lessee's accounts

2.09 But there is another aspect of the lessee's accounting to which we should more carefully direct our minds. The cash out-flows to which the lessee is committed are spread evenly through the lease term. If he had borrowed, and were repaying principal with interest in equal instalments, then at least to that extent, his profit and loss account charge would normally be greater in the lease's earlier years, and would decrease as time progressed. It is possible to imagine that a lessee could, in theory at least, set up different patterns of depreciation in order to 'tailor' his profit and loss charge as in Table 4.

		Coinciding with cash outflows		'Normal' as in para 2.06		Weighted towards front	
Yr 1	Interest	1,179		1,179		1,179	
	Depreciation	1,509		2,000		2,500	
			2,688		3,179		3,679
Yr 2	Interest	965		965		965	
	Depreciation	1,723		2,000		2,275	
			2,688		2,965		3,240
Yr 3	Interest	723		723		723	
	Depreciation	1,965		2,000		2,050	
			2,688		2,723		2,773
Yr 4	Interest	445		445		445	
	Depreciation	2,243		2,000		1,750	
			2,688		2,445		2,195
Yr 5	Interest	128		128		128	
	Depreciation	2,560		2,000		1,425	
			2,688		2,128		1,553
			13,440		13,440		13,440

Table 4

Aggregate charges in lessee's profit and loss account using different bases of providing depreciation.

All that SSAP 21 has to say about the depreciation charge is that "an asset leased under a finance lease should be depreciated over the shorter of the lease term and its useful life". (For this purpose it defines the lease term as not being limited to the primary term, see paragraph 1.08, but as also including so much of any secondary term "for which the lessee has the option to continue to lease the asset...which option it is reasonably certain at the inception of the lease that the lessee will exercise").

2.10   This is not the place to set out the whole theory of asset depreciation, but a few points can be briefly made:

•   The basis of depreciation charges should be consistent not only from year to year, but across different assets unless there are very specific reasons for using a different basis. It would thus be extremely unlikely that a lessee could justify the pattern of depreciation weighted towards the final years, shown in the left hand column above, since it would not in most cases be consistent with the depreciation provisions on other assets.

•   Depreciation is meant to reflect the consumption, by the business's use of the asset, of its earning power. This is not the same concept as writing the asset down to its realisable value on a sale. There are some assets whose earning power in their first year of use is nearly twice as great as that of their fifth year, (£2,500 compared to £1,425, in the right hand column of the table in paragraph 2.09), because of the maintenance costs that have to be incurred on a five year old asset, (and the amount of its 'down time'). But it can also be said that a lessor might not think that his own security for the fifth year's rentals was adequate, if the asset's earning power had declined to that extent; that would suggest that a five year lease would be unlikely to be offered, that three or perhaps four year leases of assets of that type would be the maximum that would be available. Therefore a steeply 'front-ended' profile of depreciation as in the right hand column may be inappropriate.

This appears to suggest that the straightline basis, or a less steeply front-ended profile, may be the most reasonable. It is, of course, always acceptable to depreciate the asset not to zero, but to a figure expected to be derived from its eventual sale, provided that:

- one can forecast its useful life with a sufficient degree of accuracy to be able to estimate the date of that sale;

- that enables one to estimate the proceeds with some degree of confidence;

- the lessee will receive something from the asset's sale – which is another way of describing a commitment by the lessor to pass back to the lessee some of the sale proceeds (it probably needs to be most, if there is to be any certainty that the amount will not prove negligible).

Capital value in the lessee's accounts – leasing from the equipment manufacturer

2.11   We have calculated the interest rate implicit in the lease, and used that as the basis of the lessee's profit and loss account charge – and similarly of his quantification for balance sheet purposes how much he is still 'indebted' to the lessor at each year end during the lease term. There are three points which need to be made in amplification of this, in this and the next two paragraphs. If we assume an equipment supplier acting also as the lessor of the asset concerned, that lessor's 'cost' would obviously be less than the selling price he would charge to normal purchasers; and it would be on that normal selling price that he would want to base his lease pricing. In the case of finance leases this is entirely acceptable – the supplier makes a 'normal' (manufacturing) profit on the item which he recognises at the time he signs the lease, and then will make a 'normal' (leasing) profit through the lease term in the way we shall be looking at in later paragraphs of this chapter. The lessee's appropriate figure to be capitalised, and to be the basis of profit and loss account charges through the lease term, would be based on the supplier's normal sales price. When we get to operating leases, the principles are completely different (paragraph 3.11). The equipment supplier is not permitted to recognise a manufacturing profit on his product when he lets it on an operating lease. And its value would in any event not appear in the lessee's accounts, (paragraph 3.09).

Capitalising the present value of minimum lease payments

2.12 The second point is slightly different – and at this stage may seem to be so much of a nicety as to be almost totally irrelevant in the real world. Certainly accountants would not in practice suggest that in the circumstances set out below, it was necessary for the lessee to do any recalculations; the size of the resulting alterations in this illustration simply would not warrant it. The point's real significance appears only later in this book. Suppose that a lessor is confident that the leased asset will realise £500 at the end of the five year lease term, and that he can safely guarantee to rebate his lessee's rentals so as to recover 'principal' of £9,500 only, together with finance charges on the full £10,000. From the lessor's point of view, he still needs to recover the same quantum of finance charges from the lessee; all that we are looking to alter is the source of the final £500 of principal repayment he obtains. But in making that alteration, we are in danger of fundamentally altering, from the lessee's point of view, the relationship of principal and interest included in the lessee's quarterly rentals.

What, strictly, the lessee should capitalise in this case is 'the present value of his minimum lease payments'. These minimum lease payments have decreased from the £13,440 shown in paragraph 2.02 to £12,940 on our assumption about the final £500. If we were to insist that the finance charge component of them remained at £3,440, then that would translate into a considerably higher rate of interest on what we would be saying was only £9,500 of principal. In these circumstances, the lessee could recalculate the present value of that £12,940, using not the misleadingly higher interest rate but only the rate of 3.357 percent per quarter, which has not of course changed. The present value for his asset comes out on this basis at £9,742, and finance charges at £3,198. The way in which these figures are arrived at is explained in paragraphs 3.03 and 3.04 below, since that is the point at which it is appropriate to explain the real significance of the discounting of minimum lease payments.

Arriving at finance charges under the rule of 78

2.13   The third point arises from the sheer complexity of the calculations we set out in paragraph 2.05 to arrive at the implicit rate – or even in cases where the lessor divulged the figure, there would be those who would not calculate the interest component of each year's rentals.

For simplicity SSAP 21 allows the 'rule of 78' as an acceptable alternative to the full 'actuarial' rigours of compound interest calculations. These alternative figures, in Table 5, are relatively simple.

	Number of rentals not yet due					Interest charge	
Yr 1 Qtr 1	19	3440	x	19/190		344	
Qtr 2	18	3440	x	18/190		326	
Qtr 3	17	3440	x	17/190		308	
Qtr 4	16	3440	x	16/190		290	
							1,268
Yr 2 Qtr 1	15	3440	x	15/190		272	
Qtr 2	14		and so on			253	
Qtr 3	13					235	
Qtr 4	12					217	
							977
Yr 3 Qtr 1	11					199	
Qtr 2	10					181	
Qtr 3	9					163	
Qtr 4	8					145	
							688
Yr 4 Qtr 1	7					127	
Qtr 2	6					109	
Qtr 3	5					91	
Qtr 4	4					72	
							399
Yr 5 Qtr 1	3					54	
Qtr 2	2					36	
Qtr 3	1					18	
Qtr 4	–					–	
							108
	190						3,440

Table 5

Calculation of the quarterly interest charges using the 'rule of 78' method for a five year lease, rentals quarterly in advance.

The aggregate interest charge is £3,440 over the full five years, and the proportion of that allocated to each quarter is simply found by multiplying 3,440 by the number of further rentals payable in future quarters, and dividing the answer by 190, the 'sum of the digits'. (The 'rule' takes its name from the fact that 78 is the sum of the digits from 1 to 12).

It is always said that the rule of 78 produces an acceptable degree of approximation for leases which are not too long, say not more than six years, and at interest rates that are not excessively high. Probably the 14.112 percent rate we have been using is towards the upper end of acceptability.

2.14   The comparison of these rule of 78 figures with those previously calculated on the actuarial basis shows the following. Just for further comparative purposes, there is also set out the results of what is referred to as the 'straightline' basis, which is no more than the illogical assumption that the interest element of each years' rentals is equal through the whole term of the lease (see Table 6).

	Actuarial Interest liability		Rule of 78 Interest liability		Straightline Interest liability	
Yr 1	1,179		1,268		688	
		8,491		8,580		8,000
Yr 2	965		977		688	
		6,768		6,869		6,000
Yr 3	723		688		688	
		4,803		4,869		4,000
Yr 4	445		399		688	
		2,560		2,580		2,000
Yr 5	128		108		688	
	—		—		—	

Table 6

Lessee's annual interest charges, and balance sheet 'borrowings', calculated under three different bases; five year lease, rentals of £672 per quarter in advance.

The author's own view is that there is no 'accounting' disadvantage in the simpler calculations in the rule of 78, but there is nevertheless a sound reason for preferring a calculation method which demonstrates just what interest rate the lease rentals imply. Having said that, the author must make it clear that we will in chapter 5 be examining lease evaluation techniques, including the question whether for that purpose the implicit rate is wholly relevant, based as it is only on the lessee's 'primary' cashflows; our conclusions may be that the implicit rate is not quite as significant an item as it might at first seem. But that is a discussion that we will come to in paragraphs 5.02 et seq, and which it would not be appropriate to anticipate here. At this point it is vital that we:

• understand the principles involved in looking at leases as if they were borrowings at interest by the lessee, and;

• understand why accounting rules suggest that that is the appropriate basis for the lessee's treatment of the asset, the liability, and the profit and loss account charge.

It is also worth stating clearly that, in this chapter so far, we have been looking from the lessee's point of view at only the simplest and most straightforward form of finance lease. What we have not yet done, but will come to in Chapter 3, is to look at the quite different situation that arises where the lease is characterised as an operating lease, rather than a finance one; and nor have we yet looked at the question also answered in chapter 3, namely where the dividing line needs to be drawn between those two categories. All of this is yet to come.

The lessee's liquidity

2.15 There is one small practical point that it is appropriate to mention before we move from the lessee's position to that of the lessor. In paragraph 2.09 we quantified what might be thought of as the lessee's 'normal' profit and loss charges during each of the five years of the lease term. It might be a realistic assumption that these would approximate to the pattern of the lessee's earnings from the use of the asset concerned. Further, that the lessee's earnings could be expected, by and large, to accrue in the form of cash. If we therefore set out this stream of cash generation, alongside the stream of cash outflows for rentals, the picture is as in Table 7.

	Inflows	Outflows	Cumulative surplus
Year 1	3,179	2,688	491
Year 2	2,965	2,688	277
			768
Year 3	2,723	2,688	35
			803
Year 4	2,445	2,688	(243)
			560
Year 5	2,128	2,688	(560)

Table 7

Calculation of improvement in the early years in the lessee's liquidity, on the assumption that the cash generated by the leased asset is similar to the profit and loss charges for a five year lease of that asset; improvement in liquidity in early years, followed by reversal thereafter.

The pattern thus appears to be, (if our two assumptions are correct that income is 'slanted' towards the asset's earlier years of use, and that that income can be equated to cash generation), that liquidity will build up during the early years of the lease. Later in the lease term, it will either build up less rapidly, or if the asset earns no more than its precise cost, as above, the earlier build-up of liquidity will be consumed. All of this ignores, of course, the fact that if liquidity does build up in the early years, the lessee may promptly use the cash concerned to expand his business by further investment in stocks, purchases of further fixed assets (– or merely by allowing the size of his debtor's ledger to increase by not collecting his debts as quickly). That would merely increase the difficulties he would face if he did need to turn these assets back into cash thereafter to meet the liquidity squeeze. The size of the numbers is perhaps not unmanageable in this particular instance, but the practical point is that the lessee does need to be aware whether his lease rentals, and earnings, are building up liquidity which will subsequently be consumed, or whether this is not the case. The point can be put more forcibly. If it is true that relatively newer assets should earn more than those a few years old, (maintenance costs and down-time might suggest that this is generally the case), then the lessee should be worried if in the early years of the lease he is not building up liquidity. The implication is that in the later years his earnings may fall short of the rentals due. Choosing the asset, and agreeing the lease terms, are not the end of the matter as far as the lessee is concerned. Watching what is happening through the lease term is equally essential.

The lessor's viewpoint

2.16 What we now need to do is to move from the lessee's viewpoint to that of the lessor. Into the same basic lease that we have used for illustration purposes so far, we can build two or three additional assumptions so as to demonstrate how the lessor operates, and what it is that motivates him:

- First we assume that the £10,000 which we have described so far as the asset's 'cost' is in fact what accountants would call its 'fair value', that is to say what a potential purchaser would have to pay to buy it. The point of this assumption is that if the lessor were also manufacturer of the asset concerned, he should use as his 'transfer price' from his manufacturing activity to his leasing activity a figure, £10,000, which allows him to recognise a proper (manufacturing) profit on that transfer.

- Secondly we assume, for the good tax reasons that will become apparent in paragraph 2.21 below, that the lessor purchases the asset on the last day of an accounting period rather than the first.

- Provided that the date of purchase of the asset and the date he 'incepts' the lease are the same, that will mean that he receives the first quarter's rental from the lessee on that last day of his accounting period. But lessors normally recognise their rentals in their accounts over the period to which they relate, not on the date on which they are due (see the technical explanation for this in paragraph 2.17 below). Therefore the lessor would, in theory, bring in 1/93 of £672 in the first period, and the remainder of that £672 in the next accounting period. For simplicity of illustration, we ignore that 1/93, and assume that the whole of the first four rental receipts are credited in the lessor's accounting period which starts the day after the asset purchase/lease inception actually took place. (The inception of a lease is the lessor's action of making it effective, by handing over the leased asset, and requiring payment of the first rental – if rentals are payable at the start of each period. Inception may thus be later than the asset purchase date, but should never precede the date of signature of the lease agreement. There is a slightly different definition of inception in the statement of standard accounting practice, SSAP 21, namely "the earlier of the time the asset is brought into use and the date from which rentals first accrue" but in normal circumstances this will be the same as our less formalised explanation).

- We make that same assumption in relation to the lessor's interest costs for the funds he borrows to acquire the asset – that no part of that interest needs to be treated as an expense earlier than the accounting period starting the day after asset purchase/lease inception.

- Since the lease was incepted on day 365 of what it is convenient to call 'year 0', it comes to an end on day 364 of year 5. We assume that immediately thereafter, on day 365 of year 5, the lessor sold the asset, and passed substantially all of the proceeds back to the lessee by way of a 'rebate of rentals'. In parenthesis, this is a transaction which significantly reduces the lessee's overall costs of the asset's provision, (that is to say of the lessee's possession and use). We did not take it into account when looking in earlier paragraphs of this chapter at those costs – from the lessee's point of view. It would not normally be a factor which the lessee could, or should, take into account in calculating the interest rate implicit in the lease, unless one were dealing with the somewhat unusual situation of a lessor guaranteeing some minimum level of rebate.

- There is a particular reason, which we will explain in paragraph 2.21, why it is convenient to assume a relatively high figure for the asset's disposal proceeds, £2,500; and why the rebate the lessee receives is therefore as high as £2,450 (98 percent).

Accounting on an accruals basis

2.17   The second of the four Fundamental Accounting Concepts (set out in Statement of Standard Accounting Practice No 2, SSAP 2) is the accruals concept. It requires that revenue and costs be "accrued" – that is to say that they be "recognised as they are earned or incurred, not as money is received or paid" – and. . . "that they be dealt with in the profit and loss account of the period to which they relate". Although the argument is occasionally put forward that a rental due on day 365 of year 0, and not in any circumstance refundable, "relates" to that day only, the better view is that it forms part of a series of rentals each of them related to three month periods starting on the days on which they are due. This is the footing on which rentals are credited in the profit and loss account on a 'time basis'. The second side of the accruals concept, equally important to the proper recognition of profits and losses, is the process of matching. The revenue and costs already referred to are to be "matched with one another so far as their relationship can be established or justifiably assumed". If rentals for a quarter are receivable at the commencement of that quarter, and interest on the borrowings for the asset purchase are payable quarterly, but at the end of the relevant quarter, it is not very difficult to justify the assumption that the company's accounts would show a truer and fairer view of its profitability if these revenues and costs were accrued and matched, than if the rental were treated as income on day 365 of year 0, and the interest as expense of day 92 of year 1.

Tax on the lessor's operations

2.18 Here, it is convenient to introduce an assumption which has implications of a rather different kind. The assumption is simply that the lessor company is profitable. When it writes the lease that we have been looking at, it will pay tax on the profits that it generates from doing so; and if, (as we may not be entirely surprised to find is the case), it incurs a tax loss in one or more years, it will reduce the tax which it would otherwise have paid on its other profits for those years. As an assumption this probably over-simplifies the positions one normally meets in practice. More often than not, one is dealing with groups of companies rather than single entities. The tax losses arising from a specific lease may reflect through into an overall loss in the computations of the company which has written that lease, in which case any reduction of a tax liability has to be looked for under the provisions which enable loss making companies in a group to 'surrender' their losses to another (profitable) company in the group – and if this is both companies' wish, to be paid for doing so. We will look at these aspects in Chapter 7 below. For present purposes it is not unreasonable to proceed on the basis of our simple assumption. However, the particular implications we will be drawing out of it do need to be thought through. When a company makes profits, the tax authorities participate. If its profits represent a return of 10 percent on the funds put

into the company by its ordinary shareholders, those shareholders are only
able to retain 6½ percent within the company – the balance is paid away
by the company to the tax collector. (Once again this is a statement which
can be criticised as oversimplified, because 'small companies' pay tax at
a rate less than 35 percent. And although 'retentions' of larger companies
bear tax at 35 percent, it can be validly argued that profits distributed as
dividends are less heavily taxed in the company's hands, while tax or absence
of it at the shareholder level is a different question. Despite this, we will
continue for present purposes to work on the assumption that our leasing
company is liable at 35 percent, and that it is that rate we should regard
as reducing its retentions. We will then explore these arguments further
in paragraph 7.32, and justify the stance we are adopting).

2.19   That participation by the tax authorities has two aspects. The one
already mentioned is the simpler – if pre-tax returns are 10 percent on
funds employed, then on the face of it one might assume that post tax
returns would be 6½ percent. But life for leasing companies is seldom so
simple. If we assumed that by investing £1,000 in a three year lease, a lessor
could generate a profit of £100 the whole of which arose and was taxed
in year 3, then it would be true that £65 would be the retained profit at
the end of year 3, and that it would constitute the expected percentage
of the £1,000. But let us suppose that through some quirk in the tax laws,
the authorities treated the company as having made, in respect of this
particular investment, a tax loss in year 1 of £100, and a taxable profit
in year 3 of £200, the net tax take over the three years would still be £65.
What would be different would be the cashflow, and the percentage earned
on funds invested. We assumed that the company was profitable overall,
and that its tax loss actually generated a saving of tax which would
otherwise have been paid for year 1 of £35. That means that between the
tax date for year 1, and the equivalent date for year 3, the authorities are
providing £35 of the finance needed for the lease, and the lessor's own
investment is correspondingly reduced by £35. That alters, (perhaps not
significantly in these particular figures), the percentage yield. But its far
more important effect would become apparent if we had made the
assumption that the £1,000 invested had come, at least in part, from a lender,
rather than from the lessor's shareholders. The tax authorities' generosity
in providing £35 of tax repayment from year 1's tax date to that of year
3 would have a considerable effect on the lessor's borrowing costs, and
thus on the overall profitability of the transaction.

The necessity for looking at the lessor's tax position on each separate lease

2.20   We expressed our assumption at the beginning of paragraph 2.18
as being that our lessor was "profitable overall". The jargon used by most

lessors would be that they had, or had access to, "tax capacity". The vital implication is that whenever they need to assess the profitability or otherwise of a prospective transaction, it is valid − indeed essential − that they look at the cashflows including those flowing from the transaction's own tax results, in order to see what borrowing and shareholder funds are required, and what return it will generate for each. Another way of thinking of this is to picture the lessor company as built of a number of 'bricks', each of them being an individual and fully self contained lease. Each brick therefore uses funds from shareholders and lenders, each has its own cashflows, which after the initial borrowing and asset purchase will mainly consist of a flow of cash from the lessee through the lessor's hands to the lessor's financier, but which will also include tax cashflows between lessor and tax authorities. Each brick should generate its own contribution to the overall profits of the lessor − and perhaps it is here that it becomes apparent that 'brick' is not a wholly appropriate word to use to describe these individual transactions which come, at the end of their lease terms, to contain no asset, no borrowing, no rights or obligations granted to or owed by a lessee, and only a small cash balance earned for the lessor company.

2.21 To work out the tax figures for our 'brick' we need to work through the tax computations which follow from our illustrative lease and which have four main strands. First, there are what the tax legislation describes as the writing down allowances on the leased asset. The lessor is the person who incurs the expenditure on its acquisition, and he is also regarded by the tax authorities as using that asset in his own trade of leasing. (Although the legislation does also recognise that the lessee has not only possession but also 'use' in his own trade. What the lessee does not do, and what prevents his being entitled to tax allowances is that he does not incur the capital expenditure on the asset's acquisition, nor does the asset ever belong to him. In parenthesis, we have also to add that there is an underlying assumption not only that the lessee does not currently own the asset, but that he has no right, conditional or otherwise, to acquire it in the future. If he did, the transaction would be likely to fall into the category dealt with in chapter 6, under the heading 'hire purchase' − and the allowances for tax would be dealt with entirely differently. This is a matter best left to be examined in chapter 6). The allowances therefore go to the lessor. In their simplest form, they are calculated at 25 percent, on a reducing balance basis, for years starting with that in which the lessor incurred his expenditure. By assuming that he incurred that expenditure on 31 December of Year 0, rather than on 1 January of Year 1, we have accelerated the allowances' availability by a full twelve months, a point which we will see (in Table 8) has dramatic effects on the tax figures in the lessor's cashflow (and was the reason for our choice of date of expenditure).

Expenditure	– year 0	£10,000
Allowance	– year 0	2,500
		7,500
Allowance	– year 1	1,875
		5,625
Allowance	– year 2	1,406
		4,219
Allowance	– year 3	1,055
		3,164
Allowance	– year 4	791
		2,373
Sale proceeds–	year 5	2,500
Claw-back of allowances	– year 5	(127)

Table 8

Writing down allowances, and balancing charge, in years 0 – 5, at 25 percent on reducing balance basis.

Those figures show that after five years' allowances (years 0 to 4 inclusive) the taxpayer has been permitted cumulative tax deductions of £7,627, and the tax authorities still regard the asset as having an 'unexpired earning capacity' of £2,373. In this particular instance that conclusion may have been justified, in the sense that after a full further year of use, (but of course there were only five years of use overall, even if six allowances could have been claimed), the asset was sold for £2,500, the implication being perhaps that its purchaser regarded it as still having a significant earning capacity at the end of year 5. The reason why we chose that level of proceeds was not, however, to justify the Inland Revenue's profile of allowances, but a more mundane one. Following the 'brick' concept, explained in the preceding paragraph, we want if possible to look at a lease all of whose 'loose ends' have been tied up by the end of its lease term (or rather by the end of the lessor's accounting period in which that lease term ended). If the sale proceeds had been less than £2,373, then the lessor would have continued to be entitled to 25 percent allowances, on a decreasing basis, on the shortfall of proceeds below 'written down value' through years 5, 6 and so on. In fact, because a reducing balance calculation always tends towards zero, without ever getting there, one would have a very loose end. Setting proceeds at a figure which produces a claw-back of allowances avoids this.

2.22 The second of the four strands in the lessor's tax computations is the rebate of rentals which the lessor gives to the lessee out of the sale proceeds of the asset. We quantified this at £2,450 in paragraph 2.16, and we said that the lessor paid it over on day 365 of year 5, out of the proceeds realised on that same day. The Inland Revenue treat the rebating of rentals as entitling the lessor to deduct the sum concerned in arriving at his profits. This can generally be expected to give him an advantage compared to the alternative possibility which would be to regard it as a reduction of the sale proceeds for which the asset had been realised. If we were to start from the asset's written down value after the year 4 allowance, as shown in the preceding paragraph, and were to assume sale proceeds of £1,000 of which £975 was rebated in year 5, we could see that the tax deductions/allowances for that and subsequent years would be as in Table 9

	Treating rebate as deductible expense		Treating rebate as reduction of proceeds	
WDV of asset	2,373		2,373	
Proceeds	1,000		25	
	1,373		2,348	
Allowance yr 5	343	343	587	587
Deductible yr 5		975		–
Total Allce/deductible		1,318		587
	1,030		1,761	
Allowance yr 6	258	258	440	440
	772		1,321	
Allowance yr 7	193	193	330	330
Value not yet allowed	579		991	

Table 9

Alternative possible treatments in the lessor's hands of rebate given to lessee on sale of asset. The righthand column treatment, regarding the asset's sale as having realised only the net amount (i.e. after deducting the rebate) is in practice never adopted.

showing that both as regards the speed of obtaining deductions and allowances, and the amount of the "asset value" not yet allowed for tax (despite the asset's no longer being in the lessor's ownership) it is preferable to treat the rebate as an expense.

2.23   The third and fourth strands in the lessor's tax computation are simply the rentals receivable, and the interest payable. The rentals we know, and the interest payable we will put in at the figures shown in Table 10 – and demonstrate later that it is correct. It is also convenient to omit, at this stage, the explanation why the lessor's tax computation seems not to look like that of any other taxpayer. Such other computations start with an accounting profit, and 'adjust' it to conform with tax rules. This explanation fits more appropriately into paragraph 2.56 below.

The first thing to be said is that the aggregate profit over the six years is £671. The net tax payable over those six years is £236, which is of course

	Year 0	Year 1	Year 2	Year 3	Year 4	Year 5	Total
Allowance	(2,500)	(1,875)	(1,406)	(1,055)	(791)	127	(7,500)
Rentals	–	2,688	2,688	2,688	2,688	2,688	13,440
Rebate	–	–	–	–	–	(2,450)	(2,450)
Interest	–	(1,045)	(790)	(574)	(338)	(72)	(2,819)
Profit/(loss)	(2,500)	(232)	492	1,059	1,559	293	671
Tax payable	–	–	172	371	546	103	236
Tax repayable	(875)	(81)	–	–	–	–	–

Table 10

Lessor's tax computation for five year lease, asset purchased day 365 of year 0, rentals £672 quarterly in advance, asset sold for £2,500 and rebate £2,450 given to lessee day 365 of year 5.

35 percent of £671. The second point is that we have constructed a lease which has no loose ends – in our figures there is no asset value carried forward at the end of year 5 for allowance in a future period, nor any other figure which has either not been received, or has not been taxed. We will find when we put the cashflow together that it ends with a profit attributable to shareholders of £671 pre-tax, £435 post-tax; we will in fact see that this latter has been 'extracted', that is to say removed from this 'brick' to go towards financing the operations of the lessor in other bricks. The lease cashflow therefore shows all loose ends tied off neatly, no asset, no liabilities, and no cash because of the extractions. But there has been an overall profit, retained within and reinvested in the continuing operations of the lessor company. That profit did not emerge on the day the lease was signed, nor on the day it terminated – it arose through the lease term. How an accountant recognises it, that is to say under what rules he decides how much is the profit of each accounting period during the lease term is an excessively complex science (or art). An examination of the principles will form the next section of this chapter.

The lessor's cashflow

2.24   Just how complex are the lessor's activities, becomes apparent when one sets out his cashflow. Table 11 is one of the two most important tables in this book, and the author makes no apology for insisting that his readers grasp how it is put together before they pass on to other matters. Of particular significance, for instance, is the reason why some of the columns' subtotals are shown at 31 December and some, seemingly, at 1 January. Even more vital are the relationships between the figures in the columns headed 'rentals extracted' and 'rentals applied to repay borrowings', which obviously total £672 in each quarter but which are not split between the 'equity' and 'external borrowing' sides of the cashflow in a haphazard way. The commentary on the format and figures is in paragraphs 2.25 and 2.26.

		Equity					External borrowing				
		Rentals extracted	Start of quarter	Equity income	End of quarter		Rentals applied to repay borrowings	Tax	Start of quarter	Interest expense	End of quarter
Y1 Q1	1500	–	1500	60	1560	8500	(672)		7828	280	8108
Q2	1560	(202)	1358	53	1411	8108	(470)		7638	273	7911
Q3	1411	(187)	1224	48	1272	7911	(485)		7426	266	7692
Q4	1272	(172)	1100	43	1143	7692	(500)	(875)	6317	226	6543
				204			(2127)			1045	30254
Y2 Q1	1143	(157)	986	38	1024	6543	(515)		6028	215	6243
		(718)									
Q2	1024	(151)	873	33	906	6243	(521)		5722	205	5927
Q3	906	(141)	765	31	796	5927	(531)		5396	192	5588
Q4	796	(131)	665	26	691	5588	(541)	(81)	4966	178	5144
				128			(2108)			790	22902
Y3 Q1	691	(120)	571	23	594	5144	(552)		4592	164	4756
		(543)									
Q2	594	(114)	480	19	499	4756	(558)		4198	150	4348
Q3	499	(103)	396	16	412	4348	(569)		3779	134	3913
Q4	412	(93)	319	13	332	3913	(579)	172	3506	126	3632
				71			(2258)			574	16649
Y4 Q1	332	(83)	249	10	259	3632	(589)		3043	108	3151
		(393)									
Q2	259	(73)	186	8	194	3151	(599)		2552	91	2643
Q3	194	(63)	131	6	137	2643	(609)		2034	73	2107
Q4	137	(52)	85	4	89	2107	(620)	371	1858	66	1924
				28			(2417)			338	9825
Y5 Q1	89	(42)	47	2	49	1924	(630)		1294	46	1340
		(230)									
Q2	49	(28)	21	2	23	1340	(644)		696	25	721
Q3	23	(23)	–	–	–	721	(649)		72	2	74
Q4	–	–	–	–	–	74	(672)	546		(1)	(53)
		(93)		4			(2595)			72	2135
							(2500)				
							2450	103	–	–	–
							(50)				
		(1935)		435			(11555)	236		2819	81765

Table 11

The lessor's cashflow, five year lease, rentals £672 quarterly in advance, taking into account sale of asset for £2,500 at end year 5, and rebate to lessee of £2,450. Financed by borrowings £8,500 at 3.57 percent per quarter, and by equity £1,500 requiring 4 percent post-tax reward. Equity cash extraction proportionate to net cash invested.

2.25 The lessor invests £10,000 in the purchase of the leased asset, but he would be unlikely to obtain the whole of that sum by borrowing. Those who lend to him expect, just as any lenders expect of any trading company, that he will put up some of the finance from his own (equity) sources. In our illustration, the lessor puts in £1,500 of his own funds, and borrows £8,500. These two separate elements of the finance are dealt with separately, but alongside each other, in the cashflow - the equity element on the left and the borrowing on the right. The borrowing section needs little explanation except to point out that the interest expense for each year is what we had earlier taken it to be in paragraph 2.23. The principal originally borrowed, increased by interest calculated quarterly on the outstanding balance, and increased also by net tax payments, is reduced by the application of a proportion of the rents, and by the excess of sale proceeds of the asset over the rental rebate given to the lessee. Summarising the totals of the columns in the cashflow gives:

Original borrowing		£8,500
Add interest		2,819
		11,319
Add tax payments years 3 - 5	1,192	
less repayments years 1 - 2	956	
		236
		11,555
Less proportion of rentals applied	11,505	
add excess of sale proceeds		
over rebate of rentals	50	
		11,555

It can be calculated relatively easily that the rate of interest the lessor is paying on his borrowings is 3.57 percent per quarter, which compounds to exactly 15 percent per annum. On the face of it, the lessor's use of equity funds appears equally straightforward.

Original injection		1,500
Add reward required (note that this is the after		
tax retention, because we dealt with the tax		
payments and repayments on the 'other side')		435
		1,935
less rentals	13,440	
less applied on 'other side' above	11,505	
	1,935	

2.26 But it is the putting of these two elements together which is somewhat complex:

• First, our calculations allow for the equity reward being required to be 4 percent per quarter, which compounds to just 17 percent per annum. (This is not a 'deductible' in computing the lessor's profits for tax purposes in paragraph 2.23).

- Secondly, the proportion of rentals applied to repay borrowings, and the balance of those rentals 'extracted' from this lease, (and passed to other uses within the company), obviously affect the two levels of outstandings; on one of which the interest rate is to be 3.57 percent per quarter, and on the other of which the equity reward is to be 4 percent per quarter.

- But there is not a total freedom over the decision whether to apply rentals to repayment of borrowing, or to extraction of equity component, because the amounts of cash extracted are required by the lessor to be proportionate to the balances of 'net cash investment' in the lease.

This last concept is shown in the final (right hand) column of the lessor's cash flow. At the ends of the four quarters of year 1, the lessor's outstanding external indebtedness was, respectively, £8,108, £7,911, £7,692 and £6,543, which total £30,254. If one aggregates all such balances of quarterly indebtedness through to the end of year 5 quarter 3, (after that the cash flow was positive through to the date of the final tax payment of £103), the total comes to £81,765. Our objective is to time the equity extractions proportionately to those balances of indebtedness as shown in Table 12.

$$\frac{30,254}{81,765} \times 1,935 = 718$$

$$\frac{22,902}{81,765} \times 1,935 = 543$$

$$\frac{16,649}{81,765} \times 1,935 = 393$$

$$\frac{9,825}{81,765} \times 1,935 = 230$$

$$\frac{2,135}{81,765} \times 1,935 = 51$$

$$= 1,935$$

Table 12

Calculations of equity extraction for lessor. Equity injected £1,500, and reward at 4 percent per quarter post tax coming to £435. Net cash investment as in righthand column of Table 11.

The accounting jargon for this is that the lessor's method of recognising profit is based on his "earning a constant rate of return on the net cash investment in the lease" to quote SSAP 21. That is what determines the levels of equity extractions on the dates the quarterly rentals are received – days which immediately follow those on which indebtedness is determined. It is of course true that not every leasing company sticks to so simple a formula; many of them build further guidelines into their computer programmes, to deal with particular aspects such as the direct expenses relating to the lease's negotiation, (incurred largely at that time, rather than throughout its term), and the risk of bad debts late on in the lease term. But these are matters we will come to below.

The lessor's pricing of prospective transactions

2.27   That exercise of working out the lessor's cash flow to give him:

• the required interest rate on external borrowing;

• the required reward on his equity component;

• the mix of borrowing and equity which the project necessitates;

• the speed of equity (plus reward) extraction which coincides with the reduction in the balance of 'net cash investment' in the lease;

can be done by trial and error – but it is hard work. Every serious lessor company has a computer programmed to perform the calculations. More fundamentally, it is that computer programme, and the cashflow which corresponds with its calculations, which then set out the basic view of what the company's activities should be, and are. It is often said that a company's information systems determine how its management runs the company, and how the company does its business. That may be more, or less, accurate in the case of other types of company, but in the case of lessors writing finance leases it is too true to be funny.

• The lessor's sales force use the computer to quote the rentals at which they can do business;

• the lessor's managers use the computer to sign up that business, or to turn it down;

• the lessor's directors use the computer's output to make their strategic, and tactical, management decisions;

which is all very well provided they have that fundamental understanding of both their business, and their customers' needs, which is not necessarily learned from computer printouts. There are a number of particular aspects of the business which we have not yet examined, or which we may have mentioned in general terms, but still need to look at in greater detail. An example of the first is the pattern of expenses incurred by the lessor in, first, signing a lease and getting it onto his books, and thereafter in administering it, paragraph 2.79. An example of the second is the lessor's credit risks, that is to say the possibility of bad debts among his lessees, paragraph 2.60 *et seq.*. We will come to these below, but it is convenient first to look at the principles for the lessor's accounting for his portfolio of finance leases.

The lessor's accounting for finance leases

2.28 When we looked, in paragraphs 2.06 to 2.08, at the way a lessee is required (by SSAP 21) to capitalise the rights and obligations he acquires under a finance lease, it was very easy to trace through the double entry book-keeping, and therefore to understand not only the transaction itself, but how it affected the company's accounts as a whole.

	Journal		Balance sheet		
	Debit	Credit	Liability	Asset	Profit & Loss
Asset acquisition	10,000			Dr 10,000	
Lease creditor		10,000	Cr 10,000		
Yr 1 Rents	2,688		Dr 2,688		
(interest 1,179)			Cr 1,179		Dr 1,179
Cash		2,688			
Yr 1 Depr expense	2,000				Dr 2,000
Depr provision		2,000		Cr 2,000	
End Yr 1			Cr 8,491	Dr 8,000	Dr 3,179
Yr 2 Rents	2,688		Dr 2,688		
(interest 965)			Cr 965		Dr 965
Cash		2,688			
Yr 2 Depr expense	2,000				Dr 2,000
Depr provision		2,000		Cr 2,000	
End Yr 2			Cr 6,768	Dr 6,000	Dr 2,965

and so on

Table 13

The lessee's liability, asset and expense as shown in his accounts for a five year lease, rents £672 quarterly in advance, no account taken of any rebate that may be received on the asset's sale.

The double entry is made abundantly clear if, as in Table 13, we 'journalise' each step, (in the boxed left hand two columns). We can then follow the effect of these entries into the lessee's balance sheet and profit and loss account year by year. Reminding ourselves of the lessee's position is actually helpful as a prelude to trying to follow through the lessor's accounting for three specific reasons — the first of which accounting literature tends to dismiss. This is that the lessee's entries above show his aspects of the 'brick' (paragraph 2.24); and it is much easier to grasp the lessor-aspects we are about to look at if we start working on his brick, on its own, rather than saying that we do not need, for instance, to worry about the lessor's borrowings and repayments lease by lease, because these are already reflected in the accounts of his company taken as a whole. The second reason why it is valid to remind ourselves of the lessee's position is that we saw in paragraph 2.07 and 2.08 that the lessee's 'capitalisation' of the leased asset followed from the extent of the rights and risks passed to him by the lessor, whilst the lessor retained, in effect, little more than the 'right' to make a financial profit from a (notional) loan to the lessee. Lenders whose trade it is to lend money do not normally show their portfolios of outstanding loans as fixed assets on their balance sheets — all of which means that the lessor does not show the leased asset as such on his balance sheet, and nor does he 'capitalise' the asset which he does reflect — it is merely a balance owed to him by the lessee. And the final point, which we will see very clearly below, is that the lessor's 'current asset' (which of course mirrors to some extent in his accounts the 'lease creditor' liability in those of the lessee earlier in this paragraph) has only one of the two

	Balance sheet				Profit & Loss
	Liability	Assets		Original Equity	
	External Borrowing	Investment in finance leases	New Cash Generated		
Asset Acquisition		Dr 10000			
external borrowing	Cr 8500				
original equity				Cr 1500	
Year 1					
rentals					Cr 2688
applied/extracted	Dr 2127		Dr 204	Dr 357	
interest	Cr 1045				Dr 1045
capital repaid		Cr 1329			Dr 1329
taxation	Cr 110				Dr 110
	Cr 7528	Dr 8671	Dr 204	Cr 1143	Cr 204

Table 14

The lessor's book-keeping entries for the single lease, referred to as 'the brick'. Five year lease, rents £672 quarterly in advance, financed by £8,500 borrowing and £1,500 equity, the former at 3.57 percent per quarter and the latter rewarded at 4 percent post-tax.

characteristics of that lease creditor, namely that it decreases in size as the lessee pays rentals of which some part is treated as principal repayment; but it does not simultaneously increase in value by any 'interest factor'. However, in relation to this current asset in the lessor's books, the rules for determining what is and what is not the principal repayment are necessarily much more complex than they were for the lessee.

2.29 The book-keeping entries for the lessor's 'brick' look like Table 14 (here the reader needs to refer back to the cashflow table for the lessor set out in paragraph 2.24)

Some of those figures need no little explanation; the balance at the end of year 1 of the original equity put into the lease can be read straight out of the lessor's cash flow in paragraph 2.24, as an example. So also can the application of rentals against external borrowings, and it is not hard to see why the extraction of the original equity, together with the reward on thereon also extracted (£204 under the heading 'new cash generated'), is shown in two separate columns above; the net profit generated out of the lease can be expected to be in cash form over the lease's full term. But that last statement highlights two figures above which do not reflect the actual cash experience of the lessor:

- First, there is a figure slightly curiously described as "capital repaid" of £1,329. From its position in the profit and loss account, (and as a reduction in the carrying value of the asset), one might think it analogous to depreciation – were the lessor to be carrying the asset as a fixed asset in his balance sheet rather than as a receivable. If that were its nature, then the lessor's pre-tax income would appear to be £314, being the difference between rental income of £2,688, and interest expense £1,045 and "depreciation" of £1,329.

- Secondly, if he had made a pre-tax profit of £314, then the tax charge of £110 shown above would represent a 35 percent burden, and the post-tax profit of £204 would make sense. But the lessor actually received a cash repayment during the year 1, (in respect of year 0's results), of £875, and in respect of the year 1 results, he expects to receive a further repayment during year 2 of £81.

We need to explain the accountants' concept of 'deferred taxation', and to expand the above figures to encompass it.

Deferred taxation in the lessor's accounts

2.30 'Deferring' taxation is a procedure required by the Accounting Bodies under Statement of Standard Accounting Practice No 15 (SSAP 15). In its simplest form, it can be explained as a method of matching (in specified circumstances) the tax charge in the profit and loss account with the income recognised in each relevant year's accounts. Thus, if a company has a 31 December accounting date, but knows that it will be receiving £1,000 of interest on a government security on the following 15 February, it will normally 'accrue' four and a half months' proportion of the interest in the accounts to December, and let the remaining one and a half months' proportion fall into the next year's accounts. If one makes the assumption that the tax authorities will assess the income for the year in which the cash is received, not the two years in which income is accrued in the profit and loss account, then one might show pre-tax income, and the tax charges, as follows:

Year 1	*– Pre-tax income*	£750
	Less tax on year 1's income	nil
		£750
Year 2	*– Pre-tax income*	£250
	Less tax on year 2's income	350
		(£100)

Because this is nonsensical, SSAP 15 requires that where there is a "short term timing difference", which will reverse in the foreseeable future, the tax charge should adjust for this:

Year 1	*– Pre-tax income*		£750
	Current tax		
	(chargeable on year 1's income)	nil	
	Deferred tax		
	(chargeable for year 2, but on		
	income recognised in this year)	263	
			263
			£487
Year 2	*– Pre-tax income*		£250
	Current tax		
	(chargeable on year 2's income)	350	
	Deferred tax		
	(release from provision made in		
	year 1 in respect of income		
	assessable in year 2, but recognised		
	in the accounts in year 1)	(263)	
			87
			£163

The charge in the profit and loss account for each year is then made up of two elements. 'Current tax' is the amount payable to the Inland Revenue, generally nine months after the balance sheet date. The 'deferred tax' charge or release brings the total profit and loss charge, (in this instance), to 35 percent of that year's (accounts) income.

2.31   But what must also be understood is that at the end of year 1, although there is no liability shown as owing to the Inland Revenue themselves, (there is no assessment at that stage, and thus no tax creditor), there is, carried in the balance sheet along with the company's other creditors a 'provision' for deferred taxation of £263. A provision is nearer to being a liability than it is to a reserve – the latter is no more than a part of the company's shareholders' funds segregated by the directors into a separate, named, account. The only things which differentiate a provision from a liability are that one or more of the following factors may be relevant to its identification and quantification. First, there may not be a legal liability to an actual creditor to whom the sum is already, (or will shortly be), payable. Secondly, there may be some necessity for assumptions about future events – for instance deferred tax will not crystallise if the enterprise incurs substantial losses in every future year, and therefore one is stating that one expects to be profitable if one creates a provision for deferred tax. Thirdly, there may be some degree of estimation in the quantification of a provision, if for instance the rate of corporation tax payable for year 2 were subsequently fixed at 30 percent in place of 35 percent, then the deferred tax provision set up at the end of year 1 would be seen to have been greater than was actually needed. The degree of uncertainty involved in these three factors is not enough, in normal circumstances, to mean that lessors can avoid establishing and maintaining deferred tax provisions, or that the balances on these accounts are not essentially similar to liabilities. There is however a question to which we will come in paragraph 7.34 below, whether such a deferred tax provision can be partial only – operated at less than the 'complete' level illustrated in the next paragraph. It would break the thread of our present examination of lessors' accounting for finance leases to introduce this philosophical discussion at this point.

2.32   In the case of the lessor we are looking at, the timing difference in respect of which we need to set up a deferred tax provision is the tax depreciation allowances given on the leased asset, which exceed the accounting 'charges'. The latter would be more easily identifiable if the lessor had treated the leased asset as one of his own fixed assets, and written it off over the period by charging 'depreciation' in his accounts. As we have seen, the lessor does in fact treat the leased asset as an amount receivable from the lessee(s), describing it as a 'net investment in a (portfolio of) finance lease(s)' (paragraph 2.28). He then regards the value of his asset as being decreased by the lessee's 'repayment of principal' (paragraph 2.29).

At this stage we have not yet worked all the way through the calculations, and therefore the reader must take on trust the level of 'repayments' in the table which follows. Secondly, a certain degree of trust is needed in relation to our being able to demonstrate below the proposition already mentioned in paragraph 2.29, that a 'repayment', and a depreciation charge on a fixed asset really do have the same effect. Trust will be rewarded. First we need to calculate the necessary deferred tax provision, including its movements during subsequent accounting periods in the lease term. This is shown in Table 15.

	Tax comp's	Accounts	Difference		
Yr 0 Tax depreciation	£2,500				
Yr 1 Tax depreciation	1,875				
Yr 1 Principal repayment		£1,329			
Cumulative to end year 1	4,375	1,329	3,046	@ 35%	1,066
Yr 2 Depr & rep't	1,406	1,701			
release from prov'n			(295)	@ 35%	(103)
	5,781	3,030	2,751	@ 35%	963
Yr 3 Depr & rep't	1,055	2,004			
release from prov'n			(949)	@ 35%	(332)
	6,836	5,034	1,802	@ 35%	631
Yr 4 Depr & rep't	791	2,306			
release from prov'n			(1,515)	@ 35%	(530)
	7,627	7,340	287	@ 35%	101
Yr 5 Depr & rep't	(127)	2,660			
sales proceeds	2,500				
release from prov'n			(287)	@ 35%	(101)
	10,000	10,000			

Table 15
Calculating the cumulative difference between capital allowances and depreciation at each year end through the lease term.

The lessor's accounting for finance leases – continued

2.33　We can now put together a better illustration (in Table 16) of the lessor's 'brick' than the one we started in paragraph 2.29.

As before, the explanation of Table 16 follows in the next two paragraphs – and it is as vital that the reader understands these figures as it was that he understood the lessor's view of his activities earlier illustrated in his cashflow in paragraph 2.24.

	Balance sheet					Original Equity	Profit & Loss
	Liabilities			Assets			
	External Borrowing	Current Tax	Deferred Tax	Investment in finance leases	New Cash generated		
Asset	Cr 8500			Dr 10000		Cr 1500	
Yr 1							
rentals	Dr 3002	Cr 875			Dr 561		Cr 2688
interest	Cr 1045						Dr 1045
repayment				Cr 1329			Dr 1329
c tax		Dr 875					Cr 875
		Dr 81					Cr 81
d tax			Cr 1066				Dr 1066
							Cr 204
extract					Cr 561	Dr 357	Dr 204
	Cr 6543	Dr 81	Cr 1066	Dr 8671		Cr 1143	
Yr 2							
rentals	Dr 2189	Cr 81			Dr 580		Cr 2688
interest	Cr 790						Dr 790
repayment				Cr 1701			Dr 1701
c tax		Cr 172					Dr 172
d tax rel			Dr 103				Cr 103
							Cr 128
extract					Cr 580	Dr 452	Dr 128
	Cr 5144	Cr 172	Cr 963	Dr 6970		Cr 691	
Yr 3							
rentals	Dr 2086	Dr 172			Dr 430		Cr 2688
interest	Cr 574						Dr 574
repayment				Cr 2004			Dr 2004
c tax		Cr 371					Dr 371
d tax rel			Dr 332				Cr 332
							Cr 71
extract					Cr 430	Dr 359	Dr 71
	Cr 3632	Cr 371	Cr 631	Dr 4966		Cr 332	
Yr 4							
rentals	Dr 2046	Dr 371			Dr 271		Cr 2688
interest	Cr 338						Dr 338
repayment				Cr 2306			Dr 2306
c tax		Cr 546					Dr 546
d tax rel			Dr 530				Cr 530
							Cr 28
extract					Cr 271	Dr 243	Dr 28
	Cr 1924	Cr 546	Cr 101	Dr 2660		Cr 89	
Yr 5							
rentals	Dr 1946	Dr 546			Dr 93		Cr 2688
		Dr 103					
net proc	Dr 50						Cr 50
interest	Cr 72						Dr 72
repayment				Cr 2660			Dr 2660
c tax		Cr 103					Dr 103
d tax rel			Dr 101				Cr 101
							Cr 4
extract					Cr 93	Dr 89	Dr 4
					Total post-tax profits		Cr 435

Table 16

2.34 The balances outstanding on the external borrowing at each year end are the same as were shown on the cashflow statement in paragraph 2.24, as are also the balances of original equity injected and not yet recovered at the ends of the relevant years. The way in which the rentals are shown as being applied to reduce external borrowings, and for equity extraction, is slightly different from the format in paragraph 2.29. A full explanation of the figures would look like Table 17.

	Year 1	Year 2	Year 3	Year 4	Year 5	Total
Rentals	2,688	2,688	2,688	2,688	2,688	13,440
less extracted as equity and equity reward	561	580	430	271	93	1,935
Applied to reduce external borrowings per cashflow para 2.24	2,127	2,108	2,258	2,417	2,595	11,505
add tax repaid	875	81				
less tax paid			172	371	546 ⎱ 103 ⎰	236
Total applied to reduce external borrowings per 'brick' in paragraph 2.33	3,002	2,189	2,086	2,046	1,946	11,269

Table 17

Explanation of the figures shown as reductions of external borrowings in Table 16.

But we have seen that to put together the above book-keeping entries, it is necessary:

- to start with the cashflow, and in particular with the column in it which shows the pattern on which the lessor wishes to take out the 'equity reward', (post tax income generated on the equity invested in the lease);

- to calculate the deferred tax provisions and releases as well as the current tax figures which the cashflow statement already incorporates;

- and then to calculate what pattern of 'repayments' has to be credited to the lessor's investment in his portfolio of leases, and debited to profit and loss account, in order to show the desired recognition of the 'equity reward'.

2.35 The foregoing becomes clear if we re-summarise (in Table 18) the profit and loss account figures from the right hand column of the 'brick' which we set out in paragraph 2.33.

This method of showing the lessor's profits, allocated between the years

	Year 1	Year 2	Year 3	Year 4	Year 5	Total
A *Rentals*	2,688	2,688	2,688	2,688	2,688	13,440
B *Sale proceeds*					50	50
C *Capital repayment*	(1,329)	(1,701)	(2,004)	(2,306)	(2,660)	(10,000)
D *Gross income*	1,359	987	684	382	78	3,490
E *Interest paid*	(1,045)	(790)	(574)	(338)	(72)	(2,819)
F	314	197	110	44	6	671
G *Current tax*	956	(172)	(371)	(546)	(103)	(236)
H *Deferred tax*	(1,066)	103	332	530	101	nil
I *Net tax charge*	(110)	(69)	(39)	(16)	(2)	(236)
J *Post-tax profit*	204	128	71	28	4	435

Table 18
Lessor's profit and loss figures re-summarised for the five years of the lease from the righthand column of table 16.

of the lease term, is known as the 'actuarial method after tax'. What we have done is:

- take the 'bottom line' (post tax profit) (J) out of the lease cashflow (paragraph 2.24);

- engross it back by a net tax charge at 35 percent (I) to arrive at a pre-tax profit (F);

- take the current tax line (G) from paragraph 2.23 – a reference back to the computations set out in that paragraph will make it clear that these liabilities and repayments are 'fixed'; none of the 'accounting' adjustments we are considering has any effect on them;

- add the interest charge (from paragraph 2.24) (E) to the pre-tax profit (F) to get to a line we call 'gross income' (D);

- the 'capital repayment' (C) is then the balancing figure between rentals and sales proceeds received (A & B), and gross income (D);

- but we can also see that the 'capital repayment' line (C) is what we used in arriving at the deferred tax line in our calculations in paragraph 2.32 (– themselves calculations which take into account the allocation of profits between years as shown above).

We said in paragraph 2.32 that we could demonstrate that a 'capital repayment' was analogous to depreciation. Part of the proof lies in the use we made of the capital repayment in the deferred tax calculations – where we compared them with the capital·allowances given for tax purposes. But the remainder of the proof is perhaps no more than the observation that the 'capital repayments' are the balancing numbers to make the profit and loss account add up. Some literature says that the whole of lessor accounting is no more than working backwards from what you want to report as the company's income. The author does not go quite as far as that. There are, as we have already seen, and as will become clearer in our further analysis below of finance lessors' operations, compelling reasons for saying that the income recognition set out is 'true and fair'. But it is also a fact that with figures as inter-related as these, one does have not only to have a clear understanding of the way in which they fit together, but of the sequence of operations necessary to compute the answers.

Net cash investment and net investment

2.36   But even if he does not necessarily think that accountants spend their time working backwards, the sharp eyed reader will already have noticed that accountants do not seem as clever as they might be in their choice of terminology:

- in paragraph 2.26 we described as the balances of 'net cash investment in the lease' the amounts owed at each quarter and year end to the lessor's external creditor, (this was the same meaning we gave to the phrase when we first introduced it in paragraph 1.12);

- whereas in paragraph 2.34 we have referred to the lessor's 'net investment' in his portfolio of finance leases – or since we were at the time only looking at a single lease, his 'net investment in the lease'.

The first is a real liability, to the lessor's provider of finance; the second is an asset on his balance sheet, being the carrying value of what he shows among his current assets namely the notional 'loan' he regards himself as having made to the lessee. All that the author can say is that this is the terminology fixed by common usage, and that we must take great care not to allow ourselves to be misled by the similarity of the phrases used to describe complete opposites. And it is of course true that the lessor's balance sheet itself reflects his external borrowings in total, and appropriately described, rather than lease by lease.

The lessor's balance sheets

2.37   After that preliminary glance at the terminology, we might look at the lessor's balance sheet numbers at successive year ends, which are as shown in Table 19. That drawn up at the end of year 0 reflects not just the use of equity and borrowed funds to acquire the asset, and the immediate reduction in the external borrowings by the application of the first quarter's rental, but also the fact that the asset's acquisition immediately gives the lessor the right to a tax recovery (with an equal and opposite deferred tax provision) as shown in Table 19. The figures at successive year ends come from the brick, Table 16.

Year 0

Shareholders funds	1,500	*Investment in finance leases*	9,328
External borrowing	7,828	*Tax recoverable*	875
Deferred tax	875		
	10,203		10,203

Year 1

Shareholders funds	1,500	*Investment in finance leases*	8,671
less extraction	561	*Tax recoverable*	81
	939		
add profit for year	204		
	1,143		
External borrowing	6,543		
Deferred tax	1,066		
	8,752		8,752

Year 2

Shareholders funds	1,143	*Investment in finance leases*	6,970
less extraction	580		
	563		
add profit for year	128		
	691		
External borrowing	5,144		
Current tax	172		
Deferred tax	963		
	6,970		6,970

Year 3

Shareholders funds	691	*Investment in finance leases*	4,966
less extraction	430		
	261		
add profit for year	71		
	332		
External borrowing	3,632		
Current tax	371		
Deferred tax	631		
	4,966		4,966

Table 19

The lessor's balance sheets drawn up at commencement, and at each successive year end through the lease term. Five year lease, £672 rentals quarterly in advance, financed by borrowings of £8,500 at 3.57 percent per quarter, and equity of £1,500 rewarded at 4 percent per quarter post tax. £50 not rebated to lessee out of proceeds of sale of asset. (Continued on next page).

		Year 4	
Shareholders funds	332	*Investment in finance leases*	2,660
less extraction	271		
	61		
add profit for year	28		
	89		
External borrowing	1,924		
Current tax	546		
Deferred tax	101		
	2,660		2,660
		Year 5	
Shareholders funds	89		
add profit for year	4		
	93		
less extraction	93		

Table 19 (continued)

The lessor's capital ratios

2.38   That may seem an excessive quantity of figures, mechanically produced, and not having a lot of meaning. But there is one particular point that does need to be brought out. It is the general shape of a lessor's cashflow that there is:

- An acceleration of cash receipts; for instance the very fact that rents are received at the beginning of each quarter is an aspect of this, but even more significant is the level of tax repayments for the first two years.

- A corresponding deceleration of at least some outflows of cash; interest is calculated at the ends of each quarter, and quite significant tax liabilities are paid nine months after the end of each of the later years.

If all goes well the lessor has (and has not extracted) the cash he needs to meet these liabilities. The other side of that same coin is to say that the lessee is still repaying, up to the end of the lease term, his (notional) loan from the lessor; the lessor can see that there is at any point enough cash still to be repaid to meet the lessor's liabilities — and that the carrying value of that notional loan demonstrates this. But it is nevertheless undoubtedly true that the lessor can clearly be seen to be becoming less well-capitalised as the lease term progresses. If we work out his ratios of equity to assets, (a quite normal way of expressing the capitalisation of a financially orientated company), in the above balance sheets the figures are as follows:

	Equity	Assets	Ratio
Year 0	1,500	10,203	14.7 percent
Year 1	1,143	8,752	13.1 percent
Year 2	691	6,970	9.9 percent
Year 3	332	4,966	6.7 percent
Year 4	89	2,660	3.3 percent

and it would be hard to describe that as anything other than a rake's progress through the lease term.

2.39   But of course this is one of those areas where it ceases to be realistic to look at the individual 'brick' – one needs to look at the company as a whole. If it wrote only leases identical to this one, and wrote the same number of them in every year, then at any year end it would have equal numbers of every age of lease still in existence, and its equity to assets ratio would simply be the average of the above:

	Equity	Assets	Ratio Total – one
lease per year	3,755	33,551	11.2 percent

which is reasonably respectable. If the company were expanding, then the proportion of newer leases to older would be better, and the ratio would be improved. As so often is the case, it is the contracting company which may appear to be in worse shape – because its decline builds upon itself in these unexpected ways. Ratios are important, but they measure only the symptoms, rather than being capable of curing the disease. The vitally important thing is that the company trades profitably, and that it is able to meet its obligations when due. There are two potential danger areas in which leasing companies may find themselves, or into which the unscrupulous may steer them. First, a company with a mature portfolio, but without material capital resources retained from earlier business done, will find itself in difficulties if it suffers any significant level of bad debts or defaults by its lessees. It is obvious from the foregoing figures that it could only meet such losses out of some form of recapitalisation by its shareholders. Secondly, in the undoubted circumstances that any such mature portfolio will carry with it significant liabilities to the Inland Revenue, (with further similar liabilities to crystallise when timing differences reverse, that is to say deferred tax provisions), managers of a company who fraudulently run away with its assets can leave the Inland Revenue with little hope of being paid. One's automatic reaction when a company fails, or is defrauded, is to assume that the Inland Revenue are preferential creditors, and are unlikely to suffer. In a lessor company their preferences may be of little value, if they have no 'security' – using that word once again in the borrowers' and lenders' sense first introduced in paragraph 1.06.

The investment period method - an alternative method of lessor's income recognition

2.40   We framed the lessor's cashflow in paragraph 2.24 on the footing that, among other things, the extraction of the equity, (that is to say the original equity, and the 4 percent post-tax reward thereon), would be proportionate to the net cash investment in the lease. This produced both:

*   the shape of the 'bottom line', which was simply the equity reward, but depended directly upon the speed of equity extraction; and

*   the shape of the cashflow itself, including the aggregate interest on the external borrowings: because equity extraction and reduction of those borrowings are interdependent, and the interest costs depend on the latter.

(We could also, as indicated at the end of paragraph 2.26, have altered the rules under which we calculated the cashflow figures; by introducing other matters in addition to proportionality into the calculation of equity extraction. This would have altered both of the 'shapes' referred to above). Alternatively we can leave the cashflow unchanged, (that is to say leave the timing and amounts of equity extraction and of reduction of borrowings unaltered, but recalculate the allocation between years of the company's profits. This is what the investment period does (we set out the calculations in paragraph 2.42) – and its rationale is the argument that 'gross income' is what should be allocated.

Gross income

2.41   We have not previously introduced or explained the phrase 'gross income', although it did appear as a caption in the profit and loss account summarisation in paragraph 2.35. It is the difference between the rental

Rentals for five years	£13,440
Excess of sale proceeds over rebate	50
	13,490
less capital repayments	10,000
Gross income	3,490

receipts for any year, and the part of these that is regarded as a capital repayment. Or in other words, if we say that the lessor's activities are analogous to those of a financier lending money to the lessee, gross income is the interest receivable by the lessor on such loans. Our example has quantified this at £3,490.

It is undoubtedly true that most leasing companies would not bring the excess of sale proceeds over rebates into their calculations, either of gross income, or for that matter of the lease cashflow itself. In relation to the 'pricing' we built into that cashflow, what we did was to say that the interest on external borrowings was 3.57 percent per quarter, the required equity reward was 4 percent post-tax, and the rentals together with the excess of sale proceeds over rebate were then calculated so as to produce this result. Most leasing companies would exclude those net sale proceeds from both their pricing calculations, and from the gross income, and post-tax income, in calculating the allocation between years. If there were net sale proceeds, they would simply be recognised in the accounts for the year in which they arose. Why we purposely took the opposite course was to demonstrate, on the 'brick' approach, how all of the aspects of a single lease could be accounted for in a self-contained manner.

2.42 Going back to the investment period method, (paragraph 2.40), it is the gross income which is allocated (in Table 20) between years using the same 'net cash investment' figures we already used in paragraph 2.26 (where we were using them to allocate equity extractions).

$$\frac{30,254}{81,765} \quad \times \quad 3,490 \quad = \quad 1,291$$

$$\frac{22,902}{81,765} \quad \times \quad 3,490 \quad = \quad 978$$

$$\frac{16,649}{81,765} \quad \times \quad 3,490 \quad = \quad 711$$

$$\frac{9,825}{81,765} \quad \times \quad 3,490 \quad = \quad 419$$

$$\frac{2,135}{81,765} \quad \times \quad 3,490 \quad = \quad \frac{91}{3,490}$$

Table 20
Calculation of the gross income figures to be recognised in each year of the five year lease term using the investment period method.

Using that allocation of the gross income between years gives a profit and loss account looking like the top presentation in Table 21. It can be seen that this is a slightly slower pattern of income recognition than that produced by the actuarial method after tax, (from paragraph 2.35), whose result it is convenient to repeat in the bottom half of Table 21.

Investment period method

	Year 1	Year 2	Year 3	Year 4	Year 5	Total
Rentals	2,688	2,688	2,688	2,688	2,688	13,440
Sale proceeds					50	50
Capital repayment	(1,397)	(1,710)	(1,977)	(2,269)	(2,647)	(10,000)
Gross income	1,291	978	711	419	91	3,490
Interest	(1,045)	(790)	(574)	(338)	(72)	(2,819)
	246	188	137	81	19	671
Current tax	956	(172)	(371)	(546)	(103)	(236)
Deferred tax	(1,042)	106	323	517	96	nil
Net tax charge	(86)	(66)	(48)	(29)	(7)	(236)
Post-tax profit	160	122	89	52	12	435

Actuarial method after tax

	Year 1	Year 2	Year 3	Year 4	Year 5	Total
Rentals	2,688	2,688	2,688	2,688	2,688	13,440
Sale proceeds					50	50
Capital repayment	(1,329)	(1,701)	(2,004)	(2,306)	(2,660)	(10,000)
Gross income	1,359	987	684	382	78	3,490
Interest paid	(1,045)	(790)	(574)	(338)	(72)	(2,819)
	314	197	110	44	6	671
Current tax	956	(172)	(371)	(546)	(103)	(236)
Deferred tax	(1,066)	103	332	530	101	nil
Net tax charge	(110)	(69)	(39)	(16)	(2)	(236)
Post-tax profit	204	128	71	28	4	435

Table 21
Lessor's profit and loss accounts compared, using investment period method and actuarial method after tax. Five year lease, £8,500 financed by borrowing and £1,500 by equity. £50 not rebated to lessee out of proceeds of sale of asset.

At a mechanical level, the investment period method necessitates our recalculating the deferred tax line, because the timing differences alter.

The investment period method's applicability where non-leasing companies engaged in isolated leasing transactions

2.43 The investment period method is founded, as is the actuarial method after tax, on the principle that the lessor should earn a constant rate of return through successive periods on his net cash investment in the lease. That is the basic requirement in the accounting bodies' SSAP 21 in relation to the lessor's accounts. What gave the investment period method its popularity in the 1970s and early 1980s, (before the tax changes in the 1984 budget), was that its use was not confined only to companies whose sole or main activity was leasing. Such leasing companies were of course accustomed to thinking, and their computers were programmed to show, that each lease was funded partly with borrowings and partly by the use of the company's own equity — and that the proportions of each were usually the same, at least at the start of each lease. Other companies which saw leasing as much a method of delaying tax payments as of earning

		Borrowing at start of period	Rental paid	Borrowing after rental	Interest payable	Borrowing at end of period
Yr 1	Qtr 1	10,000	672	9,328	317	9,645
	Qtr 2	9,645	672	8,973	305	9,278
	Qtr 3	9,278	672	8,606	292	8,898
	Qtr 4	8,898	672	8,226	279	8,505
				35,133	1,193	
Yr 2	Qtr 1	8,505	672	7,833	266	8,099
	Qtr 2	8,099	672	7,427	252	7,679
	Qtr 3	7,679	672	7,007	238	7,245
	Qtr 4	7,245	672	6,573	223	6,796
				28,840	979	
Yr 3	Qtr 1	6,796	672	6,120	208	6,332
	Qtr 2	6,332	672	5,660	192	5,852
	Qtr 3	5,852	672	5,180	175	5,355
	Qtr 4	5,355	672	4,683	158	4,841
				21,647	733	
Yr 4	Qtr 1	4,841	672	4,169	141	4,310
	Qtr 2	4,310	672	3,638	123	3,761
	Qtr 3	3,761	672	3,089	104	3,193
	Qtr 4	3,193	672	2,521	85	2,606
				13,417	453	
Yr 5	Qtr 1	2,606	672	1,934	65	1,999
	Qtr 2	1,999	672	1,327	44	1,371
	Qtr 3	1,371	672	699	23	722
	Qtr 4	722	672			
			50	nil	nil	nil
				3,958	132	
			13,490		3,490	

Table 22

Lessee's cashflow calculated (unlike that in Table 1) on a basis taking into account an additional payment of £50 at the end of the lease term, that being an analogue for the lessor's receipts of not only the £672 quarterly rentals in advance, but also the net £50 retained out of the asset's sale proceeds.

profits, tended to see the activity as ancillary to the company's main trade, and as wholly financed by borrowing. In these circumstances it is not possible to apply the actuarial method after tax, which can only be used when equity is injected and later extracted.

Further income recognition methods for finance leases

2.44   In addition to the actuarial method after tax, and the investment period method, there are two further possibilities. Each is described as a 'before tax' method, for reasons which will become apparent as we look at the calculations. The first is the 'actuarial method before tax', and its calculations come direct from the lease cashflow which omitted to take tax into account, that is to say the 'lessee-type' cashflow in paragraph 2.02. However, unfortunately, that cash flow also failed to take into account the further point which we have built into our lessor's example, namely that the final quarter's rental receipt in year 5 is boosted by the excess of sale proceeds over rebates, so that it is effectively £722 in place of £672. If we are to make all of the figurework comparable in the lessor examples we are working through, we do need to recalculate the 'before tax' cashflow appropriately, (see Table 22).

2.45   It is obvious that each year's interest will be proportionate to the average of the net cash investment, if the latter is found from the totals, per annum, of the borrowings. On that basis, it is said that a gross income line for the lease lifted from Table 22, and used as the basis of a profit and loss account as shown in Table 23 meets the requirement that that income reflects a constant rate of return on the net cash investment:

	Year 1	Year 2	Year 3	Year 4	Year 5	Total
Rentals	2,688	2,688	2,688	2,688	2,688	13,440
Sale proceeds					50	50
Capital repayment	(1,495)	(1,709)	(1,955)	(2,235)	(2,606)	(10,000)
Gross income	1,193	979	733	453	132	3,490

Table 23
Lessor's profit and loss account showing gross income derived from the actuarial method before tax figures in Table 22.

We do not need to go on to show the interest payable and the tax figures for this profit and loss account, all of which follow quite normally. The final accounting method is the 'rule of 78', the calculations for which were set out in paragraph 2.13 for the 'lessee-type' example. They also need marginal recalculation for the same reasons indicated above, and would then produce a profit and loss position as in Table 24.

	Year 1	Year 2	Year 3	Year 4	Year 5	Total
Rentals	2,688	2,688	2,688	2,688	2,688	13,440
Sale proceeds					50	50
Capital repayment	(1,402)	(1,696)	(1,990)	(2,284)	(2,628)	(10,000)
Gross income	1,286	992	698	404	110	3,490

Table 24

Lessor's profit and loss account showing gross income derived on the rule of 78 basis, (see Table 5).

The accounting choices available to lessors – the figures compared

2.46 We thus have four methods (shown in Table 25) which are said to be acceptable for lessors' calculations of the gross income line.

	Year 1	Year 2	Year 3	Year 4	Year 5	Total
Actuarial method after tax (2.35)	1,359	987	684	382	78	3,490
Investment period method (2.42)	1,291	978	711	419	91	3,490
Actuarial method before tax (2.45)	1,193	979	733	453	132	3,490
Rule of 78 method before tax (2.45)	1,286	992	698	404	110	3,490

Table 25

Comparison of lessor's gross income lines using four possible methods of accounting for a five year lease, £672 rentals quarterly in advance, and £50 not rebated to lessee out of proceeds of asset's sale.

It is necessary to make some comments on the differences, and on why one or other may be preferable in specific circumstances. The first point to be clear about is that all of these figures are analogues for interest receivable by the lessor on his notional loan to the lessee, which itself is thought of as proportionate to the lessor's net cash investment in the lease, (together in the case of the first method with his equity commitment into the lease).

Comments on the comparison of lessors' figures

2.47 However, the aggregate over the five years remains the same in every case, (the rate at which this interest-analogue calculated is appropriately greater in those instances in which the net cash investment has been reduced by what is effectively a free loan from the tax authorities):

- Therefore, if that net cash investment is not reduced by any early tax repayments, one would expect to see relatively larger 'interest' figures in the middle to later years, and relatively smaller ones at the front end. This explains why the actuarial method before tax is the most conservative of the four, recognising more income later in the lease term than the others.

- The rule of 78 is an approximation rather than a true calculation. It is a fact that it tends to recognise income earlier than the other 'before tax' method – and this would become even more apparent if it were applied to a lease term longer than we have illustrated, or at interest rates higher than we have used. It is always necessary to take care when this method is used that too much income is not released too early in the lease.

- Generally the two after tax methods can be expected to produce answers very much in line with each other, but in our example there is a particular reason for their divergence.

- That reason is the considerable difference we chose to build in between the level of interest on external borrowing (3.57 percent per quarter, this being a pre-tax rate), and the level of the equity reward (at 4 percent per quarter post-tax). In the cashflow calculations we used to illustrate the actuarial method after tax, we made the assumption that the aggregate extraction of equity amounts, (underlying equity originally introduced, plus the reward on this), would be in proportion to the application of funds to the repayment of borrowing. That assumption itself would not appear to cause any particular slanting of profit recognition towards the front end. However the second part of our assumption was that the equity reward was to be at a considerably higher rate than the interest on borrowings, 4 percent. It is when one calculates how much of a stream of extractions is underlying equity, and how much is reward at as high a rate as 4 percent per quarter, that one sees the degree to which this 'skews' profits towards the early years. This is the reason why our particular actuarial method after tax calculations produced a much more front-ended profile than did the investment period method calculations.

- Given that there will, in all cases, be an acceleration of tax writing down allowances on the leased asset in front of the lessee's 'capital repayments', the lessor's actual tax liabilities will lag behind his accounting income. (He will start off with the need to make a provision for deferred tax, and will be able to release this as the lease term progresses). But of course his tax advantage is a real one from the point of view of the cash he has available to reduce borrowings.

- If tax rates were higher than 35 percent, and/or if the writing down allowance were greater than 25 percent, then the extent of this tax advantage would be greater; or to express it differently, the speed at which the lessor was able to reduce borrowings at the front end of the lease term would be greater – and this would have the effect of increasing the proportion of income recognised at the front, and decreasing later years' income.

- Our example achieved the maximum tax advantage possible within the 35 and 25 percent tax regime, by its assumption that the lessor incurred his expenditure on the last day of his accounting period, rather than the first, thus obtaining his first writing down allowance a full year earlier than would otherwise have been the case. This point meant that our 'after tax' methods produced results which were less conservative – without that assumption, it is likely that neither of these after tax methods would have produced any significantly greater 'front ending' than the actuarial method before tax.

Finally, although the statement is made above that the two after tax methods can generally be expected to produce broadly similar results, there is one further set of circumstances in which they will not do so. The actuarial method after tax allocates the whole of the income arising from the lease over the periods in which the lessor has external borrowings. The investment period method does the same – except that for periods in which the lessor's cashflow 'becomes positive', and he is able to invest the surplus cash to earn interest income, the investment period method leaves that income in the years in which it arises. The actuarial method after tax could be seen as less conservative, in bringing that interest income forward into the earlier years of the lessor's 'negative' cashflow.

Finance leasing through an intermediate lessor

2.48 There are occasions where a finance leasing transaction may be done through a chain of two or more lessors. For convenience we could call the legal owner of the asset the head-lessor, and the company to which it leases that asset the intermediary. The intermediary itself then leases the asset on to the end-user. Two possible reasons for the establishment of such a chain are:

- The intermediary is itself in business as a lessor, but does not want to take this particular lease onto its own books – perhaps because it is unsure whether it has the tax capacity to absorb the business, or because its own borrowing capacity is near its limit. On the other hand it does not want to lose its good customer (the end-user) to the head-lessor who is a rapacious competitor.

- Alternatively, the intermediary is itself a manufacturer of the goods concerned, and wishes its customer (the end-user) to think that it is able not only to produce the goods, but also to provide financial assistance to customers who wish to obtain possession and use through leasing instead of through outright purchase. In this case the head-lessor could be the leasing subsidiary of the intermediary's own friendly neighbourhood bank.

The head-lessor accounts for his notional loan to the intermediary as a 'receivable' on his own balance sheet, as we would expect; and also accounts for the income from the finance lease in one of the ways we have been looking at in the preceding paragraphs. His business activity, and his accounting for it, is identical to that of any lessor engaged in finance leasing. Similarly, the end-user is in exactly the same position, commercially and in his accounting procedures, as any lessee under a finance lease. He capitalises the asset on his balance sheet, showing against it the obligation to the intermediary as if it were a loan received from the latter. And he debits to his profit and loss account the 'finance charges' and 'depreciation', all as explained in paragraph 2.06.

2.49 Common sense indicates that the lessee is likely to be in a neutral position, his outflows of cash to the head-lessor being matched by inflows from the end-user; perhaps the second might be marginally larger than the first, as a reward from the head-lessor for the intermediary's having introduced the business. If the intermediary is not in any real sense a link in the chain − if the documentation prevents him from suffering loss should the end-user default, and put such loss onto the shoulders of the head-lessor − then one could say that the intermediary was acting as no more than a broker bringing together the other two parties, and that the lease was in effect made direct between those two. In these circumstances it would be realistic for the intermediary to bring the 'introductory commission' into his profit and loss account, either at the start of the lease or through its term, but reasonable also that the intermediary would show neither asset nor liability on his own balance sheet. But if, on the other hand, the intermediary is firmly welded into the chain between head-lessor and end-user, then:

- As a lessee from the head-lessor, he should show on his balance sheet the notional loan received from the head-lessor.

- As a lessor to the end-user, he should show a receivable from the latter. Because the intermediary is neither the owner of the asset nor the person who incurred the capital expenditure on its acquisition, he would not be entitled to claim the tax writing down allowances on it. For this reason, it would be appropriate for the intermediary to use the 'before tax' calculations not only in calculating how much of his own payments to the head-lessor were principal and how much interest, but also to split the amounts he received from the end-user. (This is the paragraph 2.02 schedule, not that in paragraph 2.24). The asset and liability would thus match exactly in the intermediary's balance sheet, but it is not permissible under the Companies Acts for a company to net off assets and liabilities against each other.

- In his profit and loss account the intermediary would show income from the end-user, and expense to the head-lessor, the most logical levels of each being the 'gross income' as calculated under the actuarial method before tax, paragraph 2.45.

- What the intermediary would not do, however, is to double up the figures on his balance sheet by showing an asset and liability in respect of his lease from the head-lessor, and another borrowing and receivable in respect of his lease on to the end-user.

Finance leasing through an intermediate lessor when the contracts differ

2.50 But there can be occasions when the profiles of the two finance leases will be different. Suppose for instance that we have a situation like this:

- The intermediary is a lessor company, but does not want to take the lease which follows onto its own books, in part because it is uncertain of the level of its tax capacity, and in part because it is in danger of over-extending its borrowing limits.

- The lease which its end-user has asked the intermediary to write is one over five years, for an item costing £10,000, and at a quarterly interest rate which the end-user accepts will have to be 3.415 percent per quarter. Both he and the intermediary agree to take into account in their calculations an expected sale proceeds figure of £2,500, of which £2,450 will be passed back to the end-user as a rebate of rentals. All that is fairly familiar, but what is different is that this is the second item financed in this way for the end-user, and as a result of the rebate he has just received on his first lease, he wants to pay, immediately, an extra front-end rental of £2,500. (He is motivated at least in part by the belief that the deductibility of this rental payment will effectively save him having to pay tax on the rebate from the first lease). If he does pay off, at the start, a quarter of the intermediary's net cash investment, he expects, needless to say, that his rents will be reduced by a quarter from £672 to £504 per quarter.

- If the end-user put the £2,500 rebate he has received into a bank deposit, and tried to use it, and the interest on it, to pay the full rentals on a net cash investment of £10,000 by the intermediary, he (the end-user) knows that the rate of interest the bank would offer him would not be sufficient. What he is proposing, however, would save the intermediary's own bank interest, and shrink his total borrowings at least in the short term, in the way that the table in paragraph 2.52 makes clear. (The end-user makes all this sound as reasonable and persuasive as any farmer who wants to change his old combine harvester for a new model, and knows that there is still a considerable value in the old one).

2.51   There does appear to be an alternative way of achieving the transaction, which is for only two parties to be involved. We will still call them the intermediary and the end-user, but make a mental note that it is the intermediary who actually borrows to buy the asset. If the end-user wants immediate tax deductibility for the extra £2,500 at the front end, the implication is that this must be clearly described in the lease as a payment of rent – and that in turn implies that the intermediary would be subject to tax on it at the same point. This would make the lease a very tax-inefficient one, and the intermediary would probably not wish to consider it. There is then an alternative to the alternative. The £2,500 paid by the end-user could be described as a 'contribution' towards the capital expenditure to be incurred by the intermediary on the purchase of the asset. Section 154 of the Capital Allowances Act 1990 says that a "contributor" can get tax writing down allowances in respect of his contribution, and section 153 denies the recipient of such a "subsidy" the allowances on so much of his capital expenditure as is met by the subsidy. This removes the tax-inefficiency for the intermediary, but leaves the end-user writing down his £2,500 by 25 percent per year instead of getting a full deduction for the whole immediately.

2.52   So let us look at the end-user's suggestion in paragraph 2.50 to see if it does actually work, and whether it does so for all the parties. First, we are envisaging the intermediary paying rentals totalling £2,688 per year to the head-lessor but, (leaving aside the £2,500 for the moment), receiving rentals totalling only £2,016 per year from the end-user. The intermediary's shortfall is thus £672 per annum. It is easy to calculate that if the intermediary were to use the £2,500 to reduce his own borrowings, and by doing so were to save himself interest at 3.415 percent per quarter, he could make good this £672 shortfall, in part by allowing his borrowings to creep up to where they would otherwise have been, and in part by using the interest savings. The calculations show that the £2,500, together with interest of £860 on the varying amounts of it, produce the necessary £3,360, being five years at £672 (Table 26). One would need to expand the calculations onto a quarter by quarter basis, rather than summarising them by years, if the interest calculations are to be proved.

Initial reduction of borrowings	£2,500
Year 1 interest saving	293
	2,793
Year 1 cash drawn	672
	2,121
Year 2 interest saving	241
	2,362
Year 2 cash drawn	672
	1,690
Year 3 interest saving	181
	1,871
Year 3 cash drawn	672
	1,199
Year 4 interest saving	112
	1,311
Year 4 cash drawn	672
	639
Year 5 interest saving	33
	672
Year 5 cash drawn	672
Final alteration in borrowing level	nil

Table 26

Calculations to show that £2,500, with interest on it, produce a 'drawable' total of £3,360.

That does not look unsatisfactory (Table 26), although the actual interest rate we have assumed our illustrative lessors to be paying throughout all our examples has been 3.57 percent per quarter rather than 3.415 percent, (see paragraph 2.25 – exactly 15 percent per annum on a compounded basis). So the intermediary would obtain a modest advantage out of the differential in rates. We next need to think about the accounting positions of the parties, although that of the head-lessor is no particular worry; it is no different from what it has always been.

2.53 The position in the end-user's accounts is as follows. We first need to put together for the end-user a set of figures which is consistent with the basis we set out in paragraph 2.44 except that it shows his additional, up-front rental. (Those paragraph 2.44 figures will remain unchanged for the head-lessor, in the scenario we are now envisaging). The £50 difference between the sale proceeds and the rebate of rentals was dealt with in paragraph 2.44 as if it had been a straightforward 'rental' received by the lessor. Therefore, we will in these end-user's figures treat the end-user as paying an extra £50 of rentals in year 5, and as if the rebate he receives on the sale of the leased asset is £2,500 not £2,450. Unless we make these changes in the detailed way we show the parties' positions, the inconsistencies would bedevil our attempts to identify what was really happening. We can then assume that the end-user is charging as depreciation amounts aggregating £10,000, that is the cost of the new asset, and charging as a financial expense the excess of his total rental payments (including the £50) over this. The revised, before tax, cashflow which reflects all of this, including the payment of his extra £2,500 at the front end, is as in Table 27.

		Borrowing at start of period	Rental paid	Borrowing after rental	Interest payable	Borrowing at end of period
Yr 1	Qtr 1	10,000	3,004	6,996	239	7,235
	Qtr 2	7,235	504	6,731	230	6,961
	Qtr 3	6,961	504	6,457	220	6,677
	Qtr 4	6,677	504	6,173	211	6,384
					900	
Yr 2	Qtr 1	6,384	504	5,880	201	6,081
	Qtr 2	6,081	504	5,577	190	5,767
	Qtr 3	5,567	504	5,263	179	5,442
	Qtr 4	5,442	504	4,938	168	5,106
					738	
Yr 3	Qtr 1	5,106	504	4,602	156	4,758
	Qtr 2	4,758	504	4,254	144	4,398
	Qtr 3	4,398	504	3,894	132	4,026
	Qtr 4	4,026	504	3,522	120	3,642
					552	
Yr 4	Qtr 1	3,642	504	3,138	107	3,245
	Qtr 2	3,245	504	2,741	93	2,834
	Qtr 3	2,834	504	2,330	78	2,408
	Qtr 4	2,408	504	1,904	63	1,967
					341	
Yr 5	Qtr 1	1,967	504	1,463	48	1,511
	Qtr 2	1,511	504	1,007	33	1,040
	Qtr 3	1,040	504	536	18	554
	Qtr 4	554	504			
			50	nil	nil	nil
					99	
			12,630		2,630	

Table 27
Cashflow for lessee paying a rental of £3,004 at start of a five year lease, and quarterly rentals in advance thereafter of £504, with an end payment of £50.

2.54 It is when we come to the intermediary's accounts that things start to become interesting. For completeness, we set out in Table 28 how that intermediary arrives at his 'gross income', and what for want of a better term we might call his 'gross expense'. The former comes from the cashflow in paragraph 2.53, and the latter from that in 2.44.

		Income	Expense
Year 1	*Rentals*	4,516	2,688
	less capital repayment	3,616	1,495
			1,193
	less interest saving		293
		900	900
Year 2	*Rentals*	2,016	2,688
	less capital repayment	1,278	1,709
			979
	less interest saving		241
		738	738
Year 3	*Rentals*	2,016	2,688
	less capital repayment	1,464	1,955
			733
	less interest saving		181
		552	552
Year 4	*Rentals*	2,016	2,688
	less capital repayment	1,675	2,235
			453
	less interest saving		112
		341	341
Year 5	*Rentals*	2,016	2,688
	Proceeds not rebated	50	50
	less capital repayment	1,967	2,606
			132
	less interest saving		33
		99	99

Table 28

Income and expense sides of the profit and loss account of an intermediate lessor, obtaining the asset by paying rentals of £672 in advance per quarter and leasing it on for rentals receivable of £3,004 at the front end, followed by quarterly rentals of £504 per quarter. £50 of sale proceeds of asset not rebated to lessee, but a like amount not received from asset's owner. The initial rental received, to the extent not needed to pay rentals to asset's owner, deposited to earn interest – until needed to pay those later rentals.

The intermediary's accounting, both for income and expense, seems clearly to follow the rules. And the fact that he does not appear to suffer any disadvantage by following them, seems also to make it rational for him to offer what help he can to the end-user. What the latter is seeking is the commercial benefit of being able to use surplus cash from the previous asset's disposal in the most effective way – both as respects maximising his saving of rents, and optimising his tax position.

The effects of taxation on leasing through an intermediary when contracts differ

2.55   In the circumstances that the head-lessor wanted to receive 'flat' quarterly rentals of £672 through a five year year lease term, but the end-user wanted to pay an extra £2,500 at the front and then to pay only £504 per quarter, we saw over the course of the previous three paragraphs that so far as cash, and accounting, were concerned:

* the head-lessor's position was completely unaffected by this proposed change 'down the chain';

* the end-user could save finance charges to the extent of £860 (paragraph 2.52) by paying the extra £2,500 at the front;

* the intermediary's accounts, and cash, remain in perfect balance.

It is now necessary to consider the tax positions of each of the three parties. The head-lessor's computation is exactly the same (Table 29) as was set out in paragraph 2.23.

	Year 0	Year 1	Year 2	Year 3	Year 4	Year 5	Total
Allowance	(2,500)	(1,875)	(1,406)	(1,055)	(791)	127	(7,500)
Rentals	–	2,688	2,688	2,688	2,688	2,688	13,440
Rebate	–	–	–	–	–	(2,450)	(2,450)
Interest	–	(1,045)	(790)	(574)	(338)	(72)	(2,819)
Profit/(loss)	(2,500)	(232)	492	1,059	1,559	293	671
Tax payable	–	–	172	371	546	103	236
Tax repayable	(875)	(81)	–	–	–	–	–

Table 29
Tax computation for head-lessor, owning asset leased out over five years at £672 per quarter in advance, receiving sale proceeds of £2,500 and rebating £2,450 of those proceeds to the lessee.

But we omitted, (and said we had done so), when we first set out that computation to explain why it appeared different from any other taxpayer's — why it appeared not to start from an accounting profit, nor to proceed by making what adjustments to that profit the tax law requires.

2.56 The answer is simply that, in paragraph 2.23, we had not got as far as quantifying accounting profits. It is perfectly easy to arrive at the same taxable (and tax relievable) figures in an 'ordinary' computation (Table 30).

	Year 0	Year 1	Year 2	Year 3	Year 4	Year 5	Total
Pre-tax profit *para 2.35*	nil	314	197	110	44	6	671
Deduct sale proceeds dealt with in cap allces calc	–	–	–	–	–	2,500	2,500
	–	314	197	110	44	(2,494)	(1,829)
Add Cap repay'ts para 2.35	–	1,329	1,701	2,004	2,306	2,660	10,000
	–	1,643	1,898	2,114	2,350	166	8,171
Deduct Cap all'ces para 2.21	2,500	1,875	1,406	1,055	791	(127)	7,500
	(2,500)	(232)	492	1,059	1,559	293	671

Table 30
Tax computation for the head-lessor owning an asset leased out for rentals of £672 per quarter in advance, receiving £2,500 of sales proceeds and rebating £2,450 of that figure to the lessee. The computation proceeds by adjusting the profits shown under the actuarial method after tax, Table 18.

(Note that 'Capital allowances' is a collective description of the depreciation allowances permitted under tax law, of which the 'writing down allowances' referred to in paragraph 2.21 are only one form). The point of setting out that computation in that form is to remind ourselves that it, and no other, is actually specified by tax law; to quote Lord Reid in *BSC Footwear Ltd v Ridgway,* (1971) 47 TC at page 524:

"It is well settled that the ordinary principles of commercial accounting must be used except insofar as any specific statutory provision requires otherwise."

Or in other words, one first identifies profits using ordinary commercial principles, and then one adjusts them to the extent the tax law requires — by disallowing accounts depreciation, for instance, and substituting capital allowances. In the foregoing computation, the law requires that the £2,500 be taken out of the computation of profits, on the basis that it is a 'capital' item to be dealt with through the capital allowances calculation. Secondly the head-lessor has, (by regarding his asset as a receivable from the intermediary rather than an item of plant or machinery which is what he actually spent money on, and legally owns), charged what would otherwise have been called depreciation under the name of 'capital repayments'. For an asset owner entitled to capital allowances, any accounting deduction for 'depreciation' of that asset is clearly disallowable – because the capital allowances are a substitute not an addition.

2.57 We see the same process of adjusting ordinary commercial profits to arrive at tax-acceptable results for the end-user – results based on the activities he is actually engaged in, rather than the analogue 'borrowing and investing' in plant or machinery. Since we do not have a full profit and loss account for the end-user, only the deductions he shows in that account for the leased asset, it is only in that respect that we can deal with his adjustments (Table 31).

	Year 1	Year 2	Year 3	Year 4	Year 5	Total
Depreciation and finance charges para 2.53	(2,900)	(2,738)	(2,552)	(2,341)	(2,099)	(12,630)
Rebate of rentals	–	–	–	–	2,500	2,500
	(2,900)	(2,738)	(2,552)	(2,341)	401	(10,130)
Add back deprec'n	2,000	2,000	2,000	2,000	2,000	10,000
Add back finance charges	900	738	552	341	99	2,630
	–	–	–	–	2,500	2,500
Deduct rentals paid	(4,516)	(2,016)	(2,016)	(2,016)	(2,066)	(12,630)
	(4,516)	(2,016)	(2,016)	(2,016)	434	(10,130)

Table 31

Tax computation for end-user, leasing asset for an initial rental payable of £3,004, followed by quarterly rentals in advance of £504. The effect of the necessary adjustments to the profit and loss account figures is to move the end-user's tax effective figures to his rentals paid (less rebate received).

(Note that, as explained in paragraph 2.53, the above figures treat the end-user as receiving a rebate of rentals of £2,500, but as paying a rental in year 5 of £50 more than would otherwise have been the case. This keeps everything consistent, and has no effect on the tax figures). What the above appears to show is that the 'reality' of the end-user's payment profile, and its tax deductibility, are one and the same – that he is entitled to his deduction at the front end for the extra £2,500 paid at that point.

2.58 And lastly we come to the tax position of the intermediary. On the basis of the figures we set out in paragraph 2.36, he has calculated his ordinary commercial profits to be as in Table 32.

	Year 1	Year 2	Year 3	Year 4	Year 5	Total
Gross income	900	738	552	341	99	2,630
Interest received	293	241	181	112	33	860
	1,193	979	733	453	132	3,490
Less 'gross expense'	1,193	979	733	453	132	3,490
	nil	nil	nil	nil	nil	nil

Table 32
Profit and loss account of the intermediate lessor, paying £672 quarterly in advance, and receiving an initial rental of £3,004 followed by quarterly rentals in advance of £504; depositing the excess cash received to earn interest, and using these funds to make up the shortfall between outgoings and income in later quarters.

The question is then what adjustments does the tax law require should be made to these (nil) figures to make them acceptable for tax purposes? The intermediary is not an asset owner, whose depreciation charges need to be disallowed, and who need to have capital allowances substituted in their place. He is a party who has a receivable from the end-user, and a payable to the head-lessor. The total rental payments he receives from the one, and makes to the second, each have a 'capital repayment' element, as well as a finance charge element. Only the latter elements should enter into his tax computation; and that is exactly what has happened. The

	Year 1	Year 2	Year 3	Year 4	Year 5	Total
Rentals received	4,516	2,016	2,016	2,016	2,066	12,630
Interest received	293	241	181	112	33	860
	4,809	2,257	2,197	2,128	2,099	13,490
Rentals paid	2,688	2,688	2,688	2,688	2,738	13,490
Profit	2,121					nil
Loss		(431)	(491)	(560)	(639)	

Table 33
The Inland Revenue's view of the intermediate lessor's tax computation, based not on profit and loss account figures adjusted as necessary for tax purposes, but ignoring those 'ordinary commercial accounting' figures and substituting cash receipts and payments.

intermediary has calculated, on ordinary principles of commercial accounting, how much of his receipts and payments fell to be regarded as income and as expense, and those are the figures set out above. The author does not believe that the intermediary's accounting results require adjustment for tax purposes, but he does immediately have to say that that is not the view of the Inland Revenue authorities. They claim that the intermediary's profits should be computed using rentals received and paid, rather than gross income and gross expense (Table 33).

We will see when we get to chapter 7, the section of this book dealing with tax complications and particularly with anti-avoidance, that this arises from one of those contentions by the Revenue Authorities that to counteract an advantage they believe the end-user had nefariously obtained, it is necessary that they should penalise the intermediary. This is the first of a number of warnings we will have to sound at various points in this book that it may sometimes be necessary for one party to a transaction to take an indemnity from the other – to cover the possibility of the first suffering tax which, if it was chargeable at all, should have fallen on the second.

The extent of the lessor's credit risk

2.59   The lessor's asset is, principally, a right to receive a flow of rentals, and a right to the reversion of the asset. He has incurred capital expenditure on the acquisition of an item of plant or machinery, and it belongs to him as a result. That is what entitles him to capital allowances for tax purposes. But the value to the lessor of that plant is that it should metamorphose into a stream of cash through the lease term. The lessee has agreed under the lease agreement that he will pay, throughout the lease term, the rentals called for – this undertaking is often referred to as 'the lessee's covenants' – but the implication of that phrase has changed to mean something subtly different; namely it is now more often taken to refer to the lessee's creditworthiness. A lessee having 'first class covenants' is thus the equivalent of a company whose rating in the US bond markets is triple-A, or a ship which is A-1 at Lloyds. The lessee's covenants are always by far the most important assurance the lessor has. Any security he may hold as protection against a lessee's default is a less attractive route for him to contemplate; but we do need to contemplate securities and defaults. One line of the lessor's security is that he can repossess the asset and sell it if the lessee breaches the terms of the lease, for instance by failing to pay rentals at the due dates. However, let us leave on one side for the moment, the possibility of the lessor's obtaining any substantial sum from such a sale. What would be the extent of the lessor's loss if the lessee defaulted at the end of, say, year 1 of the lease term ? It is easiest to see the answer to that by looking back at the illustration of the 'brick' in paragraph 2.33. The lessor is at that point carrying his asset, (the receivable, because we are ignoring any value there may be in the tangible plant), at a figure of £8,671. We can see that if the lessor were to sue the lessee, and to be awarded damages of that figure, let us say on day 1 of year 2, that would enable the lessor to meet his liabilities, and keep his own position whole. The figures can clearly be seen in the 'brick' itself (Table 34).

Cash award from the court		£8,671
add tax repayable in respect of year 1		81
		8,752
required to pay off external creditor		6,543
		2,209
required to reinstate original equity		
contribution to extent not already extracted		1,143
		1,066
award regarded by Revenue as sale		
proceeds of item of plant	8,671	
written down value of that plant		
after allowances for years 0 & 1	5,625	
amount taxable on sale in year 2	3,046	
liability at 35%		1,066

Table 34
The lessor's position on receipt of £8,671 'stipulated loss value' on a termination of the lease at end year 1.

That last part of the figurework is a very good illustration of what a deferred tax provision is about, and how it might (but would not normally) be crystallised; but that was not the main purpose of the figures. That purpose was to demonstrate that the carrying value of the lessor's asset is more than just a balancing figure. It is the price at which he can afford to exit from the transaction. If he does exit at the end of year 1, he has made, (and extracted), the aimed at profit for that year. If he exits with £8,671, he does not suffer any immediate loss, and nor does he lose the opportunity to make future profits. His ability to engage in an immediate repeat of the original transaction, or for that matter any other transaction, is unimpaired. Therefore, £8,671 is the figure against the loss of which the lessor needs to protect himself. By the end of year 2, we could prove to ourselves that the figure had declined to £6,970 – which can be read straight out of the brick – and by the end of year 3 declined further to £4,966. There are a number of protective devices the lessor can attempt to provide. That £8,671 is not identical to the lease creditor figure of £8,491 which the lessee is carrying in his balance sheet, because his accounting is based on a different (paragraph 2.02) cashflow as we well know. But the two figures are arrived at on similar principles. Both, for instance, are net of future finance charges – for reasons which must be abundantly clear. When we get to the 'stipulated loss value' in paragraph 4.27, we will find that £8,671, rather than the lessee's figure, is what the lessor is likely to wish to write into the lease agreement.

Provisions against bad and doubtful debts

2.60 Making a provision against bad and doubtful debts is a recognition of the likelihood that debts have become, or will go, bad; and a restructuring of the lessor's balance sheet to reflect that. In accounting terms, the amount provided reduces shareholders' funds, and shows up among the company's liabilities. It is a provision, rather than a reserve, in exactly the same senses as we explained in paragraph 2.31 in relation to the deferred tax provision. (It is possible for a company to segregate a part of its shareholders' funds into a reserve for bad debts, but that is not what we are considering here. Making a provision does affect the company's capital ratios, whereas creating a reserve would not do so). There are two methods of 'provisioning', and which the lessor adopts is likely to depend on the type of leases he is writing. If there are relatively few, substantial, transactions he should determine whether a provision is necessary and if so how large it needs to be, by assessing the quality of each individual receivable. If on the other hand, the lessor has a portfolio of tens of thousands of items, each of them relatively small (the example used is generally television sets although they are likely to be rented on operating leases rather than finance leases), then there is little possibility of doing other than using past experience to maintain a provision at an appropriate percentage of the carrying value of the portfolio. If losses arising from bad debts are then charged against a provision, (and any later recoveries credited to it), the accounting implications are simply that a charge will be needed to the profit and loss account at each year end in order to build up the account's balance to the necessary level; that is true whether that level has been decided by individual assessment of receivables or as a percentage.

2.61 It is sometimes argued that unacceptable accounting answers flow from the possibility that a debtor might be identified as doubtful relatively late in the lease term. For instance, if in the lease we are looking at, the debtor defaulted after paying the rental due on 31 December of year 4, (but before the accounts for that year had been prepared, so that it was necessary to provide in those accounts for the bad debt), it is clear that the amount needing to be provided would be £2,660. The income in year 4's accounts against which such a provision can be set is £42 pre-tax, £28 post-tax. It is therefore said that the accounting policy of recognising significant amounts of income at the front end of the lease is at fault, in that it leaves insufficient income to deal with bad debts later in the term.

In the author's view this is not a correct line of argument. The accounting policy for recognising profits, and that dealing with provisioning, are separate – each must be valid and correctly operated, but that does not mean that income cannot be recognised under the first until there is no possibility whatever that the debt might go bad. The accounting method which does do that is called 'cash accounting'. Although it is vital always to know at any time, and to plan ahead, what one's cash position is, it is not generally seen as a valid formula for financial accounting, or for recognising profits – in fact the wording of SSAP 2 quoted in paragraph 2.17 above specifically proscribes it. In this discussion so far we have treated the realisable value of the leased asset as negligible, and left it out of our reckoning. In practice, of course, its value must be brought into account in deciding what level of provision is necessary. That value may be realisable by way of sale, or by re-leasing: the asset may be one whose sale (or re-leasing) value moves in line with market movements, such for instance as a ship. The provisioning exercise is not easy, and its end result can have severely distortionary effects on the overall results of the company. One method of trying to limit the size of the fluctuations is to say that a provision once made will not be reduced, even if the asset securing the debt regains its value – but this can itself produce results as arbitrary. The only really firm guideline is that whatever basis the company does choose must thereafter be applied consistently from year to year.

Tax effects of bad and doubtful debt provisions

2.62   The question is sometimes asked whether the Inland Revenue will allow a deduction for a provision, in the circumstances that they regard the lessor's asset as an item of plant or machinery, and therefore as 'capital'. Tax law is based on a rigid system of segregating capital from 'revenue', and only bringing into the income tax or corporation tax computation income and expense which are regarded as being on 'revenue account'. The answer appears to be that Inspectors of Taxes do recognise the commonsense position; the lessor in setting up a provision for bad and doubtful debts is not creating a provision against a fixed asset – neither in the sense of a depreciation provision to recognise the asset's consumption in the course of its use in his business, nor in the sense of providing for a permanent diminution in its value necessitating a reduction in its balance sheet carrying value. The provision is made against debts. Those debts may have their origin in the lease agreement wrapped around the item of plant or machinery, but that is not the same as saying that the provision is against the value of the plant. It would be a valid Inland Revenue argument that a deduction could not be allowed if its effect were to 'anticipate losses'. The concept here is that if the lessor claims that the profit he would have made next year has been lost, or reduced, the tax authorities will only allow him to recognise that fact next year, not this. If he had before his year end agreed to make a sale forward, that is to say to deliver the goods concerned after the year end, and to be paid for them on such delivery, and then the market moved in such a way that he could have asked for a larger price had he not already committed himself at the lower, then that would be a loss, or reduction of profit, for the second year not the first. The lessor's debts over which there are doubts may be due only after his year end. The total amounts so due include an element in respect of the 'repayment of principal' which was outstanding at that year end, and a second element in respect of finance charges for periods after that year end. But his provision is only made in respect of the first element. He is not anticipating a loss of future finance charges when he provides up to the carrying value of the asset in any year's balance sheet. The Inland Revenue's concerns should therefore be limited to the question whether the bad and doubtful debt provision is 'specific'. This is a reference to the wording of the Taxes Acts, which allow a deduction only for "bad debts proved to be such, and doubtful debts to the extent they are respectively estimated to be bad.." Whilst the general rule is that a company should quantify its taxable profits under ordinary principles of commercial accounting, (and providing for doubtful debts is certainly a step in the application of those principles), the Revenue say that the specific statutory wording not only permits but requires them to set aside a 'percentage' provision on the basis that it has not been made for each debt "to the extent (it has been) respectively estimated to be bad". In practice, if the lessor's portfolio cannot be dealt with on any other basis than by use of percentages, and if he can show that the percentages he uses for the various types of business have not proved on past experience to be excessive, then it may be possible to agree that that is an acceptable way in which to make allowable 'estimates'.

Currency leases

2.63   One specific form of credit risk to which a lessor can become exposed is that of currencies fluctuating against sterling, on the assumption that it is in sterling that he keeps his own accounts and looks to pay dividends to his shareholders. But the oddity about working in currencies is that real gains, deficits and exposures are very often smaller than one expects, (or non-existent), while it is the accounting exposures that give rise to problems: that is to say the difficulties may arise when one translates currencies in order to put together sterling profit and loss accounts and balance sheets, as opposed to when one converts foreign banknotes into sterling ones. In this area there is no substitute for careful rationalisation and analysis.

2.64 Let us start once again at the lessor's brick, in paragraph 2.33. If we assume that the entire lease transaction was carried out in US dollars, and that the rate against sterling was $1.50 = £1 not only when the asset was acquired, but throughout the first year, then at the end of that first year the position would be:

	Balance sheet					Profit & Loss
	Liabilities			Assets		Original Equity
	External borrowing	Current tax	Deferred tax	Invesment in finance leases	New cash generated	
End yr 1 *sterling*	Cr 7418	Dr 956	Cr 1066	Dr 8671		Cr 1143
dollars	$11127			$13007		

- The rentals receivable would be $4,032 per annum for the ensuing four years, that is $16,128 in total. In addition to that the lessor expects to retain $75 out of the asset's disposal, bringing the aggregate to $16,203.

- The lessor's external borrowings would have been $12,750 at commencement, of which $11,127 would still be outstanding. The future repayments of that principal, together with the interest on the amounts outstanding in future periods of $2,661, would be $13,788.

- The difference between $16,203 and $13,788 is $2,415, equivalent, as one might expect if the $1.50 rate held, to £1,610.

- To that £1,610 can be added the sum recoverable from the Inland Revenue by the end of year 1 of £956, to make a total of £2,566. This is the amount necessary to cover:

original equity outstanding end year 1	£1,143
post tax profits of future years	231
both of which are to be extracted in future,	
and tax liabilities of future years (£172, 371, 546 and 103)	1,192
	2,566

On the expectation that the rate will hold, therefore, one can see that the transaction results in precisely the sterling profit that had been hoped for, and that the lessor has no exposure from inflows failing to match outflows. Another way of putting that last point would be to say that the lease was self-contained, self-balanced.

The lessor loses his balance if dollars weaken or strengthen

2.65 But that is not really true. The lease is not totally self-contained in

US dollars, because the lessor made his original injection of equity in sterling, and has other obligations to be met in sterling. He relies on being able to extract his equity, and its reward, in sterling; he also has to pay his UK taxes in sterling. So, what is his exposure if the rate US dollar weakens to $1.60 = £1 on 30 December year 1 (that is to say after he has received the rental on 30 September, and been charged the interest to 30 December, both of which we have accounted for throughout as being for the fourth quarter of year 1, but before he has received the rental on 31 December which we have accounted for as being for the first quarter of year 2). Let us assume the rate remains at that $1.60 level through the rest of the lease term:

- his four years' future rentals, and $75 net sale proceeds, aggregating $16,203 as in the previous paragraph will now be equivalent only to £10,127;

- the dollars needed to repay external borrowings, $13,788, will be equivalent to £8,617;

- the difference thus falls from £1,610 to £1,510;

- he still has £956 of tax recoverable from the Inland Revenue in respect of years 0 & 1, bringing the total available to £2,466;

- but, oddly, his tax payments for future years appear to fall further than one might expect, to £994. (Alternatively, there is an argument that they do not fall that far: we will analyse this question in due time). At present we will assume that it is correct that the total of future payments will be only £994;

- the lessor does therefore improve his overall profit in sterling terms:

available as above		£1,510
add tax repayments for years 0 & 1		956
		£2,466
less tax liabilities reduced as above		994
		1,472
original equity outstanding end year 1		1,143
		329
post tax sterling profit originally		
expected	231	
increase	98	
		329

That is the 'real' position; the lessor, on our assumptions, ends up with £98 more in his pocket than he expected.

Accounting when currencies change parity

2.66 But first it is sensible to enquire what the accounts would show at the end of year 1. That year's trading profit is not altered. It was earned in dollars worth $1.50 to the £1, and was extracted out of the lease at that rate. The balance sheet at the end of year 1, if the rate had remained at $1.50 could have been straightforwardly taken from the excerpt we showed in paragraph 2.64 from the 'brick':

Asset	*— Inv in finance leases*	*$13,007 at $1.50*	£8,671
Liabs	*— Original equity*		1,143
	External borrowing	*$11,127 at $1.50*	7,418
	Tax recoverable		(956)
	Deferred tax provision		1,066
			8,671

Let us now think through the effects of the dollar's weakening to $1.60 = £1:

- First, the balance sheet figures taken from the brick above do not include any reflection of the profits we had planned to recognise in future years. The post-tax sterling figures were originally £128, £71, £28 and £4, aggregating £231. When the lease was written in dollar terms, that became $346.

- When the rate changes, we can expect $346 to produce not £231, but £217.

- That is a decrease of £14 post-tax — £22 pre-tax, with a tax saving of £8.

2.67 We need at this point to remind ourselves, briefly, what is the theory behind a deferred tax account. If, up to a balance sheet date profits have been recognised in the accounts without there being a current liability to pay tax on them, *and* it seems that such a liability will occur in the future, then we set up a provision for that future liability. (The easiest example to illustrate this concept is that of capital allowances exceeding depreciation in the early years of a taxpayer's ownership of an asset, so that he pays tax on a figure less than his accounts profits, but where one would normally expect the position to reverse in later years). The deferred tax provision at the end of year 1 is not therefore a reflection of the tax on profits not yet recognised. But if we now think that there will be an overall fall of £198 in future tax payments, of which only £8 relates to profits not yet recognised, that means that the remaining £190 of tax saving must arise out of events up to the end of year 1 (that is to say out of the parity change). It is therefore appropriate to say that the deferred tax provision at that date can be reduced by £190, because that amount of liability will now not occur in the future, (the second of the two conditions noted above which justify the provision's creation). Thus the figures at $1.60 = £1 would become:

Asset	– *Inv in finance leases*	*$13,007 at $1.60*	£8,129
Liabs	– *Original equity*		1,143
	add exchange gain		
	(credited to reserves)		112
			1,255
	External borrowing	*$11,127 at $1.60*	6,954
	Tax recoverable		(956)
	Deferred tax provision	*(£1,066 – 190)*	876
			8,129

There are two things to be said about that revised balance sheet. First, we know that the lessor's cash position will be £98 better over the entire term of the lease. The above shows a 'gain' of £112, because his pre-tax and post-tax profits will be reduced in the next four years:

$536	*pre-tax at $1.50 would have been*	£357
$536	*at $1.60 will be*	335
		22
less tax saving as calculated above		8
reduction in post-tax profits after rate change		14

2.68   Secondly, the treatment follows one of the two methods defined as acceptable by Statement of Standard Accounting Practice No 20, which deals with accounting for exchange differences. The method concerned is called the 'net investment' method (that phrase seeming to have a strange fascination for accountants, and to be used to describe all manner of totally different things; see paragraph 2.36 for the completely different concept also described as net investment, namely the 'receivable' which the lessor carries in his balance sheet). In the currency context, the net investment method accepts that if, for instance, a sterling based company has a 'branch' in a non-sterling area, the stream of profits earned by that branch needs to be incorporated into the accounts of the whole company at the rates ruling when they are earned, but that changes in the sterling equivalent of the currency 'invested' in its branch by the company's 'head office' are not a part of the company's profits or losses for the year; they are dealt with by transfer direct into or out of the company's reserves. This seems self-apparent if, for instance, one envisages as an example not a company but a professional firm with a branch in New York. In the balance sheet of that branch at each of two consecutive year ends is the same receivable of $1,000. When the dollar is at $1.60 = £1, the sterling equivalent is £625. If the dollar were to strengthen again to $1.50, the receivable's sterling equivalent would be £667. The New York branch has made no profit locally, and is in no position to make any remittance to its head office in relation to this item. It is hard to see how the change in value could be characterised as a profit for the firm as a whole. The net investment method, by saying that that change in value is in effect a revaluation of the branch (put direct to reserves in the firm's accounts) recognises the truth of the matter namely that, with a stronger dollar, future New York profits and remittances should be worth more in sterling terms, thus making a revaluation of the branch realistic. It is not necessarily so immediately obvious that this accounting method is totally appropriate where one is dealing with:

- A currency lease, which admittedly produces a stream of dollar income, but which is less obviously autonomous than a New York branch.

- A net investment which, at the end of year 1 at any rate is partly financed by the Inland Revenue, and only partly by the lessor's own equity. (The external borrowing, being in dollars, is regarded as within the 'branch' and not as being part of the 'support' from its sterling 'head office').

- A situation in which a weakening dollar could be expected to reduce the stream of income (in sterling terms), and therefore to diminish the value of the net investment; but where that effect is more than cancelled out by the expected reduction in the level of future tax liabilities on that stream of income.

However SSAP 20 does make it clear that the word 'branch' is to be interpreted widely, and that it can include a group of assets, financed in currency, producing a stream of currency income. Indubitably, a dollar portfolio of leases would be a 'branch', even if an isolated lease might be questionable.

Tax when currencies change parity

2.69   The future tax liabilities, (that is to say those not already reflected in the balance sheet figures at the end of year 1), on the assumption that the dollar remained at $1.50 = £1, were quantified in paragraph 2.64 at £1,192. This can be arrived at by adding the figures shown in the 'brick':

liability on year 2's profits	£172
liability on year 3's profits	371
liability on year 4's profits	546
liability on year 5's profits	103
	1,192

Alternatively one can arrive at it by summarising (in Table 35) the dollar and sterling figures that go into the computations themselves for those years:

four years' rentals		$16,128	(£10,752)
less four years' interest	$2,661		(1,774)
rebate of rentals	3,675		(2,450)
		6,336	
		$9,792	
equivalent in sterling at $1.50 = £1		£6,528	(£6,528)
less capital allowances written down value at end year 1	£5,625		
sale proceeds ($3,750)	2,500		
difference is amount allowable during period		3,125	
four years' taxable profits		£3,403	
liability at 35 percent		£1,192	

Table 35
Future tax liabilities of the lessor not yet reflected in the balance sheet at end year 1 of the lessor, on the assumption that the exchange rate remains $1.50 = £1.

Capital allowances under UK tax legislation are based on the equivalent sterling of the asset's original dollar cost. Although parities may later change, the capital allowances do not. It makes sense therefore to calculate

four year's rentals		$16,128	(£10,080)
less four years' interest	$2,661		(1,663)
rebate of rentals	3,675		(2,297)
		6,336	
		$9,792	
equivalent in sterling at $1.60 = £1		£6,120	(£6,120)
less capital allowances written down value at end of year 1	£5,625		
sale proceeds ($3,750)	2,344		
difference is amount allowable during period		3,281	
four years' taxable profit		£2,839	
liability at 35 percent		£994	

Table 36
Recalculation of future tax liabilities on the assumption that the exchange rate moves to $1.60 = £1.

that part of the computation in sterling rather than dollars. When the dollar weakens to $1.60 = £1, the dollar figures in the first section of the computation do not change; it is their sterling equivalents which alter. So also does the sterling equivalent of the sale proceeds (Table 36).

That £994 is the figure we gave in paragraph 2.65 as the reduced liability following the parity change. We will continue with our examination of it in the next paragraph, but then in paragraph 2.71 *et seq.* come to the question whether it may not after all be correct.

2.70 It is clear that one could put the relevant figures from the $1.50 and the $1.60 computations together in a different form in order to show why the reduction in tax liabilities is as large as it is on that quite small change in parities:

Rentals, less interest and rebate	$9,792
add sale proceeds	3,750
	$13,542
equivalent at $1.50	£9,028
at $1.60	8,464
reduction in assessable profit	£564
reduction in liability at 35 percent	£198

The capital allowances based on the asset's original cost enter into the computation of the lessor's liabilities in each computation – but because they are unaltered by the parity change, they can be left out of account in our analysis of the reduction in tax liability resulting from that change. And that enables us to see that the curious dichotomy in UK tax laws between 'revenue' items treated in one way, and 'capital' items either wholly ignored or treated quite differently, can have very strange effects on the tax liabilities of companies affected by changes in exchange rates. A tax system which accepts that all income has been devalued by a parity change, and accepts the same for some but not all of the deductibles and allowances, is more or less bound to have strange results. There are however no universal rules or short-cuts to foretell what these results may be; analysis, and more analysis, is the only solution.

Gains or deficits on the repayments of currency borrowings

2.71 Why our figure of £994 for future tax liabilities may not be correct can be explained as follows:

- At the end of year 1, the outstanding principal of the external, dollar, borrowings was: $11,127

- At a continuing $1.50 rate, that would have been equivalent to: £7,418

- When the rate moves to $1.60, the sterling equivalent reduces to: 6,954

- In the same way that turning capital assets into more cash than they originally cost gives rise to a 'gain', so does repaying borrowings for less than they originally raised give rise to a 'gain':   £464

- That has no tax effects if the borrowings were 'on capital account' because such a gain does not fall within the lessor's profits subject to corporation tax; it is a capital item, excluded from the 'revenue' income and expense in the corporation tax computation. Nor does it fall within the scope of capital gains tax which deals only with the disposal of assets, not the repayment of liabilities.

- But if the borrowings were of a 'revenue' nature, then such a gain would itself be income of a 'revenue' nature, and included in the lessor's corporation taxable profits.

So the question which we must face is whether this was, or was not, a 'capital' borrowing, a question so arcane as to be meaningless to anyone other than an accountant or lawyer who specialises in tax.

Consider the three balance sheets in Table 37.

2.72 The first represents a bank, and as can be seen, forty percent of its total business is done in dollars. Commonsense indicates that if the dollar weakens from the $1.50 at which the above accounts were prepared, to $1.60, then the sterling equivalent of both the dollar borrowings and the dollar lending would shrink to £375. The bank would have made no gain and no loss on the change itself − but if its earnings on the dollar lending were 12 percent, and its cost of funds for the dollar borrowing was 9 percent, then its future profit stream would be only £11 per annum in place of £12. In this case tax law is clear and commonsensical; the bank cannot make a gain or suffer a loss when those to whom it has lent hand back to it the same numbers of dollars (equivalent to more or less sterling), so long as the bank has an obligation to repay those same dollars to those who had themselves deposited funds with it, (although repayment of such depositors can be achieved at an equivalent sterling that is different from the original). There is thus in this case no need to enquire whether the borrowings were capital or revenue, because that question is irrelevant where gains and losses are themselves impossible. The second balance sheet shows a company which has borrowed dollars to cover part of its needs for

	£		£
1.			
Shareholders funds	100	*Land and buildings*	100
Borrowings in sterling	500	*Commercial lending*	
in dollars ($600)	400	*in sterling*	500
		in dollars ($600)	400
	1,000		1,000
2.			
Shareholders funds	100	*Land and buildings*	100
Borrowings in sterling	500	*Current assets*	
in dollars ($600)	400	*(debtors, stocks)*	900
	1,000		1,000
3.			
Shareholders funds	100	*Land, buildings and plant*	800
Borrowings in sterling	500	*Current assets*	
in dollars ($600)	400	*(debtors, stocks)*	200
	1,000		1,000

Table 37

Balance sheets of three companies showing identical sterling capital and borrowings in sterling and dollars, but where it is clear that the use of the funds has been different.

financing its ordinary trading operations, carried on in the UK, and generating sterling income. The third, on the other hand, shows that at least part, if not the whole of the dollar borrowings has been used for capital assets.

2.73   One might think that if it were clear that the use of the funds was to be ordinary trading, (on 'revenue' account), this might indicate that the borrowings were themselves of a 'revenue' nature. But no, the courts have indicated that only in very special circumstances could the use of funds have a bearing on the categorisation of the borrowing. Perhaps that reasoning has at least some connection with the fact that uses of funds must always be difficult to establish, even initially, and that they undoubtedly change through time in any normal business situation. (Note that the quality of the asset given as security for a borrowing is even less relevant in deciding whether that borrowing is on capital account or of a revenue nature). The most significant features in the categorisation appear to be:

*   The term of the borrowing. If a company borrows for, say, five years without provision for repayment during those five years, that tends to indicate that it is looking to increase its capital resources as a company, not perhaps as clearly as would be the case if it issued equity, but

nevertheless clearly enough 'capital'.

• The type of the borrowing instrument, and the terms on which the borrowing is made. One cannot lay down simple rules, for instance that a three year term loan from a bank will never be extended and must always be regarded as 'short', whereas an issue of debentures on the stock market, capable of being transferred from one investor to another, can never be abruptly terminated by the borrowing company deciding to repay, (or to purchase in the market for cancellation). But the type of borrowing can be seen as having a bearing on the question we are trying to answer.

If we come back to our particular lessor, borrowing dollars which are to be repaid through the five year term of the dollar lease whose receivable they finance, there does appear to be every indication that the borrowing must be regarded as being on 'revenue' account. The length of the term fits that interpretation, as does the repayment through the five years and so does the nature of the borrowing. The contrary arguments could be that what is being financed is not, in law and from a tax viewpoint, a receivable but capital expenditure on an item of plant and machinery; but we know that use of the funds is not really relevant. Secondly, if this were the only asset in the leasing company concerned, it might be possible to argue that it needed to supplement its capital resources from £1,500 up to the £10,000 needed for its capital acquisition by borrowing capital funds of £8,500. That is an unconvincing argument if the borrowing one is looking at is a very small part of the company's drawing down of available credit, all of it on a revolving basis, from its bankers and other regular suppliers of finance.

2.74 What we therefore seem to be arguing ourselves towards is the acceptance that the 'gain' on the repayment of the company's borrowings is therefore taxable. If that is so, then the company's total future tax payments become:

Tax liability per the '$1.60' computation in paragraph 2.69 (Table 36)		£994
add liability on 'gain' in paragraph 2.71 which is now no longer a capital item excluded from the computation, but an ordinary item of income on 'revenue' account	£464	
liability at 35 percent		163
		1,157

Before the change in parity, we thought that those future tax payments were going to be £1,192. We now think that they will be £1,157. The reduction in tax liabilities has become £35. Of that figure, we know that £8 is the reduction in respect of profits which we have not yet recognised in the accounts. Therefore £27 is the part of the reduction which we can reflect by an immediate reduction in the deferred tax provision at the end of year 1. We could rewrite the '$1.60' balance sheet from paragraph 2.66, (taking the figures straight out of the 'brick') as follows:

Asset	– *Inv in finance lease $13,007 at $1.60*	£8,129
Liabs	– *Original equity*	1,143
	less exchange deficit dealt with through	
	reserves (£78 pre-tax, £27 tax saving)	51
		1,092
	External borrowing $11,127 at $1.60	6,954
	Tax recoverable	(956)
	Deferred tax provision (£1,066 - 27)	1,039
		8,129

What is different is the exchange deficit figure of £51; when we previously tried to draw up this table, we thought there was an exchange gain of £112. Now we think that the company's tax liabilities have only moved from £1,192 to £1,157 – (not from £1,192 to £994); we find that the £163 change in the anticipated tax liabilities is exactly matched by the £163 change in the level of exchange difference, from what we previously thought was an overall gain of £112, to a deficit of £51. At least the tax figures now make sense: overall there is a loss at the pre-tax level of £100, of which £78 is in the balance sheet at the end of year 1, and £22 will trickle through the later profit and loss accounts. The tax savings match that, £35 in total, of which £27 is in the year 1 balance sheet, and £8 will be in later profit and loss accounts.

2.75   But it is possible that a fuller rationalisation might help – to pull together what has been a less than simple eight paragraphs, and which still needs one more to wrap it up. When we stand at 31 December of year 1, looking forward at the flows of cash that we expect over the next four years, the dollar components look like this:

four year's rents	$16,128		
less interest	2,661		
	13,467		
add proceeds less rebate	75	at 1.50	at 1.60
	$13,542	£9,028	£8,464
repayment of borrowing	11,127	7,418	6,954
	$2,415	£1,610	1,510

That clearly shows the loss at the pre-tax level of £100 referred to above. It is helpful, however, to appreciate that those last three lines are an amalgam of the dollars which will flow through future years' profit and loss accounts, and those that are to go into the balance sheet at end year 1. If we put the inflows and outflows into separate columns for the balance sheet at the end of year 1, and for subsequent profit and loss accounts, the table becomes Table 38.

	Balance sheet	Profit & loss	Balance sheet	Profit & loss	
dollar inflow	$13,007	$535	$13,007	$535	
dollar outflow	11,127		11,127		
	$1,880	$535	$1,880	$535	
	at 1.50	at 1.50	at 1.60	at 1.60	
equivalent inflow	£8,671	£357	£8,129	£335	
equivalent outflow	7,418		6,954		
	1,253	357	1,175	335	a
less current tax					
payable		1,192		1,157	b
(recoverable)	(956)		(956)		
	2,209	(835)	2,131	(822)	
less deferred tax					
provided	1,066		1,039		c
(released)		1,066		1,039	
original equity	1,143		1,092		d
post-tax profits		231		217	e

Table 38
Summary of the results of the parity change, splitting the loss between that to be reflected in the balance sheet at end year 1, (at the pre-tax level £1,253 – £1,175 = £78), and to be reflected in future years' profit and loss accounts, (at the pre-tax level £357 – £335 = £22).

2.76 It is vital that we understand the book-keeping which the previous paragraph's presentation makes less than totally clear. In the balance sheet column, the £8,671 shown on the line captioned 'equivalent inflow' is of course an asset, namely a net investment in finance leases. When cash does flow in, pound notes become the asset, and the corresponding credit goes to eliminate the net investment in finance leases. On that basis, the balance sheet 'inflow' and 'outflow' are eliminated by such flows of cash. The current tax asset will similarly be eliminated by a cash receipt from the tax authorities, whilst the deferred tax liability will be released as a credit into profit and loss account. All these assets and liabilities are shown as being financed at the end of year 1 by the balance of the original equity put into the lease. On the other hand, the £357 on that same 'equivalent inflow' line, but in the profit and loss column, is not (yet) in the books in any form. When cash flows in, the credit for it will go to profit and loss account.

At line (a)   the final table in paragraph 2.75 shows the pre-tax deficit for the balance sheet at £78, being £1,253 - £1,175; and the decrease in the subsequent profits of £22 pre-tax is also clear, £357 - £335.

At line (b)   the aggregate decrease in payments of tax in the future is £35, being £1,192 - £1,157.

At line (c)   it is clear that the deferred tax provision is reduced by £27, being £1,066 - £1,039.

At line (d)   one sees the exchange deficit which is charged against reserves in the year 1 balance sheet, this being the post-tax figure of £51.

At line (e)   the £14 fall in post-tax profits for subsequent periods can be seen.

All of these figures hang together in the sense, for instance, that the difference between current tax provisions and deferred tax releases gives a net tax charge which is appropriate to the pre-tax profits. But more importantly, they hang together in the sense that one can see that a parity change in the form of a weakening of the dollar against sterling will, normally:

- create an immediate exchange deficit, to the extent that sterling equity and net sterling liabilities are as a result matched by dollar assets less liabilities which fall short of the sterling amounts;

- create a future position in which sterling profits are less than they would otherwise have been, because the dollars brought back and converted into sterling produce less;

- the tax position will not always follow these two points – but if it does not, then one needs to understand why it does not do so.

We began, in paragraph 2.63, saying that there was no substitute for rationalisation and analysis. If the explanations and illustrations in these last nine paragraphs have made nothing else clear, they have at least proved that.

Regional development, and similar, grants

2.77   There was a time when the availability of such grants was seen as creating difficulties over the pricing of leases for the items of plant involved, and as having a potentially distortionary effect on the accounts of the lessor companies. The reason for this lay in the manner in which grants of the type concerned were calculated and paid:

- The authorities could only pay the asset's owner, not the user, because they needed recourse to the asset itself if the conditions on which the grant had been paid ceased to be met, and it (or part of it) had to be repaid.

- However it was clear that the lessor who received, say, £2,000 towards the cost of a £10,000 item of plant was expected to pass on the whole £2,000 in the form of reduced rentals to the lessee, and if financing a net £8,000 item cost the lessor £2,792 (80 percent) in place of £3,490, (we can over-simplify here by ignoring the difference between the lessor's external and other finance), then the lessor was expected to pass on the full £698 saving to the lessee.

- Obviously if the lessee made a larger profit as a result of paying smaller rentals, then he should pay more tax on those profits.

- In terms of the lessor's incurring smaller interest bills, and receiving smaller 'gross income', that all made sense and one could see in the lessor's computations the necessary level of fiscal transparency.

- However similar fiscal transparency seems to have been lost from sight in relation to the 'capital' element of the transaction. The lessor bore only a net £8,000 of the asset's cost, and received taxable rentals reflecting that £8,000, but was nevertheless permitted to claim capital allowances on the full £10,000 of the cost.

The result was that the tax benefit to the lessor was not simply the timing one, (his tax allowances being available in advance of the substitute 'depreciation' he needed to charge against his profits), but was the value of allowances on expenditure he had not in effect borne. The extra capital allowances frequently turned his tax line, in aggregate for all the years of the lease's term, into a recovery rather than a charge. And that in turn meant that he could price his lease so as to make a pre-tax loss, still turned by that overall tax recovery into a post-tax profit. As already indicated the problem is now smaller than previously, partly because the changes in 1984 in the rates of corporation tax and of allowances have decreased the size of the tax advantage for lessors, and partly because grants of this type have become rare.

2.78 However, the accounting distortion was, and remains, capable of solution in one of two ways:

- The grant received can be treated for accounting presentation purposes as if it were income, at a grossed up equivalent figure. Releasing this into the profit and loss account through the term of the lease in an appropriate manner, and charging against it the notional tax 'charge' by which it has been grossed up, will produce the right relationship between the pre-tax, tax, and post-tax lines in the profit and loss accounts over the years.

- What it can be criticized for itself distorting is the level of the lessor's 'gross income', since it is at that line in the profit and loss account that the engrossed grant would be included. On an 'ordinary' £10,000 lease, the lessor's gross income reported in year 1 would be £1,359 and his interest paid £1,045, (the actuarial method after tax, per paragraph 2.35). It follows that for a lease qualifying for a 20 percent grant, the similar figures for the 'non-grant' part of the lease would be £1,087 gross income, and £836 of interest paid. If at the same time the lessor were to bring in the same proportions (that is to say £1,359 over £3,400) of a £2,000 grant, grossed up to £3,077, the gross income amount would be £1,198. His aggregate gross income in year 1 from the 'grant' and the 'non-grant' leases, the former boosted by a proportion of the engrossed grant, would therefore be £3,644, and his interest expense £1,881. If the make-up of the first of these is not made very clear, users of the accounts could get a very distorted view of the volume of leasing being written.

- The alternative presentation of grants is therefore to treat the £2,000 received as non-taxable income through the period of the lease. Since the Companies Act requires an explanation of any material reasons why the tax charge in the accounts may not appear to accord with the income included in those accounts, it will be possible for a knowledgeable reader to work out the volumes of leasing gross income, and of 'grant' income, included in the profit and loss account — even if the lessor does not spell this out.

Initial direct expenses

2.79 Lessors largely involved in writing individually tailored leases will inevitably incur very substantial levels of administrative costs before such leases are incepted, as we briefly indicated in paragraph 2.27; and the costs thereafter of collecting rentals and otherwise maintaining the lease will almost certainly be small in relation. Although these initial costs could be charged to profit and loss account as they are incurred, it is an acceptable alternative to carry some proportion of them forward to each later year of the lease's term so as to be able to achieve a 'matching' with the income generated by the lease concerned. That phraseology has been chosen carefully enough to indicate that if the effort to get a lease onto the books were to prove abortive, then the whole expense attributable to it must obviously be written off straight away, and not carried forward.

Maintenance, maintenance contracts and consumable stores used by the leased equipment

2.80 It is normal for a finance lessor to require, (as one of the term of the lease agreement), that the lessee keep the equipment in good repair and serviceable condition, 'fair wear and tear excepted', and that this be done at the lessee's own expense. In the case of higher technology items, although the financial effect of this would be largely unaffected, the degree of control that the lessor would otherwise lose over the quality of the maintenance work can be preserved if it is a condition of the lease that the lessee take out a maintenance contract for the full term of the lease with an approved company, (or with the equipment supplier himself). Quite apart from the greater efficiency that the normal, low-technology, arrangement can be seen as having for both lessor and lessee, (compared for instance with the alternative position in which the lessee would himself have to be forbidden to work on the equipment's maintenance, as well as being required to call in the lessor or his agents to do this work), putting the financial and other onus on the lessee is a part of the overall pattern identified by the accountancy bodies in their phrase that the lessee "has had transferred to him by its actual owner substantially all of the risks and rewards of the asset's ownership". In the case of leases of real property, (although most of these are likely to be operating leases rather than finance leases), the lessee's obligations to maintain the fabric of any building are normally described in the phrase "full repairing lease". Notice in particular that, both for equipment leases and the full repairing leases of real property, although fair wear and tear are excepted, this is itself over-ridden by the need for the asset to be kept currently serviceable. For instance, if a building is let for 99 years, but its lifts and lift machinery have an expected life of only 25 years, the tenant can expect to foot the bill for their entire replacement at years 25, 50 and 75: at year 99, however, he will be permitted to hand back the building to the landlord with its 24 year old lifts in it – provided that they are serviceable enough to be expected to last for one further year.

2.81   There are items of equipment which are frequently the subjects of leases, which require specific consumable stores for their operation, for instance the 'copy kits' which are needed to make some photocopiers work, or the thermofax paper for fax machines. Lessees may find that the equipment supplier, who may of course not be the same person as the lessor, insists on the right to supply these goods throughout the lease term. It is desirable from the lessee's point of view, but may not always be easy unless he goes to a different supplier and lessor, to:

- ensure that the agreement does not stipulate minimum quantities of consumables which are likely to exceed his needs;

- ensure that the price can be re-negotiated if alternative consumables drop in price during the lease term;

- ensure in particular that the consumables agreement does not extend in time beyond the point at which he expects to bring the leasing agreement itself to an end.

Exactly the same principles apply, *mutatis mutandis*, to the lessee's need to look at the terms of any maintenance contract he may be required to enter into, as described in the previous paragraph.

Insurance

2.82   Finance lease agreements normally put onto the lessee the obligation to insure the leased equipment for its full replacement value, against appropriate risks:

- fire and theft, in all cases;

- third party risks in many cases, but specifically in the case of road vehicles — where it is likely to be a further term of the agreement that in no circumstances can the vehicle concerned be taken onto a public road without such insurance being in effect;

- an appropriate level of insurance against damage. In the case of road vehicles, this is clearly a fully comprehensive policy, but for other items of plant or equipment the lessee may believe that the risks needing to be covered may be restricted.

It is normal for the lease agreement also to stipulate that the lessee inform his insurer of the lessor's 'interest' (in the legal sense of that word), in the asset concerned, and that this interest be endorsed on the policy. The lessor can ask to see the policy concerned at any point, and can also ask for evidence of payment of the premium for the period current at the time of his enquiry. The lease agreement is likely to include a covenant by the lessee to indemnify the lessor against any damage suffered by that lessor from the asset's loss, or damage to it, to the extent not covered by the insurance referred to. This is of course the sanction against the lessee's failing to cover sufficient risks, as indicated in the third of the points laid out above. The provision would undoubtedly also include compensation to the lessor in the form of interest on the late settlement of any claims by the insurer − which is itself perhaps a warning to the lessee to take every step he can to ensure that the insurer is not in a position, after a disaster, of being able to dispute the values for which items have been insured. Finally, it must be pointed out that this paragraph deals with insurance of the subject matter of finance leases, and specifically of items of plant or machinery. Leases of real property are likely to be operating, rather than finance, leases; the way in which insurance of buildings is dealt with in such leases is a very much more complex matter, to which we will give some attention in paragraph 5.18 below.

CHAPTER 3

Operating leases

Definitions

3.01 The last chapter dealt with finance leases. This one deals with operating leases. We know that there are radical differences between the two classes – for instance the following two:

- The lessee who has the use of an asset under a finance lease must carry a capitalised figure on his balance sheet for it, and must also show as a 'borrowing' the amounts of rentals (excluding the finance element) he has yet to pay; the lessee with an asset on an operating lease puts nothing in his accounts other than the expense he incurs in paying rentals (but see paragraph 3.09 below for how he shows those rentals).

- The lessor writing finance leases will tend to be a financier, looking for a purely financial profit, and anxious to put onto the shoulders of others all, or as many as possible, of the non-financial risks that can result from a leasing transaction. The operating lessor, on the other hand accepts that it is out of taking some at least of these risks that he should be able to make his profit.

But at this stage the only definition we have had of where the dividing line is to be drawn has been the general platitude in paragraph 1.19 that

> "the difference between (finance leases) and operating leases is that in the latter the lessor needs to have regard to, (and is dependent upon for his profit), the residual value of the asset at the end of the term, including the prospective re-leasing of that asset".

In the United States there have been continuing, and ever more prescriptive, attempts to draw this dividing line, or rather these dividing lines. In the hands of the lessee, leases are categorised as either 'capital' leases or 'operating' leases; in the hands of the lessor, the first of these categories is further split between 'direct financing' and 'sales-type' leases. Each of these has its own detailed definitions. But certainty is still absent, and there are still people working at bending and stretching the terms and conditions in lease agreements solely to push them one side or other of the line. (From the US lessor's point of view, there are significant tax implications which follow from the question of his leases' categorisation).

3.02 The UK approach has been to outline a dividing principle, choosing generalised terminology, and to indicate that this principle should underlie the approach to be made to any particular lease agreement; but that there can be occasions when commonsense indicates that the approach has produced an answer that is wrong, and should be rejected:

> "A *finance lease* is a lease that transfers substantially all the risks and rewards of ownership of an asset to the lessee. It should be presumed that such a transfer of risks and rewards occurs if at the inception of a lease the present value of the minimum lease payments, including any initial payment, amounts to substantially all (normally 90 percent or more) of the fair value of the leased asset. The present value should be calculated by using the interest rate implicit in the lease...If the fair value of the asset is not determinable, an estimate thereof should be used."

> "Notwithstanding the fact that a lease meets the conditions (above) the presumption that it should be classified as a finance lease may in exceptional circumstances be rebutted if it can be clearly demonstrated that the lease in question does not transfer substantially all the risks and rewards of ownership (other than the legal title) to the lessee. Correspondingly, the presumption that a lease which fails to meet the conditions (above) is not a finance lease may in exceptional circumstances be rebutted."

> "An *operating lease* is a lease other than a finance lease."

Those are the definitions in SSAP 21. It is sometimes said that accountants speak, and particularly write, in hieratic language – literally 'priestly' language, capable of being understood only by other priests. We need to devote the next few paragraphs to an analysis of this definition, to see why it has been framed in the way it has, and how it works in practice.

The present value of the minimum lease payments

3.03 The first matter to which we need to give some more thought is the exact meaning of the phrase which forms the heading of this paragraph. SSAP 21, and the guidance notes on its application published by The Accounting Standards Committee are not as helpful as one might have hoped. Let us revert to the example already briefly discussed in paragraph 2.12. We there envisaged, from the lessee's point of view:

- the five year lease under which quarterly rentals in advance of £672 had been originally demanded, and for which we knew that the implicit rate was 3.357 percent per quarter;

- (we did of course know that the acquisition cost of the asset was £10,000, because this had been the whole basis of our examination of the lease concerned in the immediately preceding paragraphs);

- we then assumed that the lessor decided he did not need to price the lease to recover the full £10,000 asset cost from the lessee, because he could be sure of getting back £500 on an eventual sale. We expressed this by saying that the lessor guaranteed to rebate £500 to the lessee;

* the less than fully spelled out facet of this assumption was that the lessor wanted still to receive all twenty rental receipts of £672 each on the first day of each quarter during the lease term, but was then going to hand back £500 on 31 December of year 5.

Nowhere, yet, have we illustrated the discounting of a stream of rentals to arrive at their present value. The process has some relationship to the short-cut illustrated in paragraph 2.05 for calculating the implicit rate – where we arrived at a table of the 'principal elements' of each rental instalment. But there are fundamental differences from that in the discounting process, and it is vital that we do not confuse the two. In particular, discounting can deal with uneven streams of payments, and those that include receipts as well as payments. The theory of discounting is simple and well known:

£96.75	invested today at 3.357 percent per quarter will produce at the end of that quarter	£100.00
£93.61	invested today at 3.357 percent per quarter, will have grown to £96.75 at the end of one quarter, and if left, by the end of a second quarter	£100.00
£190.36	today will produce two receipts, each of £100, at the end of this, and the next quarter	£200.00
£100.00	for completeness, £100 in the bank will of course allow us to draw out an immediate receipt of that £100	£100.00
£290.36	will therefore produce a stream of three receipts of £100, the first immediate, the second at the end of the current quarter, and the third at the end of the next quarter	£300.00

3.04   The present values of the streams of rental payments, including the final rebate, payable on the one hand by the lessee in the paragraph 2.12 example referred to above, and of the sales proceeds on the other hand that the lessor is confident of being able to obtain in the market at the end of the lease term, are therefore as in Table 39.

That is the derivation of the figures in paragraph 2.12. In parenthesis, it might just be worth mentioning the 'rule of 70', (nothing to do with the rule of 78 in paragraph 2.13). This states that it is approximately true that if you divide the rate of interest into 70, the answer is the number of years

	Lessee	Sale proceeds	Total
Actual 'lease payments' and sale proceeds	12,940	500	13,440
Present value of lease payments and sale proceeds	9,742	258	10,000
Made up of the present values of payments due Yr 1 Qtr 1	672		672
Qtr 2	650		650
Qtr 3	629		629
Qtr 4	609		609
Yr 2 Qtr 1	589		589
Qtr 2	570		570
Qtr 3	551		551
Qtr 4	533		533
Yr 3 Qtr 1	516		516
Qtr 2	499		499
Qtr 3	483		483
Qtr 4	467		467
Yr 4 Qtr 1	452		452
Qtr 2	438		438
Qtr 3	423		423
Qtr 4	410		410
Yr 5 Qtr 1	396		396
Qtr 2	383		383
Qtr 3	371		371
Qtr 4	359		359
(rebate & sale) end Qtr 4	(258)	258	–
	9,742	258	10.000

Table 39

Present values of minimum lease payments to be made by lessee, and present value of expected but unguaranteed sale proceeds of asset.

in which a sum of money invested at that interest rate will double. £258 invested at 14.119 percent per annum, equivalent to 3.357 percent per quarter, becomes £500 in five years as we can see above.

3.05 It is clear that if the fair value of the leased asset is £10,000, and the present value of the lessee's minimum lease rentals £9,742, then that 97 percent relationship between the two indicates that substantially all the risks and rewards of ownership have been transferred to the lessee, and that the lease is a finance lease. But it is equally clear that we actually need to construct a very different illustration in order to come to the opposite conclusion:

- the asset costs £10,000, and is to be leased over five years at £598 per quarter, payable in advance;

- the lessor assumes that the residual value will be £2,130;

- on those assumptions, the rate implicit in the lease is 3.357 percent per quarter, 14.119 per annum.

The table setting out the present values now becomes Table 40.

		Lessee	Sale proceeds	Total
Actual 'lease payments' and expected sale proceeds		11,960	2,130	14,090
Present value of 'lease payments' and of sale proceeds		8,900	1,100	10,000
Made up of the present values of payments due	Yr 1 Qtr 1	598		598
	Qtr 2	579		579
	Qtr 3	560		560
	Qtr 4	541		541
	Yr 2 Qtr 1	524		524
	Qtr 2	507		507
	Qtr 3	491		491
	Qtr 4	475		475
	Yr 3 Qtr 1	459		459
	Qtr 2	444		444
	Qtr 3	430		430
	Qtr 4	416		416
	Yr 4 Qtr 1	402		402
	Qtr 2	389		389
	Qtr 3	377		377
	Qtr 4	365		365
	Yr 5 Qtr 1	353		353
	Qtr 2	341		341
	Qtr 3	330		330
	Qtr 4	319		319
(sale)	end Qtr 4		1,100	1,100
		8,900	1,100	10,000

Table 40
Present values of lessee's minimum lease payments, and present value of unguaranteed sale proceeds of the asset in a case where the rentals are £598 quarterly in advance and the asset expected to sell for £2,130 at end year 5.

3.06   There are significant differences between the operating lease in paragraph 3.05 and the finance lease in paragraph 3.04. One is that the operating lessee pays a flat rental of £598 per quarter, with no rebate received at the end. Speaking generally, this is the fundamental characteristic of the operating lease from the lessee's point of view. He expects to pay a rental which, broadly, compensates the lessor for his holding cost for the asset, plus what the lessor may expect to be the fall (if any) in the asset's value resulting from the lessee's use of it. The lessee does not expect to be asked to pay rentals which precisely reimburse to the lessor the asset's entire original and holding costs, as in the finance lease,(paragraph 2.01 et seq). It is the lessor who in the operating lease remains not only at risk, solely or substantially, for the residual value of the asset, but receives nothing from the lessee in this regard either during the lease term or at its end. But let us not devote so much thought to the lessor's residual risk that we lose sight of the commercial implications – and particularly the lessee's viewpoint on these. There is, for instance as we mentioned in paragraph 1.18, both a demand for, and a supply of, leases of aircraft for five year terms. The expected life of an aircraft could be twenty years, but many of the lessees in this market could not afford to buy such an aircraft outright, nor to take onto their balance sheets a finance lease covering substantially all of its life, and its full value. What they look for is a deal which 'rentalises' five years out of that life, that is to say which covers the lessor's holding costs during the five year term, plus what he believes will be the decline in the value of the aircraft between, say, the fifth and tenth anniversaries of its original coming into use. Such a lease would undoubtedly be an operating one, when looked at from the lessee's viewpoint. The lessor may try to limit the risk he bears – the implications of his doing so we will come to in paragraphs 3.12 and 3.13 below – or he may decide not to do so. If he does want to limit his risks, some of the ways in which he can do so are examined in paragraphs 4.09 to 4.18. Notice also, because these also differ from the previous paragraph's illustration, that:

- The lessor's expected residual of £2,130 has a present value of £1,100. It is the 'risk and reward' associated with that residual which the lessor has retained, and not transferred to the lessee.

- We can explain £1,100 as being the present value of £2,130 receivable at the end of twenty complete quarters, (calculated at 3.357 percent per quarter), in a straightforward way by saying that £1,100 invested now and compounded will produce £2,130 at that time.

- Alternatively, and it is important that we grasp these inter-relationships between the figures, we can explain it as follows. The original example in the early paragraphs of chapter 2 had the lessee paying £672 per quarter. Our present variation has him paying £598 per quarter. The lessor is therefore short, by £74 each quarter, of the sums he needs to pay off his own external borrowing. Let us assume he sets up a specific banking facility to borrow £74 per quarter, and the interest building up on these amounts, through the twenty quarters. £2,130 is the sum which will pay off that bank drawing at the end of the twentieth quarter.

Or to express that alternative differently, £1,100 is the present value of a stream of payments of £74 each quarter, and £2,130 is its value at the end of the five year term. The relationships are the same between the figures comprised in each of the three streams (of even payments) we have been considering:

	Rental	Total rentals	Present value	Final compounding
Paragraph 2.02	£672	13,440	10,000	not calculated
This paragraph				
main example	598	11,960	8,900	not calculated
notional example	74	1,480	1,100	2,130

but the relationship does not hold for the example in the previous paragraph, in which the lessee's payments were uneven in the sense that he received a final rebate of £500 after he had made his twenty rental payments of £672:

| *Paragraph 3.02* | 672 | 12,940 | 9,742 | not calculated |

The duration of the lease term

3.07 If we continue thinking about the relationship between a fair value for the asset of £10,000 on the one hand, and £8,900 on the other as the present value of the lessee's minimum lease payments, it is obvious that the duration of the lease itself will be a material factor. Table 41 sets out some possible ways the figures can be fitted together.

All of these figures are calculated at the same implicit rate of 3.357 percent per quarter. It cannot need explanation, in the final two lines, that the residual's present value, and the residual itself, will be less spaced out when the lease term is short than when it is longer. What may not have been quite so obvious before these figures had been tabulated in this way is that to achieve the limited degree of transfer of risks and rewards necessary for

Term	Five years	Four years	Three years	Two years
Quarterly rental	£598	£704	£883	£1,245
Present values of				
Year 1 rentals	2,278	2,683	3,366	4,743
Year 2 rentals	1,997	2,352	2,950	4,157
Year 3 rentals	1,749	2,060	2,584	–
Year 4 rentals	1,533	1,805	–	–
Year 5 rentals	1,343	–	–	–
minimum lease payments	8,900	8,900	8,900	8,900
Residual value estimated at end of				
lease term	2,130	1,866	1,634	1,430
Present value of that residual value	1,100	1,100	1,100	1,100

Table 41

Possible levels of lease rentals, and of expected asset sale proceeds at the end of lease terms of five, four, three and two years in order to produce minimum lease payments qualifying the lease as 'operating'.

the lease to be classified as 'operating', the size of the residual, compared to the amount of each quarterly rental needs to be not far short of:

four to one	for the five year lease	– 2,130:	598
three to one	for the four year lease	– 1,866:	704
two to one	for the three year lease	– 1,634:	883
evens	for the two year lease	– 1,430:	1,245

We are looking at figures only just on the 'operating' side of the borderline. If one sought a present value of lease payments of 80 percent of the fair value of the asset, in place of the 89 percent we have picked, then the size of the residual compared to the quarterly rentals would be even larger.

3.08   It seems clear, in view of these numbers, that one could say that the number of operating leases of plant and macl.inery which are of five years duration or more is probably small; two, three and possibly four year leases are likely to be more normal. And the reason should be reasonably clear. Lessors generally, in the case of most items of plant, are less likely to be able to see residuals for five year old items in excess of 20 percent of original cost as being sure enough for them to be happy only rentalising 89 percent or less of the asset's original cost. Perhaps there might be an exception in the case for instance of printing machinery, (which has always had in the past a long life expectancy, although who is to say whether technological change may not alter that). But there again, it is less than totally clear that there would necessarily be a significant demand from lessees for five year operating leases of long-life items such as printing presses, where it was to be expected that the lessor would either sell the press at the end of that term, or would want a substantial rental for a re-lease; the alternative from the lessee's point of view would be a longer term finance lease, giving him no greater level of rentals, but at the same time giving should he choose, (and the choice would in this case be his), the prospect of a secondary term at a rental low enough for his position to be almost indistinguishable from outright ownership. But as soon as we start trying to set out the arguments for and against operating leases, and to do so from both the lessor's and lessee's points of view, it becomes immediately obvious that there will inevitably be exceptions to each general principle one tries to identify. What about the lessee, for instance, who only wants the printing press concerned for five years, because he expects at the end of that time to need something larger and more sophisticated? One of his courses could be to start, say, an eight year finance lease, with a view to persuading the lessor to sell the asset off the lease after five years and allow him to upgrade to the new press. The disadvantages would seem to be that the lessee would, in that negotiation of the termination of his original lease and its upgrading into a new one, have to take on the residual risk on the press he was getting rid of, and secondly he would be tied into the same lessor for that upgraded lease, rather than being able to shop around. It is thus probably of only limited value speculating whether potential lessees and lessors are, or are not, going to see mutual advantages in signing particular shapes of leases. What we need to be able to see, rather, is what shapes are available — what their features are — where their risks and disadvantages may lie — so that we know what to look for if we are potential lessees, and what to market if we are lessors. A general exposition, covering both finance and operating leases, of the terms and conditions which these may usually contain ('standard terms' is an inappropriate phrase to use in the context of leasing agreements) is included in paragraph 5, from paragraphs 5.14 to 5.24.

Lessee accounting

3.09 One important general feature of operating leases is that they are accounted for in a different manner from finance leases. Without the same degree of transference of risks and rewards of ownership of the asset to the lessee, the latter does not need to capitalise that asset onto his balance sheet, and nor does he show the associated 'borrowing'. What the lessee's accounts show are:

- a profit and loss charge for rentals payable under operating leases. Even if these rentals are not payable in equal amounts at equal intervals, (for instance if there is a rental holiday, or an initial charge), the amount charged to profit and loss each year should generally be calculated on an even basis over the term of the lease;

- the profit and loss charge should be split, either in that account or in notes to the accounts, between the amounts for leased plant or machinery, and for other operating leases;

- a note to the balance sheet should set out the lessee's commitments under operating leases, specifying the amount of rentals payable in the twelve months following the balance sheet date, and splitting that total two ways: first, between rents for land and buildings and those for other items, and secondly within each of those classes between those amounts payable under leases which expire within the twelve months after the balance sheet date, those that expire within the second to fifth years, and those that expire beyond five years from the balance sheet date.

It is reasonably clear that if there are those anxious to try to put a capital value onto the assets used by a particular company, but which it holds on operating leases, the accounts disclosures will enable them to make reasonable estimates what the figures might be. Thus someone trying to compare return on assets of two companies one of which owned or finance-leased its assets, whilst the other held a substantial proportion of the assets it used on operating leases, would be able to arrive at comparable return percentages for the two. However, there is a general belief that avoiding overweighting one's balance sheet with fixed assets, and particularly avoiding being burdened with the associated debt, is an advantage. Therefore, this feature of operating leases is regarded as of general advantage; there are specific instances, particularly in relation to the capital ratios of companies in the financial services sector, where it is of vital significance. And it is also true that a large number of companies are still affected by debenture trust deeds and other borrowing agreements whose wording, (dating from before SSAP 21 introduced the requirement for associated 'borrowing' to be shown when finance-leased assets are capitalised), may have dire effects if the company does put these 'borrowings' onto its balance sheet in addition to those under the debentures, etc, referred to earlier.

Lessor accounting

3.10   The lessor accounts for assets leased out under operating leases by capitalising them onto his balance sheet, and depreciating them. If he has borrowed in order to acquire the assets concerned, then clearly that borrowing will also show on his balance sheet. It might be thought that if the same lessor owns assets subject to finance leases and reflects these as a receivable on his balance sheet (again with associated borrowings) that the difference in the case of his operating lease assets is simply one of altitude – fixed assets being generally shown nearer the top of the balance sheet than are receivables under finance leases. But the differences are wider than mere balance sheet categorisation. We have seen that the principle decreed by the accounting bodies in SSAP 21 in relation to finance leases is that lessors should recognise profit from their leases on a basis which gives "a constant periodic rate of return on the net cash investment" in the lease. SSAP 21 suggests that lessors should credit their rentals from operating leases on a straightline basis (that is to say evenly through the lease term, even if there are rental holidays, or initial payments). This is of course the same suggestion as for lessees, noted in the previous paragraph. Except for the one ancillary point mentioned in the next paragraph, the standard is however totally silent about the way that lessors should recognise profit from operating leases: the statement that the asset is to be capitalised and depreciated provides no guidance unless more can be said about the principles on which that depreciation is to be provided. There is no such elucidation. One is therefore left with the general accounting principle that a fixed asset should be depreciated over its expected earning life, from cost down to expected eventual disposal value (or to zero) in a way that matches that depreciation as fairly as possible with the earnings the asset generates. The application of that principle has always to be coloured by three further considerations: first, prudence – accountants should, if they err at all, always err on the side of caution: secondly, the necessity that if an asset can be seen to have suffered a permanent diminution in value, perhaps through obsolescence, this fact should be immediately recognised in the accounts: and thirdly, the over-riding necessity that whatever methods are adopted for providing depreciation, and for recognising profits, should be applied consistently from year to year, and so far as is appropriate, over different classes of asset. This is all generalisation; accountancy at this level is an art not a science. The standard does additionally require the lessor to make certain disclosures in his financial statements about his operating lease activities. First, he must show the gross amount of the assets subject to operating leases, and the accumulated depreciation provided against that gross. Secondly, the amount of the rentals in his accounting period from operating leases. And thirdly he must outline his accounting policy for recognising profits from those leases.

Manufacturers letting out their products on operating leases

3.11   The point referred to in the previous paragraph which the standard does stipulate, has to do with profit recognition for manufacturers who dispose of their product by way of operating leases rather than outright sale (or finance leasing). If they had made outright sales, then clearly they would have recognised their (manufacturing) profit at that point – and we have seen in paragraph 2.11 that a manufacturer who leased his product by way of a finance lease would recognise a (manufacturing) profit at the inception of the lease, and that the (leasing) profit recognised through the term of that lease would be only the 'financier's' part of the total. Manufacturers who lease out their product on operating leases should not recognise any profit on the signing of such a lease; the total profit, not segregated between manufacturing and leasing elements, should be recognised through the term of the lease or of the consecutive leases, including the lessor's eventual disposal of the asset.

The lessee's, and the lessor's, separate positions

3.12 How the parties account for operating leases as distinct from finance leases is a not unimportant feature. But we have not yet mentioned what is probably the most significant feature of the manner in which the dividing line is drawn between the two classes of lease, and the one which gives rise to the greatest opportunities for not only lessors and lessees, but others as well, to obtain advantage from leasing. If we go back to the definition quoted in paragraph 3.02 above, it said in part:

> "...It should be presumed that such a transfer of risks and rewards (that is a sufficient transfer to be classed as a finance lease) occurs if at the inception of a lease the present value of the minimum lease payments, including any initial payment, amounts to substantially all (normally 90 percent or more) of the fair value of the leased asset..."

The point to note is that the words are '*the* minimum lease payments', not the lessee's minimum lease payments. If looking at the minimum lease payments receivable by the lessor, he can say that their present value amounts to 90 percent or more of the fair value of the leased asset, then the lease is a finance lease so far as he is concerned. But if because some part of those payments to the lessor come from a third party, the lessee's own minimum lease payments to the lessor have a present value less than the required percentage, then the same lease is an operating lease so far as the lessee is concerned.

3.13 This highlights three separate points:

- There is undoubtedly some demand, although the author thinks its extent may be overstated, for arrangements which simply give the lessee the 'off-balance sheet' advantages of an operating lease, while still giving the lessor the technical benefits of a finance lease. Undoubtedly, in the rather different leasing environment in the US, and particularly with differences in tax treatment for different categories of lease, there is a demand for this mis-matching of treatment in the hands of the parties. The author's belief is that it would be truer to say in the UK that lessees more often seek operating leases for purely commercial reasons – that the terms and conditions better reflect the terms on which they wish to obtain use of the assets concerned. Similarly, the lessors' searches for reductions of risk are just that – not attempts as such to alter the categorisation of leases.

- The lessee must treat as his own any lease payments to be made not only by him, but by any associate of his. The payments to be taken into account are 'minimum' in the sense that if the lessee has the option to break the lease at a specified date, he need only count payments up to that date, (plus any related to that exercise of his break entitlement).

- A 'lease payment' includes not only rentals, but other amounts 'guaranteed' by the lessee or by third parties.

Probably the commonest third party source of lease payments to the lessor is the supplier of equipment, who is prepared to guarantee a residual value at which he is willing to repurchase equipment off the lease – normally to be able to control the second hand market in his own equipment, a control he may want as a way of exerting indirect control over the market for that equipment new. An examination of the opportunities in this area in which leases are agreements having three or more parties will form one of the main elements of our analysis of risks and rewards, examined in detail from paragraph 4.12 to the end of chapter 4. It is not only lessors and lessees, but also equipment suppliers, dealers, guarantors/underwriters, financiers and others, who may shoulder these risks, in the hopes of gaining the appropriate rewards.

Re-leasing

3.14 There is one last point specifically relevant to operating leases which we need to clear before we conclude this chapter. The lessor in an operating lease relies on being able to achieve fairly substantial proceeds for the 'residual'. By definition these will be un-guaranteed, if the lease is an operating one from his point of view. If at the end of the lease's term, the market value of the asset is low, the lessor can either sell it and incur a loss, (or make a smaller than hoped-for profit), or he can attempt to re-lease the asset in the hope that even if that re-lease does not itself produce significant income, the asset's value may have recovered by the time that second lease term expires. This is an only too familiar transaction for owners chartering their vessels in a shipping market which has historically fluctuated between boom years and slumps. But suppose that the market has moved in the lessor's favour – that the asset's value is more than the figure he had originally hoped for when fixing the rentals he thought it necessary to charge the lessee for the term just ending. It is sometimes suggested that the lessor will in such circumstances always sell his asset; and therefore that whether or not the lessee would have wished to renew his lease, the market movements have made that impossible. Stepping back to take a wider perspective, it is said that the lessee's rentals 'reimburse' the lessor for his expenditure down to the level of the hoped-for residual; if the lessor can himself then achieve by selling the asset a further 'reimbursement' which improves on what he had been aiming to achieve, he cannot but take it. A moment's thought will however show that the theory is inadequate. Certanly, if the lessor's view is that the higher than expected market value of the asset is a temporary aberration, that prices are about to fall and then to stay down, he must be likely to sell. But if he takes the opposite view, that although prices have already risen further than he had hoped, they will continue to rise even more strongly in the future, then there is no reason why he should not be willing to consider renewing the lessee's lease.

3.15　　This brings out three points. First, although the foregoing is written in general terms, and can apply to any asset leased out under an operating lease, it is particularly appropriate to the one asset which is seldom the subject of any other type of lease, namely land and buildings. We are not dealing in this book with the leasing of land, but we must bear in mind that it is only a form of operating leasing, that the principles which apply to any operating lease transaction apply also to land – with only modest distinctions. Secondly, in circumstances where a lessor may be willing to consider renewing an operating lease, there is no implication that this will be at the same, (or a lower), rent as that charged in the term just ending. Rents go up as well as down. Finally, it is tendentious to import into operating lease transactions the concepts that appear to govern finance leasing. In the latter, the lessee shoulders almost all the risks normally associated with the asset's absolute ownership (– including for instance its residual value risk). His agreement with his lessor can be fairly characterised as a merely financial one in which the lessee 'reimburses' the lessor's acquisition cost, together with appropriate finance charges, even where the lessor may be willing to take some modest risk over the residual. But being reimbursed is not normally the operating lessor's objective. He charges what he can get – and does so just as much to his lessees as to the asset's eventual purchaser. The wording in the first few lines of paragraph 3.06 – describing the different objectives of an operating and a finance lessor, was carefully chosen so that this point should not be fudged. There may be certain similarities between operating and finance leasing, (the next chapter demonstrates that), but at the same time we lose sight of the differences only at our peril.

CHAPTER 4

Risks and rewards – for the lessor, for the lessee, and for others involved

'Support' in operating and finance leases

4.01 The throw-away line on which we ended paragraph 3.13 was a reference to leases involving three or more parties – that is to say not just a lessor and a lessee, but such others as:

- the equipment supplier;

- guarantors, and/or underwriters;

- the lessor's suppliers of finance.

And the form of 'involvement' which may be most likely for all or any of these is some participation in the risks which would otherwise be shouldered by the lessor or lessee. We have seen the accounting bodies' definition of finance leasing asks whether there has been, substantially, a transfer to the lessee of the "risks and rewards of ownership of the asset". In this chapter we do not ignore the risks and rewards of asset ownership; the residual risk is unquestionably one of them and will be one of the items we examine in depth. But we are looking more widely than that, at all the other risks that leasing may involve – at the bad and doubtful debt risks of any of the parties to pick just one of those others at random. Recapitulating these main risk areas will itself indicate some of the ways in which risks can be shifted and/or reduced to levels acceptable to the parties concerned. Some forms of risk-limitation will turn what would otherwise have been operating leases from the lessor's point of view into finance leases – the classic example would be his obtaining a guarantee of a residual value. Others will leave the actual lease's status unchanged, but may change radically the relationships between the parties; and may or may not also change those parties' status so far as concerns those in the outside world, the Inland Revenue for instance. For these reasons it is appropriate to look at these matters in a chapter generally aimed at both finance and operating leases. If one considers the two categories in the broadest terms, one could say that the processes of acquiring the asset and financing it are very similar in each case; and that what appears to set the two apart is the service the lessor holds himself out as offering, his pricing of that service, and his method of recognising the profit he earns. The two lessors' rewards differ, and their risks similarly differ, at the 'sales' end of their operations. But in relation to their 'financing' and 'holding' activities, the risks in the two types of leasing are very similar. When we need to differentiate the opportunities or effects, we can do so – but in many cases we will see that it is unnecessary.

4.02 We start therefore with a recapitulation of the main characteristics of an 'unsupported' operating lease, so as to be able to indicate where and how risks can be shifted and reduced. This gives us the key to dealing in greater detail with each possibility in succeeding paragraphs:

- The lessor carries the credit risk that his lessee may default on his rental obligations. To some extent this is covered by the lessor's right to take back the asset, but does he need guarantees or other security in addition? (paragraph 4.05)

- The lessor has almost certainly had to borrow substantial sums to finance his acquisition of the leased assets. Those assets, globally as opposed to individually, will normally form part of the lender's security, as will also the streams of rental income from the leases. But should the lessor attempt to limit each separate lender's recourse to the assets and income streams which have resulted from his loans? (paragraphs 4.06, 4.07 and 4.08)

- The lessor carries the risk that the residual value, (which may be proceeds from an outright sale, or the income stream from a re-lease with sale proceeds after that), will be insufficient to give him his required profit. 'Insufficient' may not be a word which immediately conjures up the concept that the lessor may not be able to sell at all, or to find anyone to whom he can re-lease the asset. Is there a way in which he can insure – so as to get a guaranteed residual value? (paragraphs 4.09, 4.10 and 4.11)

- As an alternative to 'insurance' of residuals, is there another way in which the lessor can limit the size of his exposure by contracting, for instance, with a dealer in the assets concerned that the latter will buy them at not less than a specified (floor) price? And if this approach is adopted, will the dealer want to have an option to purchase at a specified (ceiling) price, if it should turn out that the market situation is much better than the lessor feared it might be, when the dealer does come to make his eventual disposal? (paragraphs 4.12 to 4.18 are relevant to this and the following points)

- Contracting for the sale of assets to dealers in those goods may be realistic in the case of some items – cars and other vehicles are one obvious class. There will be other items for which it will not be possible, but where the original supplier of the equipment may be prepared, or may demand, to reacquire the assets. One possible reason may be that his limiting the quantity of secondhand items available may increase both the volumes of his sales of new equipment, and the prices at which this can be sold. A second possibility is that the original supplier may wish to be able to control the re-conditioning of any secondhand items, in order to avoid product reliability doubts arising through inadequate re-conditioning.

4.03   And of course it should never be lost to sight that leasing itself, whether finance leasing or operating, is itself a form of support supplied by the lessor to the lessee:

- by allowing the latter to spread over time what would otherwise have needed to be an immediate outflow for the acquisition of the asset;

- in the case of operating leases, this 'lessee support' can be regarded as greater, in that the lessee hopes that the amounts rentalised by the lessor may reflect less than 90 percent of the asset's value, and may be very considerably less than that percentage in the case of short leases, and/or high residual assets.

If the lessor is himself a 'supporter' in this way, increasing his own risks, is he sure he is being properly rewarded for doing this ? Or, more radically, is it the lessee that our 'overly-supportive' lessor should be asking to shoulder a greater proportion of the risks rather than looking only to the other parties referred to above ? We will look in the paragraphs that follow at some of the ways in which these forms of support are frequently built into lease arrangements, whether operating or finance. And inevitably we will need to come back to some of them in Chapter 7, dealing with some of the tax uncertainties and problems.

Seeing straight

4.04   At this point it seems relevant to sound the general warning contained in an undoubtedly apocryphal story told to the author some years ago. Contact lenses, it was said, are always sold with the benefit of insurance against loss or damage, because those who might consider wearing them are so fearful of losing them that they would not be prepared to buy without such insurance. The lenses, it was said, do not last indefinitely − after a certain number of years they can be expected to tear or fray, and will need to be replaced. But, it was said, you can claim on the insurance at that point; admittedly, the policy will by then only pay out some part of the cost of new lenses, but you are nevertheless insured. The author protested that this was not what insurance was all about, that you could not insure against 'fair wear and tear' (in this instance literally). But the point is that all is not always what it seems, and particularly that it may not be what it is called by some party who sees advantage in that way of describing what he has to sell. Some part of the 'insurance' cost borne by the purchaser of the new lenses does undoubtedly cover him against the risk of their loss during their expected life. The remainder of what is described as 'insurance' is, when analysed, very much more akin to a deposit made at the time of the original purchase, which can be put towards the cost of the replacement lenses when they need to be acquired. And why should any purchaser be prepared to hand over such a deposit that number of years in advance, (incidentally tying himself to purchasing the replacements from the original supplier and not from any competitor)? "Because...(he) would not be prepared to buy without...insurance". One must always analyse what it is that one is being asked to pay for, and even dare the author say it, what it is one is oneself selling.

The lessor's protections against credit risk

4.05 The lessor always regards the quality of his lessees' covenants (paragraph 2.59) as his primary safety line; but when and if a lessee fails, he needs to have some secondary line of defence. The lessor writing operating leases is likely to be better protected by his entitlement to repossess his asset than is the lessor with an asset out on a finance lease – simply because the operating lease is likely to be of shorter duration, and the at-the-time value of the asset is likely to be greater in relation to the level of a lessee's potential default on future rentals. Paragraph 5.23 illustrates this in figures, although it has to be said that any such figures can only illustrate the facts of the particular case being addressed, and that care must always therefore be used in deciding what general conclusions may be drawn from them. But there are normally three other protective arrangements available to such a lessor. He can choose which one or more to adopt, if he believes that normal repossession, and his right to sue the lessee for unpaid rentals, are insufficient protection. First, he may obtain a guarantee of the lessee's obligations from the latter's bank, and/or a deposit of cash or security from the lessee in respect of those obligations. Not infrequently, the lessee's banker will be the parent company of the lessor – given the ownership of companies comprising a large part of the equipment leasing industry. If this is the case, the bank concerned and its leasing subsidiary will need to look carefully at their group's exposure. Secondly, the lessor may negotiate with the equipment supplier a right to resell the equipment to the latter at a specified price in the event of its having to be repossessed. The simplest form of such a contract is a 'put' option granted by the equipment supplier, under which the lessor can require such a repurchase. (The main context in which 'put' options may be granted by the equipment supplier is to protect the lessor's residual, as we will see in paragraph 4.16, rather than to protect his credit risk; but this is another, entirely valid, situation). Thirdly, the lessor may require an initial 'balloon' rental, possibly coupled with a rental holiday in the final months of the lease term. This is not uncommon in the case of the contract hiring of cars, where it can be seen as perhaps giving the lessor some protection against the substantial fall in value of the asset as the lessee drives it out of the showroom door. When credit controls were a feature of the UK economy, it was a legal requirement that a specified percentage of a car's cost be paid by way of an initial deposit when it was sold on a hire purchase contract. There is no law requiring any equivalent 'deposit' under operating lease contracts, but it is undoubtedly convenient from the lessor's point of view to require such an advance payment if the credit risk appears otherwise unacceptable.

The lessor's borrowings – and protection by making them 'non-recourse'

4.06   We know only too well that lessors are heavy users of borrowings to finance their portfolios. A default by the lessee of a single large item, or defaults by groups of less significant lessees, can only too easily put the lessor's entire operation in jeopardy – if as a result he is unable to meet all of his own obligations to his financiers. This risk is not lessened by the fact that it is often neither easy nor an economic proposition to turn portions of a lease portfolio into cash at short notice, should the lessor find himself under pressure from his creditors. (This itself is a risk we will examine in paragraphs 4.24 to 4.26). Therefore the lessor may try to find ways in which his own creditors can be persuaded not to take action against him for payment, but to look straight through him to his lessees, and to the assets acquired by means of the original borrowings. The lessor seeks to make himself 'transparent', and to say that his own creditor should have 'no recourse' to him – only, as above, to those next in line. That appears to solve one problem, but only at the risk of opening up yet more, as we will see. But first, we can note that there are three main ways in which the lessor can try to put such non-recourse arrangements in place; and the problems opened up may not be quite the same for each. First, the borrowings can be made *ab initio* on a non-recourse basis, this being a term written into the original agreement. Secondly, a similar position can be achieved if the lessor, having used temporary overdraft facilities to finance a portfolio of, say, television rental agreements, then 'sells' those agreements under a block-discounting agreement. The arrangement is not at all unlike the sale by a normal trader of his book debts under a 'factoring' deal; factoring can be done with or without recourse, although the price will inevitably be different, and so also can block discounting of leasing agreements be done without recourse. Thirdly, the lessor can achieve *de facto* financing without recourse if his company has no assets, and no substance, apart from the leased assets which he is willing to put at risk, their rental streams, and whatever contractual arrangements there may be in place for the eventual realisation of the assets' residuals. This tactic, of leaving a particular company vulnerable to creditors in an attempt to protect its associates from recourse, is one that the directors of the vulnerable lessor company will however wish to consider from a number of angles; permitting a company to go into liquidation, insolvent, is something which raises a number of questions under 1986 legislation, including the Insolvency Act and the Disqualification of Directors Act. This is neither the place, nor even the book, to try to deal with these. One difficulty over non-recourse finance is that it can be expected to cost more than borrowings in which the lender is himself better protected. This needs no explanation, but it does need saying that the costs of trying to persuade others to shoulder risks must always be kept in view.

Non-recourse finance – the tax uncertainties

4.07 But the second area of uncertainty over non-recourse finance is its tax consequences. We will come back to this in chapter 7, but it is appropriate to outline here what the problems may be. And to do this, we have first to understand the tax legislation prior to 1982 and then to see the extent to which that year's changes may, or may not, have removed the difficulties. Interest payable on borrowings is normally deductible in arriving at the corporation taxable profits of a company. It is fundamental to the profitable operation of a leasing company that it should be able to deduct its interest costs in this way. Dividends payable on the company's shares, by contrast, are not deductible. Corporation tax is paid on those profits first, and only thereafter can a dividend be paid out of post-tax profits, (it is not necessary for present purposes to become enmeshed in the line of argument that says that at least some part of the corporation tax paid by a company is not really a cost so far as it is concerned, because our imputation system of corporation tax allows it to be passed through to the shareholder as his tax; and it ceases therefore to be the company's burden). We saw the deductibility of the lessor's interest costs of £2,819 in paragraph 2.23, and the fact that the reward of £671 on the lessor's equity contribution was not deductible – £236 of corporation tax was paid on it, leaving the lessor with post-tax profits of £435. Whether he merely 'extracted' them from the lease we were looking at, or extracted them from the company by way of dividend, would have made no difference to the company's corporation tax position. It is obvious that in these circumstances, calling a payment interest could have a tax advantage unless there were tax legislation saying that what was called interest, but was in reality a dividend, should be disallowed. The wording of the provision concerned, up to 1982, disallowed 'interest' which

> "(was) to any extent dependent on the results of the company's business or any part of it, or...represent(ed) more than a reasonable commercial return..."

It was clear that the first half of this definition specifically caught non-recourse finance, since when the results of the relevant part of the company's business (consisting of leasing the asset concerned) ceased to be profitable through the lessee's default, the interest rate became zero. That was a straightforward example of dependence. But in 1982, that first half of the provision was deleted, at least in relation to payments of 'interest' to other UK companies who paid tax on these receipts. (This was not done to help leasing companies, but to stop a tax avoidance arrangement in a totally different area). But the second half of the provision still exists. We know that non-recourse finance is likely to be more costly from the lessor's point of view than would be borrowings where the lender knew that he had access, in the event of default, to the lessor's own resources and other assets. The Inland Revenue have always maintained that it is no part of their job to give any group of taxpayers any general clearance, for instance that they would never challenge borrowings simply on the basis that they were non-recourse. All that the Revenue do regard as being within their province is looking at the accounts of taxpayers, and the transactions included in them, after the year in which they have taken place. The view they take in one taxpayer's case can never be an absolute guarantee that the same result will be agreed for another; the Revenue have a general responsibility to apply the law evenly over all taxpayers, but the facts in any two cases are never identical. Although the author has not been able to trace any case in which the Revenue have argued that the extra interest costs of non-recourse finance meant that the interest concerned was at more than a commercial rate, it is not always an entirely safe course to rely on precedent. (As we will see in chapter 7, if the Revenue authorities are determined to upset some arrangements which they regard as a 'scheme' for avoiding tax, they habitually challenge every conceivable weak point − including many which the taxpayer may have thought totally unexceptionable).

4.08 However, that provision potentially disallowing the interest on non-recourse borrowings was not the end of the story. Leasing companies have always relied on being able to set tax reliefs flowing from one lease against the profits emerging in the same year from other, older, leases. But they have also relied on being able to 'surrender' an overall tax loss arising in a lessor company whose new business greatly exceeds its mature business, to another profitable company in the group. 'Group relief' depends in the normal case on the companies concerned being in a parent/subsidiary relationship, or fellow subsidiaries, in a '75 percent group'. This again necessitates the Revenue's defining what they mean by such a group, and in particular whether there are 'ownership' arrangements to which they may wish to have regard which may have been misdescribed by those who created them as borrowings rather than equity share capital. The definition of borrowings of the offensive kind describes them as not being 'normal commercial loans'. The legislation uses slightly familiar (but they are not identical) words to define the characteristics of a loan which is both normal and commercial — it must among other conditions:

> "not entitle the loan creditor to any amount by way of interest which depends to any extent on the results of the company's business or any part of it, or on the value of any of the company's assets or which exceeds a reasonable commercial return..."

No part of that definition was repealed in 1982 — it has stood unaltered since 1973. However, there is a respectable argument that non-recourse finance still does not 'de-group' a company, by needing to be regarded as additional 'equity' capital in the ownership of the lender. Therefore, it is said that such finance does not prevent it from surrendering a loss elsewhere in its group of companies. This is one of the matters we will look at in chapter 7. For present purposes we can leave the question on the footing that any tax strategy which depends on the courts accepting a 'respectable argument' may be less than a 100 percent certainty; but on the other hand it does not seem that the Revenue has yet used this de-grouping provision to attack non-recourse finance. Its seventeen years on the statute book should perhaps have given them time to decide what the provision does really mean.

The lessor's residual risk — insurance as a method of limiting or eliminating exposure

4.09 Some operating lessors regard it as an integral part of the business of writing operating leases that they themselves should be able to predict the residual value, (which throughout what follows also includes the possibility of re-leasing); because it is their business to make profits out of those residuals as much as out of the other aspects of the operating lease. Other lessors, both finance and operating, hanker for some degree of protection. We noted in paragraph 4.02 that there are two possible approaches, namely insurance, and some form of contract guaranteeing a disposal value. As we will see, the two may shade into each other, but it is helpful to deal with them in sequence, because that enables us to focus on the questions that each raises. If a lessor finds an underwriter who will issue a policy entitling him (the lessor) to claim any shortfall between a sum stated in the policy, and the actual disposal proceeds achieved for the leased asset, it is necessary to analyse what type of policy that is. The author does not believe that it has the same characteristics as an ordinary indemnity policy. If an asset is destroyed by fire, its owner would claim under his fire policy to be 'indemnified', that is to say put back into the same financial position he was in before the loss of, or damage to, his asset. One way of expressing in money what he had lost, and therefore the amount of his claim, would be the amount he could have sold the asset for in the market had it not been destroyed − its realisable value. A second, and generally higher, quantification would be what it would cost him to acquire another asset to replace the first − its replacement value. A third, higher again, is a reflection that it is seldom either easy or satisfactory for an insured individual to replace such items as non-new clothes with other non-new clothes, so that the only effective way of putting him back where he was before a fire or burglary is for the insurer to pay out on a 'new for old' basis. But none of those is similar to the 'guarantee' policy under which the underwriter we envisage is to commit himself to pay out when the asset has been neither damaged nor lost, but has merely failed to maintain its hoped-for realisable value. The risk the underwriter is being asked to take is not one that he can assess statistically. And it is not one where he can hope to make a profit merely out of his ability to spread risks between insured parties. If, statistically, one in 2,000 houses can be expected to burn down in any year, and the insurer covers all 2,000 for a premium from each owner of 0.1 percent of value, then half of his total premium income should be gross profit. A policy guaranteeing residuals has neither of these characteristics.

4.10   The risks the underwriter takes under this policy are not only quite different from those under a normal indemnity policy, they also have very different characteristics from some other forms of risk we may be familiar with. Some analysis in general terms of 'risk' is undoubtedly appropriate in this chapter, since we are trying to come to grips with a very difficult subject:

- The fire-insurer accepts bets from householders that their properties will burn down − he pays out if they do. He makes his profit by spreading his risk over enough houses. The bookmaker who accepts bets whether the stock market index will go up or go down cannot spread risks in the same way, but he matches his book by calculating the odds he can offer to those expecting a rise, and to those expecting a fall.

Our residual underwriter has neither of those courses open to him. He takes on a 'pure' risk, and has to be confident that his premium is adequate reward.

- If the fire-insurer writes a policy covering your house for a twelve month period, and it has not burnt down by the date nine months later to which he draws up his accounts, he would take credit for some proportion of the premium you had paid, saying that it was in respect of a period during which no catastrophe had occurred, and that statistically it was therefore less likely that there would be a fire in the three remaining months than it had originally been that there could be one in a full year.

Our residual underwriter is fully exposed until the asset is sold. The passage of time does not make any difference to him.

- In some areas, those who take risks not wholly dissimilar from those taken by our residual underwriter can reduce their exposures if circumstances seem to be pointing to their having got it wrong originally. Picture someone selling dollars forward, in the expectation that that currency will fall and he will be able to buy more cheaply to fulfil his obligation to deliver those dollars. If circumstances later indicate a likely recovery of dollars, he can either close out his position by a forward purchase, matching his forward sale, or he can get out by assigning to another the rights and obligations under his original forward sale.

Our residual underwriter is unlikely to be able to find counterparties with whom he can 'trade' his position. Once in, he is likely to be locked in.

- The previous two points highlight the difficulties our residual underwriter will have in knowing, at each intervening year end whether he has made a profit, or needs to provide for a substantial loss. Those with similar problems in the banking or commodity dealing areas generally 'mark to market', that is to say revalue their open exposures by reference to the costs of closing them out at balance sheet date. If there is no market in which guarantees of residuals can be traded, this route is not open to our residual underwriter. With no straightforward method, either statistical or market-related, for recognising profits, our residual underwriter is extremely vulnerable to the depredations of a taxing authority which may argue that his profits are greater than he himself believes it prudent to recognise. This is a matter we will return to, briefly, in chapter 7.

4.11   After all those difficulties facing the residual underwriter, it may be something of an anti-climax to mention that there seems also to be a doubt about the tax-deductibility in the hands of the operating lessor, of the premium he pays to the residual underwriter for the guarantee given. There never has been any difficulty over the deductibility of the premium on an indemnity policy for a capital asset. Despite the dividing line in UK tax law between expenses 'on revenue account' and those 'on capital account' (only the former being deductible for corporation tax — see paragraphs 2.62 and 2.71), it has always been accepted that a premium paid for 'protecting' the assets of a business against loss or damage is deductible. But guaranteeing an asset's realisable value puts an entirely new meaning onto the word 'protecting'. The Inland Revenue have certainly raised a warning flag that premiums paid on such policies, particularly in view of the fact that the asset thus 'protected' is a capital asset, may be expenses on capital account, and thus non-deductible.

Contracts for residuals

4.12   We now come to what must undoubtedly be seen as the most commercially significant aspect of the lessor's attempts to reduce his own risks, namely methods for his sharing the residual risk with a third party. It is convenient to start by casting the equipment supplier in that third party role. We can then envisage the pattern we referred to in paragraph 3.13 as a lease involving three parties (or more):

- The lessee who only wants to pay rentals in respect of what he sees as the lessor's holding costs for the asset and its fall in value resulting from his own use of it. He accordingly does not want the asset's entire cost rentalised (as in a full payout lease), or to be at risk in relation to the asset's residual value, by being required to pay a final balloon if it fails to realise the amount not already rentalised.

- The lessor who also wants to reduce, if not totally to eliminate, his own residual risk.

- The equipment supplier whose main objective is to sell his products, but who may see it as a necessary adjunct that he buy-in some used items in order to help his sales of new ones.

But before we go too far with this role-playing, let us pause to remember that leasing structures are almost infinitely variable; and varying them can produce the same answers sometimes, but more often will produce subtly different ones. For instance:

- we could leave the lessee unchanged but

- change the role of the lessor to that of a simple financier, lending the price of the equipment to the equipment supplier, and obtaining his repayment in part through the latter's assignment of the rental stream received from the lessee, and as to the balance (equal to the asset's expected residual) by repayment direct from the equipment supplier;

- that leaves the equipment supplier as the continuing owner of the asset throughout, and means that he is likely to be an operating lessor, with all that means for his own recognition of profit on the transaction (paragraph 3.11), and for his tax position. (In regard to the marginal level of doubt over the availability of capital allowances to a company which is both a dealer in the equipment, and a lessor of it, see the discussion at paragraph 7.24 of the *Gloucester Wagon* case).

The way in which the parties bear or share risks between themselves can be identical in the two alternatives. Their relationships with other parties in the outside world, such for instance as taxing authorities, may not be. On a cursory look, it is hard to identify the set of circumstances which would be better solved by the parties adopting the second set of roles rather than the first – but we do need to be aware that such possibilities exist – and that there are undoubtedly occasions when some flexibility in the assignment of roles can be advantageous.

4.13 Let us therefore come back to the straightforward:

- lessee willing to see rentalised his own use of the asset;

- lessor seeking to avoid residual risk and,

- equipment supplier recognising some necessity for buying in used equipment.

We have assumed that the operating lessor may not be over-keen to take onto his books substantial volumes of leasing of a particular product, if he believes that by doing so he is multiplying up to an unacceptable level his vulnerability to a collapse in its residual value. We have seen that the equipment supplier may have good reasons for wanting the right to buy-in his own products at the end of their normal lease terms; for instance to improve the possiblilities of his selling larger volumes of new items – and/or to have a better control over the reconditioning of the older items, so that doubts over product reliability are kept to a minimum. But it seems to stand to reason that the lower the figure at which the equipment supplier can buy back the equipment, the better for his profit and loss account. However, there may be a point at which the two parties can meet – a figure high enough to reduce the lessor's exposure to a level he regards as acceptable, and low enough so that the equipment supplier's main operation is not damaged. Let us assume that these two parties contract, at the time the equipment supplier originally sells the asset to the lessor, that the first will buy it back from the second, at the end of the lease term, at the price they have agreed. Does this present any problems?

4.14   The answer is almost certainly not, so long as the price the parties agree can be shown to have been, at the time they agreed it, not only negotiated at arms length, but regarded by both as a reasonable estimate of what the asset's market value might be at the later time when the sale between them is to take place. In other circumstances, there must be some degree of tax uncertainties, as follows:

*   The lessor needs to be confident that his capital allowances will be calculated on the basis of his having disposed of the asset at the contracted price and not at some other figure, substituted by the Revenue as a 'market value'. The legislation allows for such a substitution of a (higher) market value if the sale can be said to have been made at a price below the market. There is a safeguard, namely that such a lower price will not be disturbed, (for either party), if the purchaser is himself using it in his own claim for capital allowances by reference to his own acquisition of the asset: but it is unlikely that the equipment supplier will be taking the asset into a capital allowances claim, if his objective is to recondition and re-sell, or to cannibalise the asset for re-usable parts.

*   On a broader footing, the lessor's entire claim for capital allowances depends on his having both 'incurred capital expenditure on the provision of the (asset)', and that 'in consequence...(the asset) belongs to him'. There have always been fears that if a lessor contracts, at the time he acquires an asset, to re-sell it to the supplier at a nominal figure, clearly below any realistic market value, then it could be argued that he never acquired a full degree of ownership of the asset in the first place. 'Belonging' has been said to imply an ability to dispose of the asset concerned without restrictions.

*   Per contra, if the price the lessor is guaranteed by the supplier is high, it could be argued that the lessor never had any real intention of acquiring and retaining the asset to earn profits from its use, (the use he makes of it being to lease it out for rentals); that is the definition of his incurring 'capital' expenditure as opposed to any other kind. So the implication would be that he had merely paid out a lump sum to gain temporary access to the asset for a period, but could not have capital allowances on that sum.

The Inland Revenue will strenuously resist any efforts to persuade them to give clearance to proposed transactions. But it must be clear from the number of buy-back arrangements there are in existence, that realistic, commercially-based, deals are unlikely to excite them.

Contracts with dealers in the equipment

4.15   Our use of the phrase 'equipment supplier' should not make us imagine that we are only referring to manufacturers. So far as most people are concerned, the 'supplier' of a car or a van is a dealer with the relevant manufacturer's distributorship. Such a supplier is at least as keen as the manufacturer himself to achieve maximum sales. He may not be repurchasing many used vehicles for scrap, because the motor trade is geared to passing vehicles through to the outlet which is most likely to be able to re-sell them at an appropriate price. But in every other respect, a car distributor fits the profile we have in mind when we speak of an equipment supplier. There are other trades in which there is a clearer separation between those who sell new equipment, and those who recondition and otherwise deal in secondhand items. Contracts for sale of assets off leases, at guaranteed residuals, can be made with such dealers as effectively as with manufacturers or distributors of new equipment.

Put options for disposals off leases

4.16   Instead of entering into a contract binding himself to sell the asset at the end of the lease term, a lessor might protect his position by means of an option, entitling him to 'put' the asset to the grantor of that option at an agreed price at the time concerned. If, when that time arrived, the lessor found that he could realise more in the market than he could by exercising his option, he would abandon that option. If the market price was below the option figure, he would exercise it. It might seem unlikely that lessors would be able to find parties willing to write such put options, or to write enough of them to make the lessor's line of business tenable. But one possible source of such facilities could well be the equipment supplier. He might be able to tolerate a healthy secondhand market in his products – which ought not to damage the market for the new items. But a collapsed market for such used products could do nothing either for the product's reputation, or for the new sales, and supporting it might be his only course. Dealers offering put options to lessors might be more likely to seek an opportunity to profit from unexpected asset price levels, rather than merely risk losses. If a dealer offered to allow the lessor to 'put' the asset to him at £100, but himself had a 'call' option to acquire it at £200, then the dealer would lose if the market value were below £100, would gain if it were above £200, and would be in a neutral position between those values, since neither option would be exercised. So far as the lessor's minimum lease payments are concerned, the 'put' figure is clearly guaranteed but the 'call' is not; and although he may in fact obtain more by abandoning the option and selling in the market, it is the put option figure that would be counted both in categorising the lease between finance and operating, and in assessing the degree of risk the lessor was carrying.

Put options in connection with upgrading

4.17   More complex from each party's point of view are the arrangements under which the lessor may have the right to put the asset back to the equipment supplier, perhaps at different prices on various specified dates, provided he (the lessor) acquires a new asset at that time to replace the old. The equipment supplier's objective is clear; he wants to assist the lessor to encourage the lessee to upgrade his asset. Computers were the one obvious type of asset in which this might have appeared a few years ago to be in all three parties' interests; the supplier increases his sales, the lessor increases his 'book', that is to say the volume of his receivables and his potential for profit, and the lessee increases his computing power and speeds. The greater rental costs the lessee faced would have been accepted as inevitable − on the slightly jaundiced view that once one has gone in for information technology, there is never a point at which the quantity, and cost, of equipment can be stabilised. But describing the parties' positions in that way shows where the fallacy lies. If, despite increases in its speed and power, the price of new equipment does not rise, then each of the three links in the chain immediately shows its weakness:

• The equipment supplier's margins are already under pressure, and his having to buy in used items at what may now be seen as a generous figure cannot but put them under further pressure.

• The lessor can see that the proposed upgrading will do less by way of increasing his book than he could have hoped; but equally important from the lessor's point of view will be the question whether the equipment supplier is as likely to be willing to provide again the same generous guarantee of the lessor's residual value (a second time around). That leads straight back to the equipment supplier's own problems referred to above.

• Each of the above difficulties could be solved if the lessee could be persuaded that the upgrade justified a higher level of rentals − but in a competitive marketplace he seems unlikely to be easily persuaded of that.

• So perhaps a far-sighted equipment supplier and lessor may have tried to build into the original package not only the encouragement to trade in and upgrade, but also some penalty for not doing so. Perhaps the lessee was persuaded to commit himself to paying some final balloon rental on the old equipment if he did not sign a new lease calling for rentals at or above a stipulated minimum for the proposed upgrade ?

- But the lessee may still see that upgrade as too expensive, even against the alternative of being faced with that balloon penalty. And is the penalty enforceable in any event ? It must have been written into the original agreement by reference to the lessor's ability to offer upgraded equipment with closely defined specifications. Can the lessee's lawyers show that the lessor is failing to meet his side of that bargain?

4.18 As described above, each of these links seems to have its inherent weaknesses; but the company in the weakest position of all seems likely to be the lessor, unable to dispose of equipment off his leases at what he had thought was a sufficiently guaranteed residual, because he cannot afford to acquire the replacement equipment upon which those guarantees were conditional; and unable to acquire that replacement equipment not only because its conditional price makes it uneconomic for a lessee, but also because he (the lessor) cannot contemplate that replacement's own unguaranteed residuals. Finally, if the lessor's accounting policies have in the past recognised profits from the leasing of earlier generations of equipment on the assumption that the chain of trade-ins and upgrades at ever higher rents would last forever, and he has made no provision for any slowing of prices or volumes, then the lessor's position may be parlous indeed. Perhaps it should go without saying that arrangements for the sharing of residual risk should not only be satisfactory in the sun, but be stormproofed as well.

'Parties' risks'

4.19 The risks we have been considering in earlier paragraphs of this chapter could perhaps be called 'parties' risks':

- if one party defaults, where does that leave the others?

- if one party does not want to shoulder the whole of a risk, (for instance the residual risk which the lessee normally bears in a full payout lease, and which the lessee may envisage the lessor should bear in an operating lease,) can another or others be persuaded to share it?

- can either of the above matters be solved, or improved by some change in the roles which the various parties play in the total transaction? and does this have acceptable or unacceptable other consequences for any of them?

• has each party correctly identified what his true exposure is to each of the risks concerned? and are his resources strong enough to stand the strains that may be put on them – not just by the unexpected commercial out-turn, but by the possible failure of a counterparty as in the first point above?

And if each has correctly identified his risks, (not only where they are, and how large they may be, but also for how long the exposure will continue), has he made sure that he is properly rewarded for them? And has a contingency plan to mitigate the damage he might suffer if a risk were to crystallise?

Structural risks – tax rates and the tax system

4.20   But there is a whole range of further risks which are inherent in the very structure of a leasing transaction. It would be irrational to pretend that there is a clear dividing line between the classes, or that the crystallisation of a risk we have put into one class will not at the same time trigger a problem in another class. Secondly, there may be greater difficulties in achieving a fair and workable answer, or sharing of burdens, when something 'structural' occurs. And thirdly, (or perhaps it is no more than the second point in a different guise), there is often no very constructive suggestion one can make to assist the parties. It is perhaps easiest to show what these circumlocutions are trying to say by illustration. If two years into the lease we have used throughout this book to illustrate our points, the rate of corporation tax were to be increased from 35 percent to 45 percent, then the lessor's aggregate tax burden would be calculated as in Table 42.

		35% yrs 0 & 1 45% yrs 2 – 5	originally
Yr 0	Loss	(2,500)	(875)	(875)
Yr 1	Loss	(232)	(81)	(81)
Yr 2	Profit	492	221	172
Yr 3	Profit	1,059	476	371
Yr 4	Profit	1,559	701	546
Yr 5	Profit	293	132	103
Total tax		574	236
Post-tax profit		97	435

Table 42
Effect of an increase in the rate of corporation tax from 35 percent to 45 percent in respect of year 2's and later years' profits.

The figures in the left hand column were not in the mind of the lessor when he quoted a rental of £672 per quarter to the lessee; the lessor expected to be earning a reward on his equity contribution, (for his risks and his effort) of a post-tax £435, as shown on the right.

4.21 Unless they had agreed otherwise, the lessor would suffer the whole burden of the tax rate increase, and the lessee would be unaffected. The usual form of any such agreement to the contrary would be a 'tax variation clause' in the lease, saying that if the rate were to change, the lessee would pay such extra amount by way of rentals as would leave the lessor with the same post-tax profit he would otherwise have earned. Frequently, as indicated, tax variation clauses are written only one way, to ratchet up the lessee's rentals if the tax rate increases, but not to decrease those rentals if the rate were to fall. And those points themselves show how little there is to be said about changes in tax rate. There is no fair balance between lessor and lessee at which they can agree to bear the extra cost. If the lessor believes his customers will accept it, and come back for more, then he will push the burden onto his lessees. If he does not, he will grin and bear it himself, (he will be getting a 45 percent value out of allowances on the business he has just written, in the same years in which he is paying those higher tax bills on the later years' profits from this particular lease). There is another point. Even in so straightforward a case as this, it would be unusual to find a tax variation clause which specified that if the tax rate moved by x percent, the rentals would go up by £y. The reason is twofold. Tax rate changes are sometimes announced as a programme of upward movements each year over a period – but it is desirable not to have to recalculate every lease rental every year; although the lessee would much rather the rental were left unchanged, if it has to move, he would rather it moved to a new flat rate, not thereafter to be changed. Secondly, the timing of tax rate changes, (in terms of the profits to which they apply, and the date at which the higher cash sum first becomes payable), and the period necessary for the lessor to do his recalculations and agree them with the lessee, mean that it is only sensible to provide for adjustment of the rentals not already due and/or paid when these figures are agreed; it would be even less satisfactory to write a formula into the lease which created a retrospective liability for the lessee.

4.22 We have used the phrase 'structural risks' for this whole group of items which may leave the lessor exposed (or which he may seek to pass on to the lessee). That is perhaps slightly confusing, in that the second specific risk is that the structure of the tax system may be changed. A change of this type could be, for instance, from our present imputation system of corporation tax to a classical system – such a move would be likely to alter tax rates quite substantially at the corporate level, but could not be described merely as a rate change. But a structural change might also consist of legislation requiring that lessors pay tax on rentals by reference to date of receipt, rather than by reference to the period through which they accrue (see paragraph 2.17). That change would accelerate by a full twelve months our lessor's liability on £672 of rentals received on 31 December in each years 0, 1, 2, 3, and 4 – and by doing so change noticeably the profile of his cashflow. It is more common for lessors to try to protect themselves against damage flowing from a change in the structure of the tax system, and for lessees to accept that this is a reasonable burden for them to be expected to bear. Once again, the clause in the leasing agreement designed to achieve such protection for the lessor is usually written in very general phrases, and because it may be complex to calculate what change is called for in the rental level in response to some structural tax change, (and perhaps even more complex to persuade both lessor and lessee that this is the only way the clause can be interpreted), provision is usually included in the clause for the calculations to be made by an independent party, and for him or some other to act as arbitrator in any dispute that arises.

Interest rate changes

4.23   The third of the structural risks that the lessor probably faces is one mentioned right at the start of this book (paragraph 1.02). To the extent that the lessor is engaged in a financial business, he is vulnerable to changes in the rate of interest charged to him by those from whom he borrows, and may wish to pass through such extra costs (or benefits) to his lessees. In this case, it is possible, but not attractive, to make use of the same type of generally worded clause in the lease agreement as we have envisaged for tax changes, in order to have someone recalculate what change is necessary in the rentals. No attempt to 'hypothecate' particular borrowings against particular leases could be practicable, and even trying to attribute a proportion of the different types of borrowing to each lease would be difficult if not impossible; most lessors will have borrowed both fixed rate funds, and floating rate, and the proportions are not likely to remain constant. The lessor may be strongly tempted, therefore, to make use of a simple numerical formula in the lease agreement to the effect that if on a day (say) three weeks before a rental falls due, the LIBOR rate quoted by a reference bank is x percent above or below a specified rate, then that rental will be increased or reduced by £y. In this case, unlike that of the tax adjustments, each subsequent rental will have to be put up or down, (or will stay where originally fixed), in line with the same machinery for fixing it. One has to notice, however, that although the lessor might be able to protect his own position in total by such a simple arrangement, he would be doing so only at the expense of considerable inequity between the individual lessees. Early in a lease, a very much larger proportion of rentals goes towards interest on the lessor's borrowings than is the case in later years of the lease. An interest rate rise should therefore result in a larger rise in rentals for a newer lease than for an older one, in the same way that a mortgage interest rise is more painful for the recent borrower under a repayment mortgage than for the earlier borrower. It is possible to write a numerical formula which allows for this point, and achieves a greater degree of fairness between lessees, as well as producing a generally acceptable approximation of the protection needed by the lessor.

Turning a proportion of the portfolio into cash

4.24   This is not so much either a 'party risk' or a 'structural risk', as one of the ways a lessor may attempt to retrieve the position after some such risk has crystallised. The process itself is no more nor less than the lessor's assignment, for cash, of a proportion of his total portfolio of leases, the procedures for, and implications of, which we briefly looked at in paragraphs 1.09 – 1.15. But we also said in paragraph 4.06 that this exercise may be neither simple nor quick. That only disclosed a part of the problem, as we will see. The real difficulties are 'structural' in yet another sense of that word – namely that the figures simply do not seem to fit together in a satisfactory manner. We need to start digging back into the figures of the example we have used throughout, in order to explain how and why there is such a mis-fit. The 'brick' in paragraph 2.33 showed the following position at the end of year 2:

	Balance sheet				Profit & Loss
	Liabilities			Assets	Original Equity
External borrowing	Current tax	Deferred tax	Investment in finance leases	New cash generated	
Cr 5144	Cr 172	Cr 963	Dr 6970		Cr 691

Let us assume, (because this coincides with the way that these figures have been put together), that the lessor is willing to assign the lease on 31 December of year 2, in such a way that:

- the assignee will himself acquire the asset in year 2 and be entitled to a capital allowance for that year;

- our lessor will allow the assignee to have the rental due on 31 December of year 2 — which is not treated as having already been received in the above figures.

We know that if the lessor wants to 'come out of the lease whole', that is to say without loss on the exit itself, and without sacrificing any of the profits he has already made, he needs to sell the leased asset for £6,970, (this was the point explained in paragraph 2.59). (See Table 43).

Provided he gets that figure, he can use it to pay off his
external borrowing £5,144

and to meet his tax liability for year 2 which
will be recalculated as follows to take into
account his disposal in that year of the asset

Rentals received		2,688		
Interest paid		(790)		
Capital allowances				
Sale proceeds	6,970			
written down value	(5,625)	1,345		
		3,243	at 35 percent	1,135
				6,279

and he will have enough left to make good the outstanding
amount of his equity injection 691

6,970

Table 43
Illustration of the lessor's ability to 'come out of the lease whole' on receipt of £6,970 for an assignment of the lease at end year 2. Note that in computing his tax position, the whole sum is treated as being proceeds of disposal of the leased asset, but that the use of the cash is what is illustrated above.

4.25 The problems start when we think through the position of the assignee who pays £6,970 for an asset with a lease wrapped round it having three years to run, entitling him to quarterly rentals of £672, and to retain £50 out of the sale proceeds of the asset at the end of that three years. Assume for simplicity that he is prepared to take it onto his books by borrowing externally that same figure of £6,279, and committing his own equity to the extent of £691. That is not the 85:15 percent ratio we assumed lessors might take as their guideline, but we know (paragraph 2.38) that a lessor's ratios do degenerate through a lease's term; perhaps we can assume for present purposes that the assignee would take this three year lease onto his books with the ratios it would have had if he had himself incepted it two years earlier. Assume also that the external borrowing costs the assignee the same 3.57 percent per quarter, 15 percent per annum, that we have used throughout for the lessor's interest costs. The assignee's cash flow for the next three years, (it is put together in exactly the same form as our own lessor's was in paragraph 2.24), looks like Table 43.

		Equity					External borrowing				
	Rentals extracted	Start of quarter	Equity income	End of quarter			Rentals applied to repay borrowings	Tax	Start of quarter	Interest expense	End of quarter
Y3 Q1	691	–	691	3	694	6279	(672)		5607	188	5795
Q2	694	(137)	557	2	557	5795	(535)		5260	177	5437
Q3	557	(112)	447	2	449	5437	(560)		4877	164	5041
Q4	449	(91)	358	2	360	5041	(581)	(610)	3850	129	3979
				9			(2348)			658	20252
Y4 Q1	360	(75)	285	2	287	3979	(597)		3382	114	3496
		(415)									
Q2	287	(68)	219	1	220	3496	(604)		2892	97	2989
Q3	220	(61)	159	1	160	2989	(611)		2378	81	2459
Q4	160	(54)	106	1	107	2459	(618)	253	2094	70	2164
				5			(2430)			362	11108
Y5 Q1	107	(45)	62	1	63	2164	(627)		1537	52	1589
		(228)									
Q2	63	(36)	27	–	27	1589	(636)		953	32	985
Q3	27	(27)	–	–	–	985	(645)		340	12	352
Q4	–	–	–	–	–	352	(672)	471	151	5	156
		(63)		1			(2580)			101	3082
						156	(2500)				
							2450	106	–	–	–
							(50)				
		(706)		15			(7408)	8		1121	34442

Table 43

Cashflow constructed for the assignee-lessor for the remaining three years of the lease, assuming that his initial equity injection is the same as that of the assignor (£691), and that the balance of the consideration he gave for the assignment was borrowed (£6,279).

The extraction of cash on the equity side is calculated by reference to the net cash investment:

$$\frac{20,252}{34,442} \times 706 = 415$$

$$\frac{11,108}{34,442} \times 706 = 228$$

$$\frac{3,082}{34,442} \times 706 = \frac{63}{706}$$

And if one wanted to summarise the remaining figures one sees:

the assignee receives 12 rentals of £672		£8,064
plus the excess of sale proceeds over rebate		50
		8,114
which he pays out		
on purchase of the asset	6,279	
as interest on the external borrowing	1,121	
as tax on his own profits	8	
		7,408
		706
the balance being		
his original equity, now extracted	691	
together with his reward on this	15	
		706

4.26   And what is the problem ? Well, simply that the assignee's rate of post-tax reward on his equity is not 4 percent, as it was in our original lessor's cashflow in paragraph 2.24. The rate the assignee gets above is a mere 0.4 percent, post tax. The reason why the lease's profitability has dropped so disastrously is reasonably easy to see. At the end of year 2 our original lessor certainly had external borrowings totalling £6,279. That is shown by the figures excerpted above from our original 'brick'. But only £5,144 of these were interest bearing borrowings. The balance of £1,135 was unpaid tax − £172 of it being due within nine months, and the balance being further 'deferred'. On the assignment, we see that the original lessor has to pay off the whole of this 'free' loan; and the assignee then has to face the fact that the whole of his own external borrowings are interest bearing. Admittedly, the effect of his first capital allowance is that nine months after he steps into the saddle, the Inland Revenue are 'lending' him money, free of interest, but the amount is not as large, nor as prolonged − and in any event it comes only after he has been paying full interest for that nine months. The lease's whole profitability is knocked out of kilter by the effects of the assignment. And it seems obvious that in a world in which all other things are equal, the assignee would be unlikely to be keen to pay as much as £6,970 for the lease we have been looking at. That is why we can say that the figures do not fit. Either the original lessor will exit with a loss (or a considerably reduced profit), or the assignee will have to accept a lower level of profitability than one might have expected him to have been willing to do. Notice in particular that although this explanation has been wholly based on a finance lease illustration, identical principles would apply to the operating lessor's financing of his leased asset; all that tends to obscure this fact is that the operating lessor's pricing of his service to his lessee, and his method of recognising his own profits from the transaction, are less closely based on these identical (finance/operating) borrowings and equity used to acquire and hold the leased asset. But the author does once again have to say that the original illustration's figures were designed to highlight, at the risk of overstating, the original profitablity of the lease. They almost certainly overstate the fall in profitability on this assignment. Secondly, assigning the lease early in its life, when the 'tax loans' are at a substantial level will also tend to overemphasize the disadvantages of the procedure. And finally, the order in which we examined the steps in the process might mislead the reader into thinking that the acquisition of a lease, part of the way through its term, can never be profitable for the assignee. This is not correct. If the assignee pays an appropriate figure, he can make a proper level of profit. What our illustration shows is that it seems unlikely that both assignee, and original lessor, will make the profit they might have sought. Each can only do so at the expense of the other's profitability – because there is insufficient space for them both.

Terminations and stipulated loss values

4.27 The disadvantages, (probably penalties would be a better word), flowing from early termination of a lease might be thought mainly to affect the lessee.

• the lessor will repossess the asset, and demand to be reimbursed for the costs he may incur in doing this, and the loss he may sustain on realising it;

• the lessor will not only demand any rentals already due but unpaid, but may also demand all rentals which would have been payable at future dates up to what would have been the lease's normal termination;

• the lessor may also demand a penalty sum, to compensate him for the profit he would have made had the lease run its normal course;

Lease agreements often include provisions requiring all of the above, even though it is impossible not to see that the lessor is certainly double, and in some areas, treble counting the damage he may suffer. The lessor and the lawyers who drafted the lease agreement for him would insist that they would not in practice ask for the whole of the foregoing, but that it is sensible to write each provision into the lease in the above form – so that whatever are the circumstances surrounding the early termination, they can frame an appropriate claim against the erstwhile lessee. Some lessors are concerned however, and some lawyers share their concern, that a court might not be willing to enforce the penalties they called for, arising out of an agreement which so manifestly failed to hold an equitable balance between the parties. 'Stipulated loss values' are an attempt to formulate a claim by the lessor against the lessee which might be more acceptable to the courts – and which still give the lessor the flexibility in making his claim fit the circumstances. The idea is that the lease agreement contains a schedule of monetary amounts for various dates between the lease's inception and normal termination dates, such that the lessor's receipt of the relevant sum would fully cover the damage he had sustained. As an example, the original lessor in the immediately preceding example (paragraph 4.24) could have written £6,970 into the lease agreement as the stiupulated loss value at 31 December of year 2, (immediately before the receipt of the rental due on that day). If the lessee had terminated, but had paid over the £6,970, that would have enabled the lessor to pay off his external borrowing, meet the tax liability arising on the 'sale of the asset' for £6,970, and have left the lessor with the then outstanding amount of his equity contribution. He would already have made, and would retain, the profits of years 1 and 2. He would not make the profits he would otherwise have made in years 3, 4 and 5. But because he had his equity back, intact, he could re-borrow, and reinvest in a new asset and incept a new leasing transaction so as to be able to continue making profits.

4.28 If that were as far as it went, £6,970 would be the 'correct' figure to use for the stipulated loss value. We would be able to see that one suggestion that is sometimes made would in the circumstances be uncontroversial. This is the suggestion that the stipulated loss value is the asset's 'value' for accounting purposes – that is to say that if the lessor merely inserts it into his 'brick' (paragraph 2.33) as his investment in financial leases, this will automatically result in his recognising the correct level of income in each accounting period in the lease term. He does not need, on this basis, to make the calculations we illustrated in the paragraphs leading up to the lessor's profit and loss account in paragraph 2.35. But this is only true if we are confident that the calculation of the stipulated loss value has not been 'distorted' as we indicate below is likely to have been the case. Continuing with our simple illustration of the stipulated loss value of £6,970 at the end of year 2, it would be clear that that was all the lessor needed to 'keep him whole'. If he realised £4,500 from selling the asset, he would need £2,470 from the lessee. He need not for instance ask for future, not-yet-due, rentals. And he need not ask for other penalties. The problem with the calculation of stipulated loss values is the practical one that each early termination involves work and expense for the lessor, not all of the latter clearly enough identifiable to be re-charged to the lessee. Therefore the lessor will automatically build a 'cushion' into the figures in order to cover this. Secondly, the lessor will be only too well aware that there will always be some delay in his obtaining the cash from the lessee, even if the amount is clearly stipulated in the lease agreement

– so that he needs a further element of 'cushion'. The stipulated loss value quickly grows to a figure greater than £6,970. One of the consequences is that it becomes an unreliable measure of accounting results. But the more important consequence is the 'risk factor':

- So far as the lessor is concerned, has he correctly calculated the basic figure, and has he then realistically allowed for the effort and cost which an early termination will involve so that he is adequately protected against loss ?

- So far as the lessee is concerned, he presumably accepts that in the give and take of the negotiation of the lease agreement, a proper level of stipulated loss payments is one of the matters which he really should 'give' ? But is he satisfied that he understands how the lessor arrived at the figures he has put into the lease, and can therefore agree their 'propriety' ?

Step rentals and balloons

4.29 Structural risks of a rather different type arise from the actual pattern of rentals called for under the lease. We have concentrated largely on leases having a level pattern of rentals through the lease term. But we have noticed that some operating leases, (in particular contract hiring arrangements for cars to individuals or to companies whose credit is not impeccable), may involve rentals in advance and rental holidays at the end of the term (paragraph 4.05). We also noticed that what may be thought of as the classical pattern of finance lease we have illustrated requires the rentalising of the asset's entire cost, and only after that gives a rebate of rentals equal to a substantial proportion of the sale proceeds (paragraph 2.16); however, we did earlier mention that there was an alternative way of achieving a broadly similar objective (paragraph 1.05), namely that the lessor could rentalise say 80 percent of the asset's cost, and provide also that the lessee should pay a final balloon rental at the time of its disposal equal to the difference between 20 percent of its cost, and 98 percent of the sale proceeds. In mentioning that last possibility, we said that the lessor's 'security' was obviously less for the final balloon than for the earlier quarterly rentals – there was no longer an asset to repossess and sell. The same principles apply whenever a lessor may be asked to consider a pattern of rentals which leaves him, at any stage in the lease term, less fully protected than he would prefer to have been. Final balloons are extreme examples. A 'stepped' pattern of rents, the second year greater than the first, and the third than the second, may be sensible from some points of view, but does need to be looked at from the point of view of the the lessor's risk that his lessee will default.

4.30 One particular aspect of this is that the risks associated with these unusual patterns of rentals probably do require to be reflected in the lessor's accounting principles for recognising profits. The author is conscious, in writing, that it seems to contradict an earlier opinion. In paragraph 2.61, we had this to say on the subject of providing for bad and doubtful debts:

> "It is sometimes argued that unacceptable accounting answers flow from the possibility that a debtor might be identified as doubtful relatively late in the lease term. For instance, if in the lease we are looking at, the debtor defaulted after paying the rental due on 31 December of year 4, (but before the accounts for that year had been prepared, so that it was necessary to provide in those accounts for the bad debt), it is clear that the amount needing to be provided would be £2,660. The income in year 4's accounts against which such a provision can be set is £42 pre-tax, £28 post-tax. It is therefore said that the accounting policy of recognising significant amounts of income at the front end of the lease is at fault, in that it leaves insufficient income to deal with bad debts later in the term".

But there are two points. We were talking at that stage about finance leases, and most of our discussions had been about an accounting policy (the actuarial method after tax) which recognises significant levels of profit in the early years of the lease, this itself being in line with the constant rate of return on the net cash investment. That net cash investment will have a different profile if the rentals are stepped, or ballooned, towards the end of the lease term. But more importantly, it may be acceptable to use the constant rate of return as a guiding light when cash has been flowing in from the lessee on what might be thought of as a 'normal' pattern, similar to that of the vast majority of the company's other leases both older and more recent. It would be quite another thing to use that same constant rate of return principle, without adjustment, to recognise profit on a lease when no rentals, or only negligible sums, had been received in cash. Secondly, the lessor's extra degree of credit risk on the stepped or ballooned rentals could be reflected, perhaps, in some higher level of provisioning for doubtful debts − that is precisely what the diminished level of security in the lessor's hands might suggest.

Statutory risks

4.31 The third class of risks, besides 'party' and 'structural' ones, are the statutory risks. It is not appropriate to attempt to give an exhaustive list, and one example will therefore suffice to illustrate the fact that lessors must not overlook the fact that they remain the legal owners of the leased assets, even though they may have transferred 'substantially all the risks and rewards of ownership of the asset' to the lessee. And lessees must accept that as a result of that substantial transfer, they are likely to be regarded as the asset's 'operator'. The example is that the obligations and liabilities of the owner of an asset under the Health and Safety at Work legislation cannot be transferred by the asset's legal owner to any other party. Be warned, and investigate what other risks there may be in your proposed activities.

Risks - an overview

4.32   Going back for a moment to the subject referred to in paragraph 4.29, namely unusual rental profiles, we used at one stage to see special transactions relying to a considerable extent on such profiles – usually very heavily tax based leases, in which the availability of substantial tax allowances seemed to be of greater moment to some of the parties than any profit which the deal might have provided overall. To the extent these rentals might be thought to create excessive credit risks for the lessor, the lessees were sometimes asked to make cash deposits into accounts on which the lessor could call in the event of any such default. That gave the lessor total risk elimination – but... The 'but' must remind us that leasing is a business, and that all the parties involved in it, and in businesses which use its products, or supply goods and services to lessors, are in their various businesses for profit. There is no business which does not involve risk. One can buy one's way out of it, (or most of it), but the likelihood is that the costs of doing so will eliminate the profit one hoped to make. What this chapter is all about is not the elimination of risk. Transactions which are free of risk, and in which profit seems unimportant are neither business nor leasing, (which explains incidentally why the Inland Revenue have challenged over the years a considerable number of the types of transaction referred to in the first paragraph above). We must always, as a matter of course, in every proposed deal:

- identify where the risks lie;

- decide whether they would be better shared with some other party (or possibly transferred to his shoulders);

- identify what the costs are of sharing those risks, or laying them off, as above;

- and perhaps most importantly of all, not only identify but attempt to quantify, the exposures which we have accepted we should continue to carry.

That is all a positive exercise; defensive may be a word that can be applied to parts of it, but negative is not an apt term. The result of this positive exercise, and indeed of leasing as a whole, is the second word in the heading of this chapter – 'reward' is what we are after, and we get there by taking only measured risks; certainly not by avoiding all risk.

Leveraged leases

4.33   The word 'leveraged' used in connection with management buy-outs is taken to mean that those backing the managers with loan capital have been willing to lend considerably more than the level of equity that those managers have themselves contributed. It is therefore easy to assume that every lease we have so far considered is 'leveraged', and indeed that leasing companies are themselves highly leveraged businesses. This is not, however the meaning in the United States of the phrase 'leveraged leasing'. The transaction is quite common there, whilst being virtually unknown in the UK; such is one result of our tax system. The parties whose positions are leveraged, in the sense of their being willing to take an extra degree of risk in the hope of reaping an extra level of reward, are the financiers. They lend to the lessor, not only forgoing any recourse against the lessor, but with only restricted recourse to the lessee's income stream and the asset in the lessee's hands. On successful completion of the lease term, however, the leveraged financiers are entitled to participate in the asset's residual. The arrangement is frequently used for major project financing – and the leveraged lenders are described in the plural because it is more usual for the role to be undertaken by a consortium than by a single individual or corporation. The arrangement's relevance to this book, and this chapter in particular, is merely the demonstration that there are those who welcome the opportunity to take risks, viewing the correctly assessed risk as the opportunity for profit.

CHAPTER 5

Lease evaluation

The potential lessee's question

5.01 The question most often asked by those wondering whether to lease assets, or to acquire them by purchase or hire purchase, is 'Which is the cheaper ?'. The purposes of this chapter are:

- to show that while that question appears on the surface to be valid, it cannot be given a valid answer unless it is first rephrased, secondly set in the context of the business's existing (and proposed future) operations, and thirdly examined in relation to the specific lease agreement and its alternatives;

- rephrasing the question is partly a matter of defining whether immediate cashflows are so critical a factor that the medium or longer term must be assumed to be capable of being handled at that time – or whether the questioner is seeking an all-round, longer term, look at his enquiry;

- we will see below how vital it is to consider any possible leasing transaction within the business context rather than outside it, as an unrelated, theoretical, possibility;

- and we have once again to point out that not only can lease agreements differ widely in cost and other provisions, but that some of those other provisions have generally to be regarded as traps for the unwary. We will indicate some of the worst of these.

The implicit rate re-examined

5.02 The first part of our rephrasing of the lessee's question must be to clarify which flows of cash, in and out, he wishes to compare with which other flows, in order to decide relative 'cheapness':

- One possibility which was the one adopted in the lessee's cashflow set out in paragraph 2.02, (on which we based the calculation of the implicit rate), is to look simply and solely at the rental outflows.

- Another would be to take into account also the expected rebate of rentals related to the asset's eventual sale off the lease – or if it seems more likely that the lessee will wish to retain that asset into a secondary term of the lease, the rentals during that term and the rebate when the lessee does eventually ask for the asset to be sold. This would have given us a totally different 'cost' for the asset.

- Yet another would be to take into account the flows of cash to and from the tax authorities resulting from the lease rentals, and from any alternative, in order to make the comparison one which sets 'like with like' on a more complete basis.

Let us leave aside for the moment the asset's sale proceeds and the lessee's rebate of rentals, and concentrate on the third approach – taking an 'after tax' viewpoint. In the leasing possibility, the rentals are the only outflows, and tax reliefs on them can be taken as notional receipts nine months into the following year, (because we assume that they reduce what would otherwise have been larger tax payments at those dates). This would then compare with the borrowing, and asset purchase, possibility, where the primary outflows would be the principal and interest to service the borrowing, but the tax reliefs would be rather different, namely relief for the interest but not the principal, together with capital allowances on the cost of the asset.

5.03   Having identified the alternative cashflows as above, we can then discount them back to a present value, using a realistic rate of discount. Whichever alternative results in the lower present value must be the better choice. But notice three points about this process:

- The cashflows themselves do not alter as a result of our choice of discounting rate. We have a notional lender who has agreed (we are still using the figures from the example in paragraph 2.02) to lend us £10,000, to be repaid by 20 instalments of £672 per quarter payable in advance. That embodies an interest rate of 3.357 percent – the implicit rate. We can choose to discount that back to present value at 3 percent per quarter, or at 3.5 percent; those choices do not alter the proportions within each £672 instalment which are deemed to be interest, or to be principal. Only the lessor's renegotiation of the level of the rentals could do that, or in our notional borrowing case, the deemed lender's renegotiation of the £672 instalments he is prepared to accept for the loan's repayment.

- If we choose a discount rate which is somewhere near realistic, we should arrive at a present value for the inflows and outflows on the lease alternative of something over £6,500. The reason is that the primary outflows will discount back to £10,000 or thereabouts, namely the value of the asset. The secondary inflows, (the tax reliefs), will discount back to a figure less than £3,500, because of the inbuilt delays each year in the giving of these reliefs. In the case of the notional borrowing and asset purchase, we would expect to find that the present value was less than that in the lease alternative if the tax reliefs are available on an overall quicker footing, but not otherwise. To the extent that we are dealing with uneven flows in the case of these tax reliefs on a notional borrowing etc, the rate of discount is somewhat more sensitive − but we will come to that after we have looked at our first set of figures worked out in the next paragraph.

- It is correct to say that the rate implicit in the lease as calculated in paragraph 2.05 is 3.357 percent. What does not follow from that is that if a potential lessee can borrow funds at 3.35 percent, he should borrow and should purchase the asset; whilst if he can only borrow 3.36 percent the lease is the better alternative. The implicit rate should never be mistaken for the after tax borrowing rate on which we need to base our evaluation techniques. That is why we said in paragraph 2.14 that in the context of lease evaluation, the implicit rate is not quite what it is sometimes thought to be.

5.04 Thus if we use a discount rate of 3.57 percent per quarter, we can compare the present values of the cashflows of the lease used as our principal example, with the present values of what would be the cashflows on an equivalent borrowing and asset purchase. In the lease, the rentals are £672 per quarter. A full year's rentals are therefore £2,688, and the value of tax relief on this amount at 35 percent is £941. In a borrowing and purchase situation, the cash outflows for principal and interest on the borrowing are the identical sums of £672 per quarter. The interest

	Lease		Borrowing/purchase		
	Rentals	Expense for tax	Principal & interest	Interest expense for tax	Capital all'ces
Year 1	2,688	−	2,688	−	−
Year 2	2,688	2,688	2,688	1,179	2,500
Year 3	2,688	2,688	2,688	965	1,875
Year 4	2,688	2,688	2,688	723	1,406
Year 5	2,688	2,688	2,688	445	1,054
Year 6	−	2,688	−	128	3,165
	13,440	13,440	13,440	3,440	10,000

Table 44

Comparison of leasing with borrowing/purchasing; amounts and timing of primary cashflows, and amounts on which tax relief is due with timing of that relief.

component within this comes from paragraph 2.02; and the capital allowances assume that the asset is disposed of for nil proceeds at the end of year 5, (an assumption which is consistent with that used for the 'lease' figures, where we are at this stage ignoring the sale of the asset, and the rebate receivable by the lessee). The comparative figures to be used in arriving at cashflows, which can then be discounted back to present values, can be summarised as in Table 44, (the tax deductibles being given a value not for the year to which they relate, but in which the tax relief will crystallise into a reduction of liability).

We know that tax relief should be available for every £1 of outflow, and the above demonstrates that this is the case.

5.05 If we now use a discount rate of 3.57 percent per quarter to put present values on each of these outflows, and on the values of the tax reliefs, (35 percent of the amounts of the tax reliefs shown above), the figures are as in Table 45.

As we expected, the present values of the primary outflows of cash do come to approximately £10,000, and the values of the tax reliefs to something less than £3,500. In fact, because the tax reliefs for the borrowing/purchase alternative are available marginally quicker than those for the leasing alternative, it is clear that the former is 'cheaper' — if one does want to answer the lessee's original query in the form in which he originally asked it. But we will have more to say about that in the next few paragraphs.

Leasing — the preferable course for the tax-exhausted ?

5.06 Whether or not there is a clear message for the lessee in the figures in the preceding paragraph and in Table 44, there certainly is one for us. It is often said that leasing is the preferable choice for companies which have tax losses, (the jargon in our paragraph heading is to describe this as tax-exhaustion), 'because they cannot absorb the capital allowances which they would get if they were to purchase the asset, whereas in the leasing alternative the company is effectively 'selling' those allowances to the lessor company for a rental which is calculated to take them into account'. The second half of the sentence (within the quotes) is absolutely true, and fails absolutely to lead to the conclusion drawn from it in the earlier part of the sentence. To absorb the capital allowances, together with the deductibility of interest payments, if the company purchases the asset, it needs to have £13,440 of taxable 'capacity', that is to say profits which would otherwise have been exposed to tax, over the five years. On the other hand, if it were to lease the asset, it would need £13,440 of taxable capacity to absorb the deductions available for the rentals paid. There is a marginal

Discount factor		Lease		Borrowing/purchase		
		Rentals	Expense for tax	Principal & interest	Interest expense for tax	Capital all'ces
1.0000	Yr 1 Qr 1	672		672		
0.9655	Qr 2	649		649		
0.9322	Qr 3	626		626		
0.9001	Qr 4	605		605		
		2,552		2,552		
0.8691	Yr 2 Qr 1	584		584		
0.8391	Qr 2	564		564		
0.8102	Qr 3	544		544		
0.7823	Qr 4	526	(736)	526	(322)	(685)
		2,218		2,218		
0.7553	Yr 3 Qr 1	508		508		
0.7293	Qr 2	490		490		
0.7041	Qr 3	473		473		
0.6799	Qr 4	457	(640)	457	(230)	(446)
		1,928		1,928		
0.6564	Yr 4 Qr 1	441		441		
0.6338	Qr 2	426		426		
0.6120	Qr 3	411		411		
0.5909	Qr 4	397	(556)	397	(149)	(291)
		1,675		1,675		
0.5705	Yr 5 Qr 1	383		383		
0.5508	Qr 2	370		370		
0.5318	Qr 3	357		357		
0.5315	Qr 4	345	(483)	345	(80)	(189)
		1,455		1,455		
0.4462	Yr 6 Qr 4		(419)		(20)	(494)
		9,828	(2,834)	9,828	(801)	(2,105)
		6,994		6,922		

Table 45

Discounting to present values the primary payments and tax reliefs in the lease and comparing these with the equivalent present values for borrowing/purchase.

acceleration of the availability of these deductions in the 'purchase' alternative, given the particular assumptions we have made about asset disposals, and discount rates. But it is only marginal. What cannot be justified in any way are either of the two implications that the quotation appears to contain, that:

- A lessee is not entitled to a tax deduction for his rentals paid – and is thus 'worse off' in this regard than an asset owner, because the latter does get capital allowances on the asset's cost. (But, the implication continues, the lessor may be prepared to pass on some of the benefit of the allowances to the lessee in the calculation of the rentals.)

- And/or, the relief for capital allowances is given so enormously much faster than that for rental deductions that unless the company has vast tax capacity in year 1 it will lose out on the capital allowances – but would be able to absorb the rental deductions.

There may have been some truth, not as much as was often claimed, in the second proposition before the tax changes of 1984. But that fact does not seem to the author grounds for being tolerant with those who are still offering advice that is now seven years out of date.

Discounting to present values – further examined

5.07 The next point that we need to grasp is the significance of the discount rate we choose. In paragraph 5.03, we discounted back to present day values at 3.57 percent per quarter the primary outflows of £672, whether in the form of rentals paid or of instalments of principal and interest on a borrowing, and discounted similarly the values of the tax reliefs. The figures we ended up with were as in Table 46.

	Lease		Borrowing/purchase		
	Rentals	Expense for tax	Principal & interest	Interest expense for tax	Capital all'ces
Present value of all flows at 3.57% per qr	9,828	(2,834)	9,828	(801)	(2,105)
		6,994		6,922	

Table 46
Recapitulation of comparative present values for leasing and for borrowing/purchase, using a discount rate of 3.57 percent.

and it would appear that the advantage lay with the borrowing/purchase alternative; and that the quantum of that advantage was £72 in present values. If we use a higher discounting rate, we would expect the present values to be less, as in Table 47, from which it seems that the advantage still lies with the borrowing/purchase alternative, the quantum being £74 in present value.

	Lease		Borrowing/purchase		
	Rentals	Expense for tax	Principal & interest	Interest expense for tax	Capital all'ces
Present values					
at 3.75%					
per qr					
Yr 1	2,546		2,546		
Yr 2	2,197	(727)	2,197	(318)	(676)
Yr 3	1,896	(628)	1,896	(225)	(438)
Yr 4	1,636	(542)	1,636	(146)	(283)
Yr 5	1,412	(467)	1,412	(78)	(183)
Yr 6		(403)		(19)	(475)
	9,687	(2,767)	9,687	(786)	(2,055)
		6,920		6,846	

Table 47

Comparison of present values for leasing and for borrowing/purchase, discounted at 3.75 percent.

If we use a lower discount rate, the figures become as in Table 48 and the advantage still lies with borrowing/purchase, this time the quantum of that advantage being £70 of present value.

	Lease		Borrowing/purchase		
	Rentals	Expense for tax	Principal & interest	Interest expense for tax	Capital all'ces
Present values					
at 3.25%					
per qr					
Yr 1	2,564		2,564		
Yr 2	2,256	(753)	2,256	(330)	(700)
Yr 3	1,986	(662)	1,986	(238)	(462)
Yr 4	1,748	(582)	1,748	(156)	(305)
Yr 5	1,536	(512)	1,536	(85)	(201)
Yr 6		(450)		(22)	(530)
	10,090	(2,959)	10,090	(831)	(2,198)
		7,131		7,061	

Table 48

Comparison of present values for leasing and for borrowing/purchase, discounted at 3.25 percent.

Thus, if we are using the process of discounting to present values merely to compare the attractiveness of two possible courses of action, the rate we use will not normally be critical. That could be untrue if the profiles of outflows and inflows are different to an extreme extent, but where (as here) they are not substantially dissimilar, discounting to present value is a remarkably robust process at any reasonable discount rate.

5.08   The comparison between leasing and borrowing/purchasing survives our changing the data in the alternatives we are looking at. For instance, let us feed into the leasing example an assumption that the lessee receives £2,450 by way of rebate of rental at the end of year 5, (actually shown below as received not on 1 October in year 5 but on 1 January in year 6); the corresponding assumption in the borrowing/purchase alternative has to be that the asset is sold for that sum at the end of year 5, so that the capital allowances are reduced from £3,165 to £715 − the value of these at 35 percent being respectively £1,108 and £250. The last example in the preceding paragraph, using the 3.25 percent discount rate, would then change to that shown in Table 49 (in fact it is only the 'year 6' line which changes).

	Lease		Borrowing/purchase		
		Expense	Principal	Interest expense	Capital
	Rentals	for tax	& interest	for tax	all'ces
Present values					
at 3.25%					
per qr					
Yr 1	2,564		2,564		
Yr 2	2,256	(753)	2,256	(330)	(700)
Yr 3	1,986	(662)	1,986	(238)	(462)
Yr 4	1,748	(582)	1,748	(156)	(305)
Yr 5	1,536	(512)	1,536	(85)	(201)
Yr 6	(1,290)	(40)	(1,290)	(22)	(120)
	8,800	(2,549)	8,800	(831)	(1,788)
	6,251			6,181	

Table 49
Comparison of present values for leasing and for borrowing/purchase, changing the assumptions in both cases to show a rebate of rentals and sale proceeds of the asset of £2,450 on 1 January year 6, (taken into account in the capital allowances calculation in respect of year 5).

Once again, the comparative advantage of the borrowing/purchase alternative remains rock steady at £70.

Discounting dissimilar cashflows to present values

5.09 Although the discounting process is undoubtedly the best means available for comparing leases which have dissimilar cashflows, one has to be a bit more circumspect about the choice of a discount rate. In paragraphs 3.03 to 3.06 we compared a finance lease and an operating lease:

- the finance lease was one with which we have become somewhat familiar, quarterly rentals in advance of £672 for a five year term;

- the operating lease was one on which the rentals were £598 per quarter in advance for a five year term, this being the level needed to rentalise £8,900 out of the asset cost of £10,000.

We can give these two leases equal present values by making different assumptions about the rebating of rentals to the lessee at the end of the five years:

- In the finance lease, we make the familiar assumption that the lessor gives the lessee a rebate of £2,450.

- In the operating lease, the lessor has rentalised £8,900 of the asset's cost, and has failed to rentalise £1,100. That latter figure is the equivalent of sales proceeds at the end of the lease term of £2,130, (this point was explained in paragraph 3.05). If, having failed to rentalise an amount equivalent to £2,130 of the sale proceeds, the lessor retains that and rebates £320, we will find that the two cashflows discount back to the same figure.

5.10 The figures are set out in full in Table 50. The discount rate is 3.57 percent per quarter.

The present values of the rentals and rebates of rentals are equal. Notice that the actual rentals less rebates in the two leases are different. The size of that difference is £650. One can see in the above table that this is:

Difference between rebates	*(£2,450 − £320)*	=	£2,130
less difference in rentals	*(20 x £74)*	=	1,480
			650

but readers with long memories will remember the statement in paragraph 3.06 that if the lessor in the operating lease (in order to service his own external borrowings) borrowed from a bank the £74 shortfall in each quarter's income through the five years, at an interest rate of 3.57 per quarter, £2,130 would be the sum needed to pay off that borrowing at the end of the five years; or to put it another way, £2,130 is the 'end value'

Discount factor			Finance lease		Operating lease	
			Rental	Present value	Rental	Present value
1.0000	Yr 1	Qr 1	672	672	598	598
0.9675		Qr 2	672	650	598	579
0.9361		Qr 3	672	629	598	560
0.9057		Qr 4	672	609	598	541
			2,688	2,560	2,392	2,278
0.8763	Yr 2	Qr 1	672	589	598	524
0.8478		Qr 2	672	570	598	507
0.8203		Qr 3	672	551	598	491
0.7936		Qr 4	672	533	598	475
			2,688	2,243	2,392	1,997
0.7679	Yr 3	Qr 1	672	516	598	459
0.7429		Qr 2	672	499	598	444
0.7188		Qr 3	672	483	598	430
0.6954		Qr 4	672	467	598	416
			2,688	1,965	2,392	1,749
0.6729	Yr 4	Qr 1	672	452	598	402
0.6510		Qr 2	672	438	598	389
0.6299		Qr 3	672	423	598	377
0.6094		Qr 4	672	410	598	365
			2,688	1,723	2,392	1,533
0.5896	Yr 5	Qr 1	672	396	598	353
0.5705		Qr 2	672	383	598	341
0.5519		Qr 3	672	371	598	330
0.5340		Qr 4	672	359	598	319
			2,688	1,509	2,392	1,343
0.5167	Yr 6	Qr 1	(2,450)	(1,265)	(320)	(165)
		Total	10.990	8,735	11,640	8,735

Table 50

The finance lease where the rents of £672 per quarter are rebated to the extent of £2,450, compared to the operating lease with rentals of £598 and a rebate of only £320. The rents under the former are less because the lessor's net cash investment reduces faster; but the present values of the two are equal.

of a stream of receipts of £74 per quarter. The reason why the lessee finds himself paying a net £650 more under the operating lease than the finance lease is simply the 'time value of money'; because the lessee has benefitted in the operating lease from this £74 per quarter reduction in rentals, he has to pay its cost. If one wanted to continue the analogy above, namely that the lessor did actually set up a bank facility, one could say that the lessee is effectively having to make good the bank interest which the lessor incurs on these borrowings. However one prefers to explain it, the fact is that the lessee under the operating lease does pay £650 more than he would under the finance lease; and as we see in the next paragraph, he gets tax relief on that extra amount.

5.11 In the previous paragraph the cashflows which we discounted back to an equal present value were only the primary flows, that is to say the rentals and rebates. If we are to make a full comparison of the finance and operating leases, we need to look at each on an 'after tax' basis, that is to say also to put a present value on the values of the tax deductions for those rentals. The position then begins to look somewhat different (Table 51).

	Finance lease				Operating lease			
	Rent	P.V.	Value of tax relief	P.V.	Rent	P.V.	Value of tax relief	P.V.
Yr 1	2,688	2,560			2,392	2,278		
Yr 2	2,688	2,243	(941)	(747)	2,392	1,997	(838)	(665)
Yr 3	2,688	1,965	(941)	(654)	2,392	1,749	(837)	(582)
Yr 4	2,688	1,723	(941)	(573)	2,392	1,533	(837)	(511)
Yr 5	2,688	1,509	(941)	(502)	2,392	1,343	(837)	(446)
Yr 6	(2,450)	(1,265)	(83)	(39)	(320)	(165)	(725)	(339)
	10,990	8,735	(3,847)	(2,515)	11,640	8,735	(4,074)	(2,543)

Table 51
The comparison from Table 50 of finance and operating lease rentals and present values is now extended to include the values of the tax reliefs resulting from those primary cashflows.

Although the present values of the primary flows are equal, the present values of the tax reliefs favour the finance lease. But the reason for this is not simply that the discounting of equal amounts of tax reliefs, given at different dates, produces this result; it is clear that the amounts of the tax reliefs differ – which is of course what we noted in the previous paragraph. The values of the tax reliefs are:

> *Finance lease – net rentals £10,990 at 35%*   *£3,847*
> *Operating lease – net rentals £11,640 at 35%*   *£4,074*

The timing of these tax reliefs is not such that their present values coincide. One would not expect that to be the result given the fact that the tax reliefs are, all of them, delayed by between 21 months and 9 months after the dates of the primary payments.

The significance of the discount rate

5.12   In paragraphs 5.09 to 5.11 we have been comparing two different cashflows, a finance lease and an operating lease respectively, by discounting them back to present value at 3.57 percent. That rate was in fact the precise one used originally to equate the two leases − or rather, to equate their rental and rebate cashflows (paragraph 3.05). If we use a different rate, we would not expect the two present values of the rentals/rebates to remain equal; when the profiles are different, the rate which makes their present values equal must by definition be unique. The present values of the secondary (tax relief) cashflows were already unequal when discounted at 3.57 percent. If we use a different rate, it is likely that they will remain unequal, (although there is, somewhere, a discount rate which would level them up). But the question is whether we can still draw some safe conclusions from figures discounted at the different rates we choose. The best way of trying to answer that may be by looking at some different calculations:

Discount rate *3.57 percent*	Finance lease		Operating lease	
	P.V. of rentals	P.V. of tax relief	P.V. of rentals	P.V. of tax relief
Totals per paragraph 5.11	8,735	(2,515)	8,735	(2,543)
		6,220		6,192

apparent bias in favour of operating lease £28.

Discount rate *3.25 percent*	Finance lease		Operating lease	
	P.V. of rentals	P.V. of tax relief	P.V. of rentals	P.V. of tax relief
Yr 1	2,564		2,281	
Yr 2	2,256	(752)	2,007	(669)
Yr 3	1,985	(662)	1,766	(589)
Yr 4	1,747	(582)	1,554	(518)
Yr 5	1,537	(512)	1,368	(456)
Yr 6	(1,292)	(40)	(169)	(347)
	8,797	(2,548)	8,807	(2,579)
		6,249		6,228

Table 52
Present values discounted at 3.25 percent of the rentals and tax reliefs of the finance and of the operating lease respectively.

If we choose a lower discount rate, the present values will alter as shown in Table 52. The apparent bias in favour of operating lease changes to £21.

The lower discount rate makes the primary cashflows of the operating lease appear more expensive; a gap of £10 has opened up between the figures of £8,797 and £8,807. At the same time, the lower discount rate has widened the gap between the benefits of the tax reliefs. That advantage was £28 in favour of the operating lease (£2,515 compared to £2,543) when we used the 3.57 percent rate. It is now £31 in favour of the operating lease, (£2,548 compared to £2,579). But despite these two movements in opposite directions, the overall bias remains towards the operating lease.

5.13   If we use a higher discount rate than 3.57 percent, the figures move in the opposite direction, but the overall bias remains unchanged (Table 53).

Discount rate *3.75 percent*	Finance lease		Operating lease	
	P.V. of rentals	P.V. of tax relief	P.V. of rentals	P.V. of tax relief
Yr 1	2,546		2,265	
Yr 2	2,197	(727)	1,955	(647)
Yr 3	1,896	(628)	1,687	(558)
Yr 4	1,636	(542)	1,456	(482)
Yr 5	1,413	(467)	1,257	(416)
Yr 6	(1,173)	(36)	(153)	(311)
	8,515	(2,400)	8,467	(2,414)
		6,115		6,053

Table 53
Comparison of present values of rentals and tax reliefs, discounted at 3.75 percent, for the finance and the operating lease.

The apparent bias in favour of the operating lease is now £62: the primary cashflows now show an advantage in that direction of £48, (£8,515 compared to £8,467), whilst the tax reliefs still show an advantage in the same direction, albeit narrower at £14.

One's conclusions must not be drawn in too general terms. Since it is clear that when we are looking at the cashflows of two leases which are not diametrically different in profile, the discount rate is unlikely to be critical – if a 'middle' rate leads one relatively clearly in one particular direction, using a higher or a lower rate, but one that is still realistic, is not likely to change that. But one cannot say that the discount rate is not important:

• if one is comparing leases with very different profiles, for instance one with substantial front end advance rentals, and another with stepped rents;

• if the use of a 'middle' rate appears to leave the comparison evenly balanced, one would need to be very careful over drawing a conclusion from using a higher rate, or from using a lower one.

Terms and conditions that might be thought usual

5.14 The lessee's question quoted in paragraph 5.01 was 'is leasing cheaper?' That can be answered — the method of arriving at a sensible answer being the use of discounting to present values outlined in paragraphs 5.02 to 5.13. But when mentioning our lessee's question we signalled a strongly held view that it needed broadening; that whether to lease or not must always be examined in its business context, from all the angles which apply in the particular business. It is to that exercise that we shall devote the remaining paragraphs of this chapter. It is 'evaluation' in the wider sense of that word, deciding whether the lease on offer provides not just the best value, but the best fit, for the business's needs. And the significance of this paragraph's heading is that we must never think that anything in leasing is 'standard' — still less 'normative'. Some of the markers were laid out in general terms in our introduction (Why lease ? paragraph 1.18). It would do no harm to recapitulate them here because each can, or may be agreed not to be, a term or condition of the lease contract being considered by our particular lessee.

'Quasi-borrowing' orientated considerations

• Should rentals be calculated on the basis of fixed rate finance, or floating ?

• Does the lessor require further security in addition to his right to repossess the asset ?

• At what interest rate is he willing to calculate the level of the rentals ?

• Is there an accounts-presentational need to avoid showing a fixed asset, and a borrowing, on the lessee's balance sheet ? If so, can the lease be structured as an operating one from from the lessee's point of view ?

Commercially orientated considerations

• Is there some over-riding reason why the intending lessee must, or may not, acquire legal ownership of the asset? It was not that long ago, for instance, that there were obstacles in the way of foreign companies acquiring interests in real property in England, and a restriction still applies in many countries overseas. Leases, rather than freeholds, are all that are available for land whose development is being fostered under many government, local authority, and development agency schemes – but the question often affects other assets in the same way as it can affect land. The best way of approaching this question is to think the matter through in the light of the aspects we were addressing in paragraphs 1.16 and 1.17; if he is not a 'freeholder', is there a serious disadvantage in our lessee spending money on ('purchasing') an asset which will 'revert' to the freeholder at the end of his lease ? If the answer is yes, then what possibility is there of his persuading the freeholder to spend that money and rentalise it ?

- Is it important that the intending lessee have the right effectively to 'dispose of' the asset, (or his leasehold rights and obligations) during what would be the lease's primary term as well as thereafter ? This is a question to which we will return in the next paragraph but one.

- Who should bear the residual risk ? We have dealt with this exhaustively in chapter 4. It is a fundamental factor in considering possible lease terms, but there is one particular aspect of it which we may not have sufficiently highlighted. The lessor under the full pay-out lease in paragraph 2.16 not only made his lessee bear the full residual risk, but rentalised the full £10,000 cost of the asset; it was only when the asset was sold that the lessee was entitled to 98 percent of its proceeds by way of a rebate of rentals. We had however mentioned in paragraph 2.12 the possibility of a lease under which the lessor rentalised only £9,500 out of the asset's cost, and would retain £500 (or more) out of the asset's disposal proceeds, in order to achieve his aimed at profit. (We examined this lease further in paragraph 3.04, and concluded that it was a finance lease rather than an operating one). Different again was the operating lease in paragraph 3.05, where the lessor rentalised only £8,900 of the asset's cost, and did not expect the lessee to bear any part of the asset's residual risk. The point which we may not have clearly enough spelled out in all this is that it might be usual for the first of these leases to permit the lessee a secondary lease term at a nominal rent; it would not be normal for the third to contain any such provision – certainly not at a nominal rent; and in relation to the second lease, although the lessor might be prepared to provide for a secondary term, he would only do so if some way could be found of safeguarding his required disposal proceeds, bearing in mind that the asset would continue depreciating in value during any such secondary term.

- But in the general connection of the risks the lessee may or may not want to take on, there is the even more fundamental question illustrated in paragraph 1.18 by reference to the five year old jumbo jet; Do you want to purchase outright an asset whose cost reflects its expected fifteen remaining years of useful life, or do you want to 'purchase' only the possession and use of that asset for, say, the next twelve months? This is not primarily a question where the residual and other risks will lie, it is much more relevant to ask what is feasible ? And what strain does it put on the balance sheet ?

• Is it essential to have replacement equipment available when the asset is 'off the road' ? And if so, can this be achieved better (or only) under leasing arrangements ?

• Is it essential to tie up in advance the arrangements for trading-in the asset, possibly also involving upgrading to a newer generation ? And again can this be better (or only) achieved by leasing ?

An option to acquire the asset as a term of the lease ?

5.15   This is not a nonsense question. What we said in paragraph 1.19 was:

> 'although for tax reasons it is unusual for the lessee to be given any option
> to acquire the leased asset, there are some leases in which this option is given.
> (More often options for an eventual repurchase may be held by another
> party...)'

The tax reasons are a matter which we alluded to briefly in paragraph 2.21, and which we will be looking at in greater detail in the next chapter dealing with 'hire purchase'. At this point it is sufficient to say that a lessee who has the right to purchase the asset is the party whom the Inland Revenue regard as entitled to the capital allowances on the capital expenditure he incurs on its acquisition, and that the lessor who has granted such an option denies himself those allowances by having done so. But that does not mean that lessees should never consider demanding such options – demanding in effect that their leases be converted into hire purchase deals. For instance, the printer who wants a new press, but can only afford it over a period of say three years is most unlikely to want the continuing expense and restrictions throughout its remaining, say, forty years of life that a secondary term under a finance lease would involve. Why not pay for it over three years in a way which gives absolute, unrestricted, ownership at the end of that payment period ? Obviously the cashflows alter radically, as we will see in the next chapter, when the entitlement to capital allowances moves from lessor to lessee; and this will affect the level of rentals. The evaluation exercise will be based on that altered cashflow, but the commercial 'fit' may be better than could be provided by means of a straightforward lease. The purchase option is a course which we must always remember is available, even if there may not be so many transactions in which it is appropriate as those for which it can be ruled out.

The ability to dispose of the asset

5.16 An effective ability to dispose of the leased asset during what might be thought of as a typical primary term under a finance lease can be written into a lease agreement in one of a number of different ways, the principal ones being:

- The lease could be written as an operating lease, with the lessee given the option to terminate at selected dates.

- Within a finance lease structure, it is possible to provide for break-dates, at which the lessee can escape on payment of the stipulated loss values, (paragraph 4.27) or their equivalent in terms of balloon rentals; the lessee would undoubtedly want to have any such payments reduced by amounts equal to the whole, or a substantial proportion, of any disposal proceeds obtained by the lessor for the asset.

- The lessee can be given the right to upgrade, at specified dates, to a newer generation of equipment provided through the same lessor. We looked in paragraphs 4.17 and 4.18 at some of the parallel arrangements between the lessor and the equipment supplier dealing with such upgradings.

- The lessee's interest can be made assignable; this is far from being a usual arrangement in equipment leases, as opposed to those for real property. It would be realistic to assume that if the lessor agreed to its being written into the lease terms, he would do so only for an 'assignee previously approved by the lessor, such approval not to be unreasonably withheld' to use the standard American phraseology.

- The lessee may be given the right to carve out a lesser interest in the subject matter of the lease (paragraph 1.08).

Insurance

5.17 It is usual for equipment lessors to require their lessees to insure the equipment leased under finance leases against normal risks, as explained in paragraph 2.82, and to supplement that provision with a covenant by the lessee to indemnify the lessor against damage to the asset, this being intended to be done by using the insurance proceeds, but constituting a sanction against any lessee who failed to insure adequately and effectively. Where equipment is leased under operating leases, it is frequently the case that the lessor himself insures it, and that this is reflected in the rentals charged to the lessee. But one must be careful not to generalise; there are all sorts of reasons why different arrangements may be necessary. To give one such example, where fleets of business cars are provided on contract hire, there is a choice between insuring all the fleets globally in the provider's policy, or having each employing company insure the cars hired to its own employees, obviously claiming that they are safer drivers than are those of other companies; or having each employee insure his own vehicle. That last may sound the least attractive on a number of counts, but if there are instances, (as there usually turn out to be), where the car concerned is used not only for the employer's business and his employee's private purposes, but also on occasion for some other business of the employee or his wife, then individual insurances may be the only way in which one can ensure that the cover is complete.

5.18   The insurance position for real property is different again. We must still beware of generalising, but one common structure would comprise:

- an undertaking by the tenant to pay as consideration for 'the demise' of the leased premises 'further rent' equal to the insurance premiums payable by the landlord;

- a covenant by the landlord to insure the premises, the insured sum being equal to the entire costs of rebuilding or replacing the premises in a new condition, plus an amount equal to three years' rents. That three years rental is to be paid by the insurer to the landlord entirely for his own purposes – as will be clear below;

- if the premises are damaged or destroyed to an extent which renders them impossible of use by the tenant, the latter is entitled to a *cesser* of rent during the period commencing at the date of destruction and ending when the restored premises are again fit for use and occupation;

- that *cesser* would not be granted if it were any negligence by the tenant that caused the landlord's policy to be vitiated – and in such a case, the tenant covenants to indemnify the landlord against the costs of rebuilding (as well as being required to continue paying his rents during that rebuilding).

One implication of the above appears to be that although the tenant has 'an interest' in the real property under the terms of his lease, he has no 'insurable interest'. We defined the latter in general terms in paragraph 1.01 by saying that only if someone suffers loss as a result of the happening of any of the perils insured can he validly insure himself against such loss. Absent negligence, the tenant does not suffer loss in relation to the rebuilding costs, because his entire obligations to keep the premises in repair, and to deliver them over to the landlord at the end of the lease, are covered by the landlord's having himself covenanted to insure, and to reinstate out of the proceeds of that insurance. Secondly, the tenant suffers no loss out of having to continue paying rent for unavailable premises, since this is waived during the (likely) rebuilding period. Thus the tenant not only does not need to insure, but cannot do so validly. That in turn means that the landlord's insurance would not be jeopardised by the existence of other cover taken for the same risks. From the landlord's point of view, the legalities are very elegantly, as well as quite adequately, covered. From the tenant's point of view the financial risks are removed, but the hassle-potential is very considerable. When storm damage, for instance, has to be made good, it will be necessary:

- for all the tenants to agree on, say, two builders from whom estimates can be obtained for the repairs;

- for the landlord to be persuaded that either of those builders will do an adequate, and reasonably priced, job;

- for the landlord to submit the claim to his insurer, and obtain his go-ahead;

- almost certainly for one or more of the tenants to pay the builders in advance of being able to conjure the insurance proceeds out of their landlord;

- and for the landlord and/or the insurers to satisfy themselves that the work has been satisactorily carried out.

It could be much easier if the tenant, or one out of their number, was appointed by the landlord as his agent, with freedom to handle these matters, and authority to deal with his insurers and the other tenants, without the need for the amount of to-ing and fro-ing indicated.

Maintenance contracts and consumable stores

5.19 We looked at these two subjects in paragraphs 2.80 and 2.81; in the context of evaluating the 'fit' of a proposed lease, there is little to add to what was said there, but it could be helpful to recapitulate it:

- For high technology equipment leased on a finance lease basis, it is usual to find that the lessor requires that maintenance and repairs be carried out by staff approved by the equipment supplier, familiar with the equipment and trained to effect the necessary repairs. One of the most difficult matters to judge in advance of signing a lease for such equipment is whether the associated maintenance contract provides value for money, but it is probably fairer to view the lease and the contract as a single overall package – unless the whole is accepted (or can be renegotiated), the equipment will simply not be available at all.

- For other finance-leased equipment, the lessee must usually undertake to keep it 'in good and serviceable condition, fair wear and tear excepted', and can use his own staff, or others chosen at his discretion, to achieve this.

- Essentially that same (second) set of requirements apply to real property leased on a 'full repairing basis', including applying to the equipment that may form an integral part of such property, such for instance as lift machinery in an office building. Keeping such machinery 'serviceable', if it has a twenty five year life, may involve its complete replacement three times during the term of a ninety nine year lease, but should not require that the twenty four year old lifts are replaced with new on the lease's expiry, if they can still be persuaded to work.

- As regards consumable stores, for instance the 'copier kits' needed for the operation of some photocopiers, the warning we gave in paragraph 2.81 was against the lessee committing himself to quantities greater than he would need, and particularly against his allowing those commitments to extend in time beyond the point at which he expected to terminate the lease of the equiprrent concerned. Each is a trap into which some unwary lessees have fallen.

Liquidity

5.20 We made some simplistic comments in paragraph 2.15 on this aspect of the possible 'fit' of a leasing arrangement. The problem is that no general comments can be other than simplistic − it is only when one has access to the projections of sales and cashflows for the particular business that one can begin to look sensibly at this question. With that disclaimer, however, what we assumed in paragraph 2.15 was that the income from the use of a machine over a period cf five years from its date of purchase might be very roughly proportionate to the annual charges which would show in the profit and loss account as a result of that machine's ownership. If we assume that, for an outright purchase, those charges might themselves equate to the pattern of interest expense in the lessee's cashflow in paragraph 2.02, with straightline depreciation, then we are saying that the income that this purchased machine could be expected to generate would show something like the profile set out below. It is in the nature of leasing arrangements that rentals are usually level − the principal exception consisting of the rebate given on sale of the asset where its estimated proceeds have not been allowed for in the calculation of the rentals. Therefore, one could show one's expected cash outflows against the projections of cash inflows arrived at as above:

	Inflows		Outflows	Cumulative surplus
Year 1		3,179	2,688	491
Year 2		2,965	2,688	277
				768
Year 3		2,723	2,688	35
				803
Year 4		2,445	2,688	(243)
				560
Year 5	2,128		2,688	
less rebated	(2,450)		(2,450)	
		(322)	238	(560
		10,990	10,990	

That is the same table as was originally set out in paragraph 2.15, except that we have inserted into it the rental rebate. Including this in the 'outflow' column produces an obviously sensible answer, in that the cash the lessee would otherwise have seen paid away as rents in the fifth year is decreased by the figure of £2,450. However, in the 'inflows' column, the answer becomes obviously nonsensical, in that the rebate cannot be expected to result in the lessee's revenues from the machine turning negative in his final year of possession and use. This merely serves to underline the warning given at the beginning of this paragraph that one cannot pluck cash inflows out of the air – they must be more solidly based than that. But that does not mean that the pattern of increase in liquidity that the leased asset can be expected to generate in its early years, with the slowing (or even reversal) of that generation in later years, should not be best-estimated at the time the 'fit' of the leasing deal is under examination.

Tax deductions

5.21 We know what the rules are for the tax deductions available to a lessee; he deducts the rents he pays. If he has an operating lease, he deducts them in the same pattern in which they are debited in his profit and loss account; this is normally on an even basis through the term (even if the rents are not paid in equal amounts) as explained in paragraph 3.09, and would normally be on an accruals basis for the reasons explained in paragraph 2.17. If on the other hand he has a finance lease, his profit and loss account will show debits for 'finance charges' on a notional loan, and for 'depreciation'. In his tax computation, the former has to be struck out because of the merely notional character of the loan, and the latter is struck out because the Inland Revenue would not accept that an asset only notionally owned could qualify for tax allowances of any kind, still less for a schedule of depreciation chosen at the lessee's option. In place of these disallowed deductions, the only rational (and factual) amounts the lessee can be permitted to deduct are his rentals paid. This is what we showed as being the position in paragraph 2.57. Evaluating the 'fit' of a lease in this regard therefore involves taking into account the values to the lessee of his entitlement to deduct rentals – in comparison with what would be the pattern of deductions and allowances were the asset to be provided in some other way. We have already put these figures into the comparative cashflows we were discounting earlier in this chapter.

Maximum terms of years which can be realistically envisaged

5.22   Finally, we come to a point that may, but will not always, be relevant to a potential lessee's consideration of a possible leasing arrangement. This is the question how far the cost of providing the asset can be spread into future years, or to word it differently, what is the maximum lease term for which he can reasonably ask. If he is comparing the possible lease with an alternative possible borrowing and acquisition, the question in that latter case becomes one of the level of interest charges, coupled with the maximum period over which the lender will wish to see his lending repaid. Once again, generalisations are only valuable to the extent they show what criteria are likely to apply to the actual facts in the actual business's circumstances; but some of those criteria have already been indicated in paragraph 3.07. What we were there considering was the minimum expected levels of residual which would enable a lessee to obtain equipment on an operating lease over various periods. Summarising those figures to highlight the aspect we are now interested in, they were:

	Five years	Four years	Three years	Two years
Cost of equipment	10,000	10,000	10,000	10,000
Residual	2,130	1,866	1,634	1,430

What we said in paragraph 3.07 was that those residuals could be discounted back (at a discount rate of 3.357 percent per quarter) to a present value of £1,100 at the inception of the lease; and that that latter figure, compared with the equipment's cost, enabled the lease to be written as an operating one so far as the lessee was concerned, so long as the lessor did not want the lessee to guarantee the residuals, nor did he want to have them rentalised. If we make some daring, because over-generalised, assumptions what those residual figures imply in terms of further expected useful lives of the equipment beyond the ends of the lease terms set out, they might be something like the following – which would in turn show that it could be rational to suggest that the maximum term for an operating lease would be approximately the percentage shown of any asset's expected useful life.

	Five years	Four years	Three years	Two years
Residual	2,130	1,866	1,634	1,430
Further useful life	2 yrs	18 mths	1 year	9 mths
Lease term as a percentage of total useful life	71 %	73 %	75 %	73 %

All of this is so broadly and generally estimated that one certainly cannot assume that those percentages show a curve rising to a peak at three years, and then falling. All that they do show is that it is unlikely that operating leases will be available over periods exceeding 70, or at most 75, percent of the expected useful life of the asset. Notice that there is no suggestion that an asset which over a period of, for example, four years has declined in value from £10,000 to £1,866 will have no value at all after a further eighteen months; but we do assume that its useful life as a business asset will have come to an end, because of the level of costs, and the amount of 'down-time' that might be expected if the attempt were made to continue using it.

5.23 When we turn from operating leases to finance leases, the reasoning set out above becomes subtly different. But it is still easiest to explain the thought processes by starting from the operating lease example. One of the factors which is always relevant, in operating leases as well as finance ones, in deciding the maximum term that a lessor can offer is the 'security' for future rentals provided by his right to repossess and sell the asset. But it is obvious as soon as we make that statement that a lessor does not expect that the realisable value of the asset will provide him one hundred percent cover. If we calculate a simple 'lessee' cashflow (Table 54) for the four year lease referred to in the previous paragraph, (that is to say based on the operating lease data in paragraph 3.07), it rentalises over four years £8,900 out of the £10,000 cost of the equipment; the balance of £1,100 which the lessor does not rentalise is made good to him in the form of the residual value realised at the end of the fourth year, £1,866, the present value of which is £1,100.

We know that the 'outstanding indebtedness' shown in the lessee's cashflow is not the same as the amounts of the 'stipulated loss values' which the

		Borrowing at start of period	Rental paid	Borrowing after rental	Interest payable	Borrowing at end of period
Yr 1	Qtr 1	8,900	704	8,196	275	8,471
	Qtr 2	8,471	704	7,767	261	8,028
	Qtr 3	8,028	704	7,324	246	7,570
	Qtr 4	7,570	704	6,866	230	7,096
			2,816		1,012	
Yr 2	Qtr 1	7,096	704	6,392	215	6,607
	Qtr 2	6,607	704	5,903	198	6,101
	Qtr 3	6,101	704	5,397	181	5,578
	Qtr 4	5,578	704	4,874	163	5,037
			2,816		757	
Yr 3	Qtr 1	5,037	704	4,333	145	4,478
	Qtr 2	4,478	704	3,774	125	3,899
	Qtr 3	3,899	704	3,195	107	3,302
	Qtr 4	3,302	704	2,598	86	2,684
			2,816		463	
Yr 4	Qtr 1	2,684	704	1,980	66	2,046
	Qtr 2	2,046	704	1,342	44	1,386
	Qtr 3	1,386	704	682	22	704
	Qtr 4	704	704	–	–	–
			2,816		132	
			11,264		2,364	

Table 54

Cashflow for the lessee in an operating lease designed to rentalise over 4 years £8,900 out of the asset's original cost of £10,000. Interest implicit in the lease is 3.357 percent per quarter.

lessor needs to receive from the lessee in the event of an early termination (paragraph 4.27); and we know that the latter are a fair measure of the lessor's credit exposures at each intermediate date (paragraph 2.59). But the indebtedness shown above does give us an approximation of the lessor's credit exposures.

On the other hand, if the value of the asset was £10,000 at the start of year 1, and will be £1,866 at the end of year 4, then one could estimate its intermediate realisable values on a curve of something like the shape in Table 55.

This does incidentally show the truth of the statement made in paragraph 4.05, that lessors writing operating leases are likely to be better protected

	End year 0	End year 1	End year 2	End year 3	End year 4
Asset value	10,000	5,200	3,300	2,300	1,866
Indebtedness as above	8,900	7,096	5,037	2,684	nil
Shortfall of asset value below indebtedness	n.a.	1,896	1,737	384	n.a.

Table 55

Comparison of estimated asset values with approximate indebtedness figures of lessee, for a four year operating lease designed to rentalise £8,900 out of an asset cost of £10,000.

in this regard than those writing finance leases. If the lessor had been rentalising £10,000 instead of £8,900, the level of the lessee's indebtedness at the ends of years 1 and 2 would have been higher than £7,096 and £5,037; and the shortfall of asset value below indebtedness would have been even greater.

5.24   But the purpose of that last table, comparing indebtedness and asset values, was to bring out once again the importance, (and in the context of the longer finance leases this is absolutely vital), of the lessee's 'covenants' – the concept we first examined in paragraph 2.59. This is the value to the lessor of the assurance the lessee is able to provide that the leased asset will indeed metamorphose through the lease term into an uninterrupted stream of lease rentals – that there will be no occasion for the lessor to have to repossess and sell the asset. If the lessee under a finance lease is one whose covenants are regarded as first class, then it is probable that, (if that lessee wants such a thing), he could obtain a finance lease covering say 85 percent of the expected useful life of any leased asset. If his covenants are less good, then the proportion of the asset's life for which it might be possible to obtain finance lease facilities might be nearer the 75 percent of useful life which we concluded in paragraph 5.23 was the probable upper limit in the case of operating leases. The author must, however, repeat yet again his warnings about these numbers being based on generalisations rather than on the particular facts of individual cases. All that they really show is some thought processes, and the approaches which it is likely that lessors may take to decision making. Whether the lease then offered fits the lessee's requirements is his decision.

CHAPTER 6

Hire purchase

Terminology

6.01   We will use the phrase 'hire purchase' to cover all arrangements under which the owner of an asset grants not only possession and use to another, but also gives him the option to acquire the asset on the completion of the hiring period. This transaction can be distinguished from 'credit sale', in which the owner transfers title to the asset to the purchaser at the outset, but allows that purchaser to pay in instalments over a period. In law, the most significant difference is of course that ownership, and therefore the right to repossess, remains in the hands of the original owner until and unless a hire purchase contract is completed; following a credit sale, the only right the original owner has is that of being able to sue for payment of any outstanding amounts of the purchase price – he has no entitlement to seize the asset in the event of the purchaser's failing to keep up his payments. If we were using the term 'hire purchase' in its strict sense, we would be dealing only with assets of a value of £15,000 or less; the purchaser is in these cases given further protections, written into the hire purchase law. For instance, the vendor's rights to repossess cease to be exercisable after two thirds of the price has been paid. For the purposes of this book, we can notice that there are these differences between the transactions which are 'hire purchase' as legally defined, and other 'leases with purchase options' which we are bringing within the scope of our rather wider definition of 'hire purchase'. The distinction is one with which we need not further concern ourselves, since our examination of hire purchase transactions in this book will basically involve business assets, at costs generally in excess of the limit referred to. When we were dealing with leasing, it was natural to refer to the two parties to a lease agreement as the lessor and the lessee. The equivalents in a hire purchase deal could, possibly, be referred to as hirer and hiree, but the second does not actually exist as an English word – and the first more usually refers to the person enjoying possession and use than the person granting it. It is altogether more convenient to refer to the two parties as the 'vendor' and the 'purchaser' – making the assumption that the latter will in due course exercise his option to acquire the asset.

171

Similarities with leasing

6.02   There are fundamental differences between hire purchase and leasing, as we will see in the next paragraph. But at the same time, there are also certain similarities, and it is useful to mention these first:

- a hire purchase contract can give the purchaser 'financing' assistance, equivalent in type to the assistance he would obtain under a finance lease;

- alternatively, it is possible to structure a hire purchase deal so as to equate to an operating lease – with the option granted to the 'purchaser' to acquire title not set at a purely nominal sum (so that it is more or less certain that he would wish to exercise that option), but for a more significant figure.

Under the first, it is true to say that the 'purchaser' has not only possession and use of the asset, but even more of the asset's risks and rewards of ownership than we have seen (paragraph 2.06) a finance lessee has in a leased asset. On this footing, the case for the purchaser's capitalising the asset on his balance sheet, and showing equivalent borrowings, is just as strong as it was for the finance lease. But correspondingly, the vendor has effectively transmuted his ownership of the asset into a right to a stream of hire receipts, and a final option receipt, all more correctly shown on his balance sheet as hire purchase receivables than as a physical asset. The alternative form of the transaction is one under which the payment of hire provides the payer with possession and use of the asset, but where its owner must be regarded as not having shed the risks and rewards of his ownership. It is tempting to complete that sentence by saying that the owner has not shed his risks and rewards because there remains a substantial degree of uncertainty whether the purchase option will be exercised at any stage. But that would not be entirely correct. The Statement of Standard Accounting Practice (SSAP 21) outlines the position more fully. The definitions of a finance lease, and of an operating lease, (which we quoted in paragraph 3.02), are drawn so as to include not only those normal 'leases' in which the lessee is given no option to purchase, but also those 'hire purchase' contracts in which he has such an option. What differentiates the hire purchase contract, which must be regarded as a financing arrangement, from the other contract which is similar to an operating lease, is not the likelihood or otherwise of the option being exercised; it is whether the owner has transferred substantially all of the risks and rewards of ownership of the asset. That word 'substantially' is to be interpreted in this case in exactly the same way as it was in the normal leasing context. If the present value of the minimum hire payments (excluding the payment on exercise of the option, which is not 'guaranteed' in SSAP 20's terms) is at least 90 percent of the asset's fair value, then the hire purchase contract is *prima facie* a financing one. If that fair value is less than that 90 percent then *prima facie* it is not. Hire purchase contracts which have the same characteristics as operating leases are not common. We need to look briefly at their implications in the paragraphs that follow, but will be devoting considerably more time and attention to those normal contracts which are of a financing type.

Differences from leasing

6.03 The fact, mentioned in the preceding paragraph, that the vendor does in a normal (financing) hire purchase contract transmute his asset into a right to a stream of hire receipts, leads us straight into a list of differences between leasing and hire purchase:

• The lessor under a finance lease has an asset from which he obtains his profit 'by keeping it in his own possession' (we would say 'ownership'). The trader who sells goods in the ordinary course of his business obtains his profit from those goods 'by parting with them, and letting them change masters'. These venerable phrases come from Adam Smith's *Wealth of Nations*, and are his definition of the difference between 'fixed capital' and 'working capital'. A more modern word for the latter would be 'stocks', (or perhaps 'net current assets', since it must embrace raw materials and work in progress, and debtors less creditors, as well as stocks of saleable products).

• This highlights the fact that the hire 'vendor', even had he not hired (and granted a purchase option over) the asset to the 'purchaser', would have been very unlikely to have regarded it as a fixed asset. The assets which vendors are likely to dispose of by hire purchase will almost always be 'stock' rather than capital items.

• In the hands of the purchaser, the question whether the asset is capital or not is of course purely dependent on the use to which he puts it, and his intentions as regards its retention or disposal. But the very fact that he has contracted to 'acquire' it over a period rather than outright is a reasonably clear pointer to his regarding it as a fixed asset.

• If we do assume that the purchaser should, as above, capitalise onto his balance sheet his 'risks and rewards of ownership of the asset', we do have to recognise that this process requires that we fasten onto substance, and ignore form, to an even greater extent than we did in our capitalisation of finance leased assets on the lessee's balance sheet. But what focuses our attention on this 'form versus substance' question is that in this case the Inland Revenue authorities also appear willing to adhere to substance, and ignore form.

The entitlement to capital allowances for tax

6.04 Once again, that last point leads us straight onto what is probably the most significant difference between leasing and hire purchase, namely the tax positions of the parties. It is convenient to start with the entitlement to capital allowances, but this, as we will see, is only one facet of the regime which applies to vendor and purchaser, and which is completely different from that for lessors and lessees. The Capital Allowances Act 1990 (section 60) provides that where a person carrying on a trade incurs capital expenditure on the provision of machinery or plant for the purposes thereof under 'a contract providing that he shall or may become the owner of the machinery or plant on the performance of the contract', then two things are to follow:

- the machinery or plant shall be treated as belonging to him, and not to any other person, at any time when he has the benefit of the contract;

- all capital expenditure in respect of that machinery or plant to be incurred by him under the contract after the time when the machinery or plant is brought into use, shall be treated as having been incurred at that time.

The 'contract' referred to clearly includes any hire purchase transaction of the type we are considering. The usual way in which such contracts combine the requirement that the 'purchaser' should pay instalments of 'hire' through a stipulated period, and that he may opt to acquire the asset, is to state that that option can only be exercised if all the payments of hire have first been paid. He can then exercise his option if he wants to. It cannot therefore be said that it is the contract which provides that he shall become the owner. But it is true that the contract provides that he 'may' do so; the phrase 'on the performance of the contract' is thus a reference to his completion of his payments of hire, which is itself the necessary pre-condition to his being able to exercise the option. One of the necessary conditions for the availability of capital allowances is that the asset must, as a consequence of the incurring of capital expenditure on its provision, belong to the person who incurred that expenditure; we saw that in paragraph 4.14. The section in the Capital Allowances Act quoted above gets over the difficulty that it is only later, if and when the purchaser opts, that the asset comes to belong to him; it is deemed to have belonged to him throughout the time he 'had the benefit of the contract'.

6.05 Deeming that the asset subject to a hire purchase contract belongs to the purchaser, when the fact is that it belongs to the vendor, is the first of the ways in which the Inland Revenue abandons form for substance. Of equal significance is their willingness to give a realistic meaning to the phrase 'capital expenditure'. What the purchaser agrees under the contract is that he will make a series of hire payments, those payments to provide him with possession and use of the asset, but no more. If he had hired the asset under an operating lease, the Inland Revenue would have accepted quite happily that similar payments were made 'on revenue account' – that is to say that they were not capital expenditure but deductible in arriving at the payer's profits. When they are made under a hire purchase contract, they can be regarded as 'capital', and thus as qualifying for capital allowances. Thirdly, the Inland Revenue deem those hire payments to have been incurred no later than the date on which the asset is brought into use in the purchaser's trading activities. What all this means for the purchaser's claim for capital allowances, and his entitlement to deduct other expenses in arriving at his profits, can best be understood by reference to some figures for a typical hire purchase transaction.

The hire purchaser's cashflow

6.06   The format of the cashflow that follows in Table 56 will be familiar,

	Borrowing at start of period	Rental paid	Borrowing after rental	Interest payable	Borrowing at end of period
Yr 1 Qtr 1	10,000	991	9,009	302	9,311
Qtr 2	9,311	991	8,320	278	8,598
Qtr 3	8,598	991	7,607	255	7,862
Qtr 4	7,862	991	6,871	230	7,101
		3,964		1,065	
Yr 2 Qtr 1	7,101	991	6,110	205	6,315
Qtr 2	6,315	991	5,324	178	5,502
Qtr 3	5,502	991	4,511	150	4,661
Qtr 4	4,661	991	3,670	122	3,792
		3,964		655	
Yr 3 Qtr 1	3,792	991	2,801	92	2,893
Qtr 2	2,893	991	1,902	63	1,965
Qtr 3	1,965	991	974	32	1,006
Qtr 4	1,006	991	15	–	15
end qtr 4	15	15	–	–	–
		3,979		187	
		11,907		1,907	

Table 56
Cashflow – hire purchase treated as a borrowing by the purchaser to be repaid by equal instalments, quarterly in advance, comprising principal and interest at 3.357 percent per quarter. There is also a final payment shown above at £15.

and the only comment to be made on it at this stage is that it is for a shorter period than the leases with which we have been dealing in earlier chapters. This is typical in hire purchase contracts, as we noted in paragraph 1.19. One part of the reason no doubt has to do with the vendor's security – if he has to repossess and sell a vehicle on which a private individual, (not engaged in a trade), is unable to continue his payments, the shorter contract is likely to give the vendor a greater degree of protection. Historically, it was also true that government required at one time that hire purchase contracts might not be longer than certain maximum numbers of months, this being a way of limiting the amount of borrowing in the economy. But there is another, tax, reason to which we will come in paragraph 6.10 below.

The final payment of £15 made at the end of the fourth quarter of year 4 is the payment called for on the purchaser's exercise of his option to acquire the asset. His hire payments thus total £11,892, and the option payment brings that up to £11,907. The present value of all of those payments, discounted at the rate implicit in the hire purchase contract is £10,000 – which of course means that the present value of the 'minimum hire payments' (excluding the £15) is marginally less than that figure. The finance charges included in the hire payments come to £1,907. The reason why this is less than two thirds of the figure of £3,440 we saw in the lessee's cashflow in paragraph 2.02 is simply that the above 'borrowing' is repaid over three years rather than five. The implicit rate is the identical 3.357 percent per quarter, 14.119 percent per year.

The calculation of capital allowances

6.07 Allowances are given on capital expenditure, and they start, generally, from the date it is 'incurred'. We have noted in paragraph 6.05 the Inland Revenue's willingness to accept the purchaser's payments as being in the nature of capital, and also noted that the legislation deems such capital expenditure to have been incurred no later than the date the asset was brought into use in the purchaser's trade. If we were to assume that the asset came into use during the course of the second quarter of year 1, that would mean that:

- the rental due at the beginning of the first quarter would be treated as having been incurred on at the beginning of that quarter;

- the rental due at the beginning of the second quarter would similarly be treated as having been incurred on the date it was due;

- the whole balance of the purchaser's capital expenditure would be treated as having been incurred on the day in the second quarter of year 1 on which the asset was first used.

If all those three dates fell into the same accounting period of the purchaser, his capital allowances claim would be unaffected; it would simply show the aggregate expenditure as having been incurred in that period. If on the other hand the first two payments were made in one accounting period, and the third date fell in the next, then the claim for the first of those periods would include only those first two payments, and the whole balance would be treated as further capital expenditure on the asset in the second period – the allowances on it commencing a full year later than those on the original two payments. But if we make the simpler assumption that the asset comes into use on 1 January of year 1, (and that that is also the date on which the initial instalment is due under the hire purchase contract), then we can treat the aggregate capital expenditure as having been incurred on that date. The question we have not yet faced is what is that capital expenditure ?

6.08   The answer is that the purchaser can choose whether to treat it as £10,000 or as £11,907. If he opts for the first, then he will be allowed to deduct the finance charges year by year as he bears them. The comparative figures thus become those in Table 57.

	Capital expenditure £10,000	Interest expense	Total	Captial expenditure £11,907
Allowances and deductions				
Year 1	2,500	1,065	3,565	2,977
Year 2	1,875	655	2,530	2,233
Year 3	1,406	187	1,593	1,674
Year 4	1,055		1,055	1,256
Year 5	791		791	942

Table 57
Total tax deductions available to the hire purchaser treating, on the one hand, capital expenditure as £10,000 and the balance of the contract figure as interest on an actuarial basis, and on the other, treating the contract figure as wholly qualifying for capital allowances.

At that point the written down value of the asset, on which the purchaser will be able to claim allowances for future years, is £2,373 in the left hand column, and £2,825 in the right. It is therefore obvious that all future allowances will be greater in the right hand column than the left, although the size of this difference will narrow as each year passes. But that will never outweigh the advantage presented by the left hand basis of claim in the first years. Arithmetically that must always be the conclusion whatever figures are used. In our particular example the £1,907 finance charges are fully relieved in the left hand column very early in the period, whereas in the right hand column they form part of the total sum to be relieved over the asset's life (or longer) on a 25 percent reducing balance basis. (But there is an uncertainty over the tax position on cars: see paragraph 7.02 below).

The rule of 78 — its applicability to the purchaser's deductions and to the vendor's income

6.09   It is always open to the purchaser to claim his deductions for finance charges calculated by the rule of 78, rather than actuarially as we made our calculations in the cashflow in paragraph 6.06. The figures would then be as in Table 58.

	number of future instalments					*attributable finance charges*
Yr 1 Qtr 1	11	11/66	×	1,907	=	318
Qtr 2	10	10/66	×	1,907	=	289
Qtr 3	9	9/66	×	1,907	=	260
Qtr 4	8	8/66	×	1,907	=	231
						1,098
Yr 2 Qtr 1	7	7/66	×	1,907	=	202
Qtr 2	6	6/66	×	1,907	=	173
Qtr 3	5			and so on		145
Qtr 4	4					116
						636
Yr 3 Qtr 1	3					87
Qtr 2	2					57
Qtr 3	1					29
Qtr 4	–					–
	66					173

Table 58

Rule of 78 calculations to arrive at the split between years of the finance charge element within the hire purchase contract figure.

We know that the rule of 78 tends to produce a marginally more 'front-ended' profile than the actuarial method, and that is what these figures show. It must therefore be better from the purchaser's point of view to use these calculations of finance charges instead of those illustrated in the previous paragraph — but he is unlikely to grow rich out of differences in the timing of tax deductions as small as these are shown to be. The vendor does not get capital allowances on the asset he is hiring out. He is regarded for tax purposes as having made a sale of the asset when he enters into the hire purchase contract, so that any manufacturing or 'dealing' profit becomes taxable at that point. The finance charges included in his hire receipts are taxed over the term of the deal on the basis of the rule of 78, so that the £1,907 of financing income in the above deal would become taxable in his hands at the identical times it became deductible for the purchaser. The status in the tax computation of the vendor of amounts owing by the purchaser is that these are current, trading, debts; this means that should a purchaser default, the vendor can claim to deduct for tax purposes any loss he may incur, (after bringing in any recoveries he is able to achieve by repossessing the asset and in any other way). Correspondingly, the vendor's ability to deduct for tax purposes provisions against bad and doubtful debts is just the same as that described for the lessor in paragraph 2.62.

Are there tax uncertainties ?

6.10   In a situation in which the Inland Revenue accept:

- substance rather than form in the categorisation of hire payments as capital expenditure;

- the taxpayer's entitlement to calculate his deductions for finance charges under a simple 'convention' which is known to provide a marginally accelerated rate of deduction than is perhaps justified;

and they do so in the context of legislation which then permits the tax allowances to be claimed on that capital expenditure sooner than the taxpayer has really incurred it, should we worry that they may renege on one or both of these concessions ? The answer seems to be that there are two areas of doubt. The first relates to hire purchase transactions which extend over an abnormally long period. Consider, for instance, the tax deductions available to a UK airline which leased a jet airliner from its American manufacturer, on an operating lease for a term of ten years, the manufacturer allowing in his calculation of the rentals that the residual value at the end of that period would be, say, 40 percent of original cost. The lessee would deduct, through the ten year term, rentals reflecting the even spreading through that period of 60 percent of the aircraft's cost, plus the whole of the lessor's holding costs for the ten years. Then assume that the American manufacturer offers as an alternative that same lease but with a purchase option written in for the UK airline to acquire the airliner at the 40 percent value at the end of the ten years. Straightaway the transaction is a hire purchase one for tax. (It may not be a finance-type hire purchase deal under the definition in SSAP 21, but that is irrelevant). The pattern of deductions available for the finance charges, and the capital allowances claimable on expenditure all deemed to have been incurred at the start of the ten year term, would be considerably more favourable to the purchaser than would the pattern of lease rental deductions with which we are contrasting this possibility. What the Inland Revenue have said in the past is that in a hire purchase transaction of more than about five years, the financing element of each hire payment forms so much larger a proportion, and therefore the 'capital expenditure' proportion is so much smaller, (and this is obviously accentuated even more where the purchase option requires a payment of 'fair value' rather than a purely nominal sum), that they cannot necessarily agree that the hire payments can be regarded as containing an element of capital expenditure. If they maintain this view, the purchaser would get deductions for those rentals only as and when he paid them, and the capital expenditure deemed to have been incurred at the start of the ten year period, and therefore to qualify from then for capital allowances, would be only the option price. It was thought at one time that this view might be codified in the form of a statement of Revenue Practice, but this has never emerged. It remains the case, however, that it is unlikely to be safe to assume that the Inland Revenue's relaxed attitude to hire purchase deductions and allowances would apply to deals extending over much longer periods than those typical in the UK hire purchase industry.

Back-to-back deals, or hire-purchase-in lease-out (HILO)

6.11 Doubts over the tax position also arise in back-to-back arrangements; these tend to be viewed by the Inland Revenue as no more than devices to obtain tax advantages. The best way to illustrate the structure of such a deal is to assume, first, that our purchaser contracts to acquire on hire purchase on day 365 of year 0 an asset costing £10,000. The hire payments which we will assume at this stage are £672 per quarter payable in advance, and the transaction is to extend over five years. On day 364 of year 5, the purchaser can exercise his option to acquire the asset for a nominal sum, but we will treat this as so small that we can ignore it for present purposes. At this stage, the purchaser's cash outflows are £2,688 per annum for five years. But we next assume that immediately after he has himself exercised his option to acquire the asset, he arranges for it to be sold, and the proceeds he realises from that sale are £2,500. He incurs a cost of £50 in connection with this sale. The capital allowances and deductions to which all of the foregoing entitles him are identical to those set out earlier in this book in connection with a lessor's outright purchase of a similar asset (Table 59).

	Capital allowances per paragraph 2.21	Finance charges per paragraph 2.13	Total
Yr 0	2,500	–	2,500
Yr 1	1,875	1,268	3,143
Yr 2	1,406	977	2,383
Yr 3	1,055	688	1,743
Yr 4	791	399	1,190
Yr 5	(127)	108	
Costs		50	31
	7,500	3,490	10,990

Table 59

Tax reliefs available during a five year contract term to the hire purchaser of an asset costing £10,000 and which he sells at the end of the term for £2,500, including reliefs for the finance charges on a rule of 78 basis (paragraph 2.13) and relief for selling costs of £50.

If we then assume that our purchaser leases the asset out to a lessee, under a full pay-out lease identical to the one outlined in paragraph 2.16, then his cash inflows would be £2,688 per annum in each of the first four years, and that same £2,688 reduced by a rebate of rentals of £2,450 in the fifth year. His cash inflows would thus exactly match his outflows.

6.12   What would be out of line would be his taxable income from the lessee, and the tax deductions and allowances we have already calculated, as we show in Table 60.

	Income	Deductions and allowances	Acceleration of reliefs in front of income	Value of reliefs at 35%
Yr 0	–	2,500	2,500	875
Yr 1	2,688	3,143	455	159
			2,955	1,034
Yr 2	2,688	2,383	(305)	(107)
			2,650	927
Yr 3	2,688	1,743	(945)	(331)
			1,705	596
Yr 4	2,688	1,190	(1,498)	(524)
			207	72
Yr 5	238	31	(207)	(72)

Table 60

Taxable income and tax reliefs compared for the hire purchaser who also leases out the asset concerned, showing the acceleration of reliefs in front of income at the start of the five year term, reversing in the later years.

If one were to discount the (35 percent) values of those accelerated tax allowances, one could arrive at a present value which the purchaser could afford to pay as an additional, front-end, 'deposit' under his hire purchase contract, and still be better off as a result of the deal than he would have been without either the hire-purchase-in, or the the lease-out. On a jaundiced view, our purchaser would in this case be doing no more than purchase tax reliefs – (and it is a well known fact that the Inland Revenue seems chronically to suffer from hepatitis). But there could be other reasons why the purchaser might want to take the lease receivable onto his balance sheet, with its (nearly) matching hire purchase creditor. The most usual one being his wanting to make use of every available source of financing in order to be able to meet the needs of his lessee customers – needs from which he can earn profits.

The purchaser's accounting

6.13   As already indicated, a purchaser would be expected to account for the asset he was acquiring under a finance-type hire purchase agreement by capitalising it onto his balance sheet at the present value of minimum hire payments, charging off the finance charges implicit in those hire payments to profit and loss account, and depreciating the asset in a way consistent with his other, similar, fixed assets. The actual method of computing what are each year's finance charges can be either the actuarial method before tax, or the rule of 78. The former has been the method we have used in our examples of lessee accounting, for instance the original lessee cashflow calculation in paragraph 2.02. However, what we are envisaging at the moment is a hire purchase transaction in which our purchaser pays not only the £672 per quarter hire charges through a five year period, and a final expense of £50 incurred in connection with the asset's sale, but also pays an additional, front-end, deposit – which we have not yet quantified. That deposit would certainly seem to be a part of the minimum lease payments; and therefore to suggest that each of the asset, and the 'borrowing' would enter the purchaser's balance sheet at a figure in excess of £10,000.

The vendor's accounting

6.14   It will be no great surprise that the vendor under a finance-type hire purchase contract also accounts in a similar way to a lessor. But we are in this example (Table 61) looking at that lessor himself, since it is on a lease out that he is 'disposing' of the risks and rewards of ownership. The profit he makes, and the way he accounts for it through the years of the transaction can best be explained by reference to a lessor cashflow. That sentence was quite carefully worded, to say that it is the explanation, not the book-keeping, that can be derived from this cashflow.

		Equity					External borrowing				
		Rentals extracted	Start of quarter	Equity income	End of quarter		Rentals applied to repay borrowings	Tax	Start of quarter	Interest expense	End of quarter
YI QI	304	–	304	12	316	10,000	(672)		9,328	313	9,641
Q2	316	(42)	274	11	285	9,641	(630)		9,011	303	9,314
Q3	285	(38)	247	9	256	9,314	(634)		8,680	293	8,973
Q4	256	(36)	220	8	228	8,973	(636)	(875)	7,462	251	7,713
				40						1,160	35,641
Y2 QI	228	(33)	195	8	203	7,713	(639)		7,074	238	7,312
		(149)									
Q2	203	(32)	171	7	178	7,312	(640)		6,672	225	6,897
Q3	178	(29)	149	6	155	6,897	(643)		6,254	210	6,464
Q4	155	(26)	129	6	135	6,464	(646)	(137)	5,681	190	5,871
				27						863	26,544
Y3 QI	135	(24)	111	4	115	5,871	(648)		5,223	175	5,398
		(111)									
Q2	115	(23)	92	4	96	5,398	(649)		4,749	159	4,908
Q3	96	(21)	75	3	78	4,908	(651)		4,257	143	4,400
Q4	78	(18)	60	2	62	4,400	(654)	122	3,868	129	3,997
				13						606	18,703
Y4 QI	62	(16)	46	2	48	3,997	(656)		3341	112	3,453
		(78)									
Q2	48	(14)	34	2	36	3,453	(658)		2,795	93	2,888
Q3	36	(12)	24	2	26	2,888	(660)		2,228	74	2,302
Q4	26	(10)	16	1	17	2,302	(662)	338	1,978	66	2,044
				7						345	10,687
Y5 QI	17	(8)	9	1	10	2,044	(664)		1,380	46	1,426
		(44)									
Q2	10	(6)	4	1	5	1426	(666)		760	26	786
Q3	5	(5)	–	–	–	786	(667)		119	4	123
Q4	–	–	–	–	–	123	(672)	528	(21)	(1)	(22)
end	–	–	–	–	(22)	(22)	(50)	72	–	–	–
		(11)		2						75	2,313
Totals		(393)		89				48		3,049	93,888

Table 61

Cashflow for a hire vendor assuming his receivable (investment in finance leases) can be quantified at £10,304, and that that is financed by borrowings of £10,000 and an equity contribution of £304.

6.15 The general format of this lessor's cashflow appears to be just what we might expect the lessor's computer to produce, for pricing and for accounting purposes, but it is important that we recognise what it purports to represent:

- the lessor has set up a receivable (investment in finance leases) at a figure of £10,304;

- against that he has set up a 'borrowing' of £10,000 and an equity contribution of £304;

- the interest he pays on the borrowing through the five years totals £3,049;

- but he is able to extract, in addition to the interest mentioned above, the following amounts:

original equity contribution	£304
reward thereon at 4 percent post-tax	89
tax payable on that reward	48
	441
add interest as above	3,049
	3,490

- that total of £3,490 is of course the difference between the total rents he will receive from the lessee, (including the £50 on the asset's sale), and what we originally assumed to be the asset's cost of £10,000; but it is no better than fiction to assume that the lessor can reduce his interest costs to an extent that will enable him to extract a total of £441 out of the lease.

It is not the figures, but the underlying concepts, that are valid and important in this cashflow. What it does show is that there is scope for making a profit out of the combined (hire-purchase-in, and lease-out), transaction because although the main inflows and outflows of rents and hire are equal and opposite, there is a considerable interest free inflow from the Inland Revenue in the early years, only paid back in later years. If we assume that we can earn profits from using that cash, (and note that that is not quite the same thing as saying the profits emerge in the form of savings of interest payable; because we only have notional borrowings not real ones in this deal), then it is these profits we want to account for on a rational basis through the five years. The cashflow sets those profits at a post-tax figure of £89, and shows how this would be spread, (and extracted), if it were in fact the reward at 4 percent on an equity injection of £304. But there is no such equity injection. The cashflow needs to be rewritten as shown in the next paragraph (Table 62).

Revised cashflow for the hire-purchase-in lease-out

6.16 What we have done in the cashflow statement in Table 62, compared with the previous version in paragraph 6.14 (Table 61), is to:

- preserve the 'equity reward' of £89, and its spread through the years;
- eliminate the equity contribution itself;
- but show that the interest costs on the 'borrowing' and the amounts of rents applied towards repayment of that 'borrowing' are increased by £304 from the previous figures.

		Equity					External borrowing				
		Rentals extracted	Start of quarter	Equity income	End of quarter		Rentals applied to repay borrowings	Tax	Start of quarter	Interest expense	End of quarter
Y1 Q1	–	–	–	12	12	10,000	(672)		9,328	344	9,672
Q2	–	12	–	11	11	9,672	(660)		9,012	333	9,345
Q3	–	11	–	9	9	9,345	(661)		8,684	320	9,004
Q4	–	9	–	8	8	9,004	(663)	(875)	7,466	276	7,742
				40						1,273	
Y2 Q1	–	8	–	8	8	7,742	(664)		7,078	261	7,339
		40									
Q2	–	8	–	7	7	7,339	(664)		6,675	246	6,921
Q3	–	7	–	6	6	6,921	(665)		6,256	231	6,487
Q4	–	6	–	6	6	6,487	(666)	(137)	5,684	210	5,894
				27						948	
Y3 Q1	–	6	–	4	4	5,894	(666)		5,228	193	5,421
		27									
Q2	–	4	–	4	4	5,421	(668)		4,753	175	4,928
Q3	–	4	–	3	3	4,928	(668)		4,260	157	4,417
Q4	–	3	–	2	2	4,417	(669)	122	3,870	143	4,013
				13						668	
Y4 Q1	–	2	–	2	2	4013	(670)		3,343	123	3,466
		13									
Q2	–	2	–	2	2	3,466	(670)		2,796	104	2,900
Q3	–	2	–	2	2	2,900	(670)		2,230	82	2,312
Q4	–	2	–	1	1	2,312	(670)	338	1,980	73	2,053
				7						382	
Y5 Q1	–	1	–	1	1	2,053	(671)		1,382	51	1,433
		7									
Q2	–	1	–	1	1	1,433	(671)		762	28	790
Q3	–	1	–	–	–	790	(671)		119	4	123
Q4	–	–	–	–	–	123	(672)	528	(21)	(1)	(22)
end	–	–	–	–	–	(22)	(50)	72	–	–	–
		2		2						82	
Totals				89			13,353	48		3,353	

Table 62

Cashflow, revising that in Table 61, based on a nil equity contribution and 100 percent borrowing, but continuing to show the 'equity reward' and its extraction at the levels derived in paragraph 6.15.

The make up of the figures in Table 62's tax column is as in Table 63.

	Acceleration per paragraph 6.12	Tax on equity reward	Total
Year 0	(875)	–	(875)
Year 1	(159)	22	(137)
Year 2	107	15	122
Year 3	331	7	338
Year 4	524	4	528
Year 5	72	–	72

Table 63
Make up of the tax figures shown in Table 62.

Accounting for the hire-purchase-in lease-out transaction

6.17 At this point, we need to pause in this welter of figures, to make sure we know where we are headed:

• a purchaser of an asset under a finance-type hire purchase contract would normally capitalise it onto his balance sheet, and show a corresponding 'borrowing';

• a finance lessor normally shows the asset whose risks and rewards he has substantially transferred to another on his balance sheet as a receivable, described as 'investment in finance leases', and he also shows a corresponding borrowing;

• to show the combined transaction, it would obviously not be correct to double up both the assets and liabilities. What would seem more sensible is to show a single liability, namely the hire purchase transaction in the form of a 'borrowing' from the vendor, and a single matching asset, that is to say the lease transaction in the form of a receivable from the lessee;

• since we have made no equity contribution to the setting up of the transaction, it would follow that in the commencing book-keeping entries, the receivable and the 'borrowing' would be equal and opposite;

• it also seems quite clear that the lease receivable should enter the books at £10,000; but should the hire purchase 'borrowing' show at a higher figure, if we are making a front-end, additional, deposit on top of the quarterly £672 hire payments ? Or alternatively, is that deposit more fairly to be regarded as an additional element of the finance charges? The author inclines to the latter view.

Putting all of that together, we can derive a 'brick' from the cashflow in the previous paragraph to show:

- the hire purchase borrowing starting at £10,000, and giving rise to the interest charges set out in the previous paragraph's figures;

- the receivable, also starting at £10,000, and then being 'repaid' at such a rate that the aimed at profit is released into the profit and loss account each year through the five year period;

- the interest free cash made available by the Inland Revenue.

6.18   That brick is set out in Table 64. There is really only one area in which comments are needed on it:

- The interest costs on the hire purchase 'borrowing' are included in it, quantified at £3,353 as in paragraph 6.16. This can be seen from that paragraph's calculations to represent an interest rate of 3.690 percent per quarter on the balances 'owed' to the hire purchase vendor.

- The gross income is the excess of the lease rentals over the starting value of the receivable, namely £3,490.

- The excess of the income over the expenditure is thus £137, which emerges as a tax liability on the transaction of £48 and a post-tax profit of £89, available for extraction.

- But it is obvious that each of these figures is derived from the others – that it can be suggested that none (except the gross income) is based on any reality. That is a line of argument which we need to think through, and dispose of, in the next paragraph.

6.19   Let us take stock once again:

- We have a transaction in which the capital elements of the 'hire' paid to acquire an asset match, both in timing and amount, the capital elements of the receipts of rentals from the leasing out of that asset.

- The gross income, that is to say the finance charge elements, of the rental receipts totals £3,490.

- We are actually paying away, in the form of the finance charge elements of our hire payments, exactly that same £3,490 – and once again, the timing as well as the amounts exactly match. (There is a margin of uncertainty over that statement, in that if we did in fact pay an additional, front-end, deposit under the hire purchase contract, this would be additional to the £3,490, and would create a loss of the total matching. So far, although our discussions have alluded to it, our figures have not actually included any such front-end deposit).

- But it is a fact that the deal generates cash in its early years, in the form of an interest free loan from the Inland Revenue; and this is only repaid in the deal's later years.

	Balance sheet						Profit & Loss
	Liabilities			Assets		Original Equity	
	External Borrowing	Current Tax	Deferred Tax	Investment in finance leases	New Cash generated		
Asset	Cr10000			Dr10000			
Yr 1							
rentals	Dr 3531	Cr 875			Dr 32		Cr 2688
interest	Cr 1273						Dr 1273
repayment				Cr 1353			Dr 1353
c tax		Dr 875					Cr 875
		Dr 137					Cr 137
d tax			Cr1034				Dr 1034
							Cr 40
extract					Cr 32	Cr 8	Dr 40
	Cr 7742	Dr 137	Cr1034	Dr 8647	=	Cr 8	
Yr 2							
rentals	Dr 2796	Cr 137			Dr 21	Dr 8	Cr 2688
interest	Cr 948						Dr 948
repayment				Cr 1698			Dr 1698
c tax		Cr 122					Dr 122
d tax			Dr 107				Cr 107
							Cr 27
extract					Cr 21	Cr 6	Dr 27
	Cr 5894	Cr 122	Cr 927	Dr 6949	=	Cr 6	
Yr 3							
rentals	Dr 2549	Dr 122			Dr 11	Dr 6	Cr 2688
interest	Cr 668						Dr 668
repayment				Cr 2000			Dr. 2000
c tax		Cr 338					Dr 338
d tax			Dr 331				Cr 331
							Cr 13
extract					Cr 11	Cr 2	Dr 13
	Cr 4013	Cr 338	Cr 596	Dr 4949	=	Cr 2	
Yr 4							
rentals	Dr 2342	Dr 338			Dr 6	Dr 2	Cr 2688
interest	Cr 382						Dr 382
repayment				Cr 2295			Dr 2295
c tax		Cr 528					Dr 528
d tax			Dr 524				Cr 524
							Cr 7
extract					Cr 6	Cr 1	Dr 7
	Cr 2052	Cr 528	Cr 72	Dr 2654	=	Cr 1	
Yr 5							
rentals	Dr 2135	Dr 600			Dr 2	Dr 1	Cr 2738
interest	Cr 82						Dr 82
repayment				Cr 2654			Dr 2654
c tax		Cr 72					Dr 72
d tax			Dr 72				Cr 72
							Cr 2
extract					Cr 2		Dr 2
	=	=	=	=	=	=	=

Table 64

The 'brick' for the hire purchaser, simultaneously disposing of his asset by means of a finance lease, but able to generate a post tax profit of £89 out of the differences in the secondary (tax relief) cashflows.

• If this cash were to be invested in a discrete account for the period the company has it in its possession, then it would be perfectly easy to see that the interest received on that account would be the 'profit' generated by the transaction. But that is not what happens in practice.

• The surplus funds are simply utilised for the general purposes of the company – either to reduce its other borrowings, or as equity available for other deals. This obviously suggests that the 'brick' we are looking at should be 'rewarded' for having made available its Inland-Revenue-originated funds to the other 'brick' within the company that uses them; and that the recipient part of the organisation should pay for them.

• It is precisely that that we see happening in this case. £137 pre-tax has been treated as being the 'value' of use of the Inland Revenue's funds over the years the company has them. It is the 'reward' taken by, and extracted from, this 'brick'. And it should be the 'cost of funds' used elsewhere in the company, in some other brick or bricks where the funds are used.

6.20   But we have to recognise that there are two practical difficulties. First, is £137 pre-tax the right level ? We got to that figure by deducting interest costs of £3,353 (calculated at 3.690 percent on what would notionally have been interest bearing borrowings, after deducting interest free Inland Revenue funds), from the gross income, again related to notionally interest bearing outstandings. The profit level depends on our having used an appropriate percentage for the interest payable. The second practical difficulty is in fact the reverse side of that same coin. If the company has not been able to make profitable use overall of the Inland Revenue's funds, then there is no overall profit to attribute to this 'brick'. The only way in which one can prove the truth or otherwise of that proposition is to compare:

• the aggregate number for the profits derived separately from each 'brick'; with

• the company's profits derived on a global basis.

Accountancy is an art not a science, and the difficulty of getting at a 'precisely accurate' profit figure along either route is not dissimilar from the problems surrounding the weighing of the ship's cat. (Remember ? Work out the weight of the ship with the cat on board, and then chuck it overboard and work out the ship's weight a second time ? Not recommended as the most likely method of achieving a sensible answer). But with all those reservations, putting a value on the use of the freely available funds, and recognising that this is a 'profit' which our hire-purchase-in, and lease-out, deal has generated is still the least worst course to adopt. And with all due respect to the Inland Revenue's views on transactions which they may wish to regard as no more than tax avoidance, the author believes that this particular one will have had a considerable value to any reader who has followed thus far; in providing an extra depth of understanding of the workings, the thought processes, and the accounting methodologies, of leasing and hire purchase companies.

CHAPTER 7

Taxation

Capital allowances

7.01   We have so far obtained a general acquaintance with:

- the necessary conditions to be met if allowances are to be claimed (s.24(1) CAA 1990); there must be capital expenditure on the provision of machinery or plant by a trader wholly and exclusively for the purposes of his trade, and as a result of that expenditure the machinery or plant must belong to him (paragraphs 2.21 and 4.14);

- the rather different conditions necessary for a hire purchaser to obtain allowances on the asset he is acquiring (s.60(1) CAA 1990): that his capital expenditure be not only on the provision of machinery or plant by a trader for the purposes of his trade, but that it be under contract providing that he shall or may become the owner on the performance of the contract (paragraph 6.04);

- the calculation of a 25 percent writing down allowance, on a reducing balance basis, on such expenditure on a single asset − and the balancing charge (clawback of allowances) made for the year in which that asset is sold for more than its 'written down value' (paragraph 2.21).

But capital allowances are unfortunately a considerably more complicated field than that might indicate. It is probably sensible to start with the fact that allowances are not, generally, given asset by asset; 'the pool' is the phrase which indicates that the allowances which a company claims as a deduction in arriving at its taxable income are calculated globally (all references in the following are to the Capital Allowances Act 1990).

That shows two things. First that capital allowances, just like the whole subject of taxation, are very tightly defined and controlled by the relevant legislation; some of it we will look at, but without doubling the size of this book we could not comment on all of it. Secondly, to the extent the figures are put together globally, it may be less likely that a balancing charge (clawback of allowances) may occur. £2,500 disposal proceeds of the leased asset we have used in our example throughout this book may be the largest component of the £3,298 disposal value above, and may be greater than the written down value of that asset itself, but it does not give rise to a balancing charge in the company's (total) computation.

*The 'pool' value brought forward, i.e. expenditure of previous periods not
yet allowed for tax (the aggregate of written down
values brought forward)*   £19,672

Expenditure in the period   9,834

Subtotal – 'qualifying expenditure' for section 25(1) CAA 90   29,506

*deduct 'disposal value' (calculated under s.26 CAA 90) of assets ceasing in
the period to qualify for allowances (by reason of an
event defined in s.24(6))*   3,298

*The amount on which an allowance is to be given
(s.24(2) CAA 90)*   26,208

Writing down allowance at 25 percent   6,552

The 'pool' value to be carried forward for next year's claim   19,656

Separate pools

7.02   But although a leasing company will have a 'general pool' in which
one might expect the greater part of its capital expenditure, and capital
allowances, to be dealt with, it is likely also to have a number of 'separate
pools', and the rationale for their having been originally legislated into
existence is far from standard. One such example is that:

•   Each 'expensive car' has to be dealt with in a separate pool. (Expensive
    in this instance still means costing when new £8,001 or more; which
    is the level to which the definition was raised in the Finance (No 2)
    Act 1979. Since neither car tax nor VAT can be recovered by a company
    which pays them on its acquisition of a car, the £8,001 figure is inclusive
    of these).

•   The reason for dealing individually with each such car is that the writing
    down allowance on each is limited to £2,000 per annum, regardless how
    much the car originally cost, until such time as its written down value
    falls below £8,000. The allowance is only thereafter calculated on the
    normal reducing balance basis.

•   There are included in the form of notes in parenthesis at the end of
    this paragraph, in order not to interrupt our discussion of separate
    pools, two further tax disadvantages of the leasing or hire purchasing
    of cars costing over £8,000.

•   But this penalisation is to some extent redressed by the other implication
    of the separate pool provisions. This is that the disposal of the asset
    will produce a 'balancing adjustment' of some sort, because the pool
    is separate precisely to prevent its continuing to exist empty. Thus when

an expensive car is disposed of, its owner is entitled to an immediate 'balancing allowance' if the disposal proceeds fall short of the written down value of the car. The way in which this is provided in the law is that the disposal is to be regarded as the cessation of the 'separate trade' in which its owner is deemed to have been using the car. When a trade ceases, the trader obtains a balancing allowance if his proceeds fall short of 'qualifying expenditure': that is different from the position of the continuing trader who would merely continue to be given 25 percent allowances on the amount by which his qualifying expenditure in a general pool exceeded disposal value, (even if the asset being disposed of happened to be the only one in the pool).

That is the most clearly visible, and perhaps most logically based form of the separate pool. Cars costing £8,000 or less are to be dealt with, in aggregate, in another separate pool, the rules for which are exactly the same as those indicated above for the individual pools for each expensive car.

(Notes on further tax disadvantages of leasing or hire purchasing cars costing over £8,000:

The lessee is, by virtue of s.35(3) CAA 1990, not entitled to deduct in arriving at his own taxable profits the whole of the rentals he pays for such a car. The proportion he is permitted to deduct is:

$$\frac{\text{£8,000 plus half the excess cost above £8,000}}{\text{the full cost of the car}}$$

and it will be clear that this represents an outright denial of tax relief on the remainder of the rentals — not just a slowing of the pace at which they can be deducted. In paragraph 6.08 we mentioned that the Inland Revenue appeared willing to permit taxpayers acquiring assets by hire purchase to choose whether:

• to claim capital allowances on the full contract cost; or

• to claim those allowances on the asset's cash price, and to treat the excess of the contract cost over that cash price as 'interest' deductible on the basis of a rule of 78 calculation.

In the case of cars costing more than £8,000, the Inland Revenue appear to be using the existence of this optional treatment to argue as follows:

• the wording of s.35(3) reads 'where apart from this subsection, the amount of any expenditure on the hiring of a motor car the retail price of which when new exceeds £8,000, would be allowed to be deducted in computing for the purposes of tax the amounts of profits or gains of any trade, that amount shall be reduced...' — notice that the section is very specific in attacking only expenditure on hiring;

- the consideration paid by a hire purchaser contains an element of hire as well as an element of capital expenditure, as is clearly shown by all three of the name of the transaction, the Revenue's optional treatment adopted by a majority of taxpayers, and common sense;

- the second and third of these points each reinforce the view that the capital expenditure element is the cash cost, and that the balance is a hiring charge;

- even if a taxpayer does not use the Revenue's optional treatment, that hiring charge 'would (have been) allowed to be deducted' had he done so. The subjunctive shows that s.35(3) is addressing the potential deductibility rather than the actual deduction claimed.

Therefore the section is intended to create a disallowance of some part of such a hiring charge in the case of cars whose original cash cost was over £8,000. Should a taxpayer attempt to argue that no part of what he paid was in fact hiring; that all of it constituted capital expenditure, and was thus outside s.35(3), the Revenue's response would be that what is capital and what is revenue is a question of law which the courts have reserved to themselves (*per* Lord Denning in *Heather v PE Consulting Group Ltd* [1973] 1 All E R 8); but that in that same judgment Lord Denning indicated that the courts would normally give great weight to the views of accountants; one could hardly wish for a more categoric statement of accountants' views than a SSAP – and SSAP 21 does not permit the capitalisation of the full contract cost, only the present value of the minimum lease payments (equating cash price).

These are powerful arguments. It seems to the author that the taxpayer's response to the first set of arguments attributed above to the Inland Revenue should be:

- it is accepted that the substance of the transaction, not its form, is that there is a capital element within the contract price;

- but that substance, backed up by the scheme of capital allowances in s.60 CAA 1990 (see paragraph 6.04 above) shows clearly that the part of the contract price which is not capital expenditure is a financing charge, not a hiring charge. One should certainly give great weight to the views of accountants who say clearly that that is what it is – and whose views on the years in which it must be expensed are totally irreconcilable with the suggestion that it could be a hiring charge;

- the view that hire purchase is, in substance, purchase with an extra charge built in for the privilege of paying by instalments is universal, and its fairness has been reflected by the legislature's enactment of laws protecting hire purchasers against unwarrantable repossession (but not giving any equivalent protection to lessees, because hiring is totally different from hire purchase);

- but perhaps most embarrassing of all to those who might argue the view ascribed above to the Inland Revenue, is the question whether they can seriously argue that the same sum, arising from the same contract, is financing income in the hands of the hire vendor, taxable on a rule of 78 basis, while being a hiring charge so far as the purchaser is concerned ?

In sum, the author believes those who take the view ascribed to the Inland Revenue are wrong).

Assets leased to lessees whose trading activities are outside the scope of UK tax

7.03   Before March 1984, a lessor could obtain a 'first year' allowance of 100 percent for the year in which he acquired plant for leasing; and against that, his rental income would come into charge to tax only over, say, the next five years. If the lessee were himself obtaining tax deductions for those rentals which coincided in time with the lessor's taxability, but the lessee were also bringing into charge to tax the profits he was generating from the possession and use of the machine, then the UK authorities could justify the accelerated (100 percent first year) allowances given on the asset's acquisition as 'an incentive to British industry to re-equip'. But it was much harder to see why UK leasing companies should receive such favourable incentives for leasing for instance a production line to General Motors in the US. Accordingly, in 1980 first year allowances were prevented from being given for what we will call for simplicity 'plant leased abroad'. Two years later, the authorities took a second bite at the same cherry, cutting the rate of writing down allowances on such plant from 25 percent to, generally, 10 percent but with an excessively complicated rider that no allowances whatever could be given on plant leased abroad on certain longer types of lease. What had incensed the authorities about these last mentioned leases, referred to in the jargon as 'double dips', was that it had been found possible to structure them in such a way that not only did the UK lessor obtain accelerated tax allowances, but the overseas lessee could qualify at the same time for tax incentives in his own jurisdiction, (for instance investment tax credits in the US). First year allowances were legislated out of existence in the UK in March 1984, and investment tax credits were removed in the US in 1986, but there still exist in s.42 CAA 1990, in all their glory, the provisions restricting to 10 percent the writing down allowances on plant leased abroad – and cutting out all allowances for leases which fail to meet the requirements which would keep them clear of the 'double dip' provisions. It is only sensible to essay a simplified summary of this exceptionally complex legislation – which itself is not made easier to comprehend by having been found in 1986 to be defective in certain respects, and rewritten for expenditure after that date alongside the previous, defective, provisions still retained in the legislation for expenditure incurred earlier.

7.04   In the light of the warning given in the previous paragraph that what follows is no more than a summary of anti-avoidance legislation, and one written in simple terms, it is vital that the reader check how the various terms used below are in fact defined in that legislation, and how its provisions mesh together, before reaching any conclusion on the answer to a particular problem. The basic provision is s.42(1) and (2) CAA 1990, which reduces from 25 percent to 10 percent the writing down allowances:

- on expenditure on machinery or plant for leasing, where the lessee (meaning the end user, ignoring any intermediate lessees) is outside the scope of UK tax (i.e. is neither a UK resident, nor a non-resident carrying on a trade here through a 'branch');

- excepted from the above is machinery or plant used for 'short term leasing' (meaning either leasing for periods not generally exceeding 30 consecutive days to any lessee and not generally totalling 90 days in a year to any one lessee, or meaning short lets in between longer term leases to UK based lessees);

- also excepted are ship and aircraft chartering, and container leasing, where the charterer (or equivalent) is carrying on an activity which includes not only making the ship etc available to a non-resident user, but retaining responsibility for its crewing, navigation and management.

This provision necessitates that expenditure qualifying for 10 percent allowances be dealt with in a pool separate from any that we have considered so far, (but this is to be a single pool containing all assets thus leased abroad, not individual pools for each asset). When and if the leasing of all the assets at that time in this separate pool comes to an end, then there will be a balancing allowance or charge calculated by reference to the disposal values of those assets. There are further provisions designed to:

- substitute open market values in place of any other figures which may have been adopted as the sale values of items of plant sold to connected parties;

- safeguard the Revenue authorities in cases where an asset previously used by its owner for some other purpose, or leased out in an inoffensive manner, comes thereafter to be leased in the above, objectionable, way. For instance, the owner and operator of a shipping trade normally has to put each of his ships into a separate pool (s.31(2) CAA 1990); when each ceases to be used in that trade, a balancing allowance or charge is calculated - but its amount is not given to, or charged against, the trader, it is merely added to or deducted from the amounts in his other pools. However if the reason a ship 'ceases to be used' in such a way as to qualify for ordinary allowances in its separate pool is that it starts to be leased abroad, this enables the Revenue to transfer an appropriate value into the overseas leasing pool.

7.05   We have to say something about the type of leases abroad which are denied any allowances of any sort. The legislation is to be found in s.42(3) CAA 1990. It takes the form of five possible provisions that might be found in a lease, any one of which will cause that lease to fail to qualify for allowances:

• there can be a gap of more than a year between consecutive rental payments;

• any payments other than 'periodical' ones are due under the lease (for example, front-end or final balloons would disqualify);

• any payment, expressed as an amount per month for the number of months for which it is paid, is different from any other payment so expressed (for example, stepped rents would disqualify, but there is a saving where rentals are adjusted under a tax-adjustment or interest rate-adjustment clause, or where insurance premiums charged on to the lessee alter);

• the lease can exceed 13 years, or is capable of being extended to exceed that term (both this and the previous provision would seem to disqualify leases which entitle the lessee to extend into a secondary term);

• the lessor could receive from the lessee a 'payment of an amount determined before the expiry of the lease, and referable to a value of the asset at or after that expiry, whether or not the payment relates to a disposal of the asset' − (one of the necessary conditions for the US investment tax credit was that the lease must contain a 'fair value option' exercisable by the US lessee; there were ways of ensuring that this did not of itself disqualify the UK lessor from obtaining allowances, by ensuring that either he was not its direct recipient, or the lessee not its direct payer, or it was related to something other than an actual transfer of ownership).

Even paraphrased as above, those restrictions can be seen to be very onerous. It is extremely difficult to draft a lease which does not contravene one or more of them. But if UK lessors wish to lease plant abroad, they must either find lessees prepared to pay rentals reflecting the non-availability of any allowances, or must pay the most close attention to s.42(3) CAA 1990.

Short life assets

7.06 There is a happier side to the calculation of capital allowances through separate pools. The concept of 'short life assets' was introduced in 1985. It will have been clear from our explanation of the general pool in paragraph 7.01, that tax allowances could lag behind a taxpayer's depreciation in his accounts, (the latter reflecting in his eyes his real position), and that this could be an ever increasing process. Consider for instance a tailor who buys one sewing machine every year, for £1,000 each, and sells them for £200 in the fifth year of their lives. Early in the fifth year of his operation, but after he has bought that year's machine, he will have a pool of £3,051, (being one machine at £1,000, another at £750, and others at £563, £422 and £316). When he receives £200 for the sale of the oldest machine his pool goes down to £2,851, and the writing down allowance he gets on that figure is £713. The depreciation he needs to charge in arriving at what he sees as his real profits is £800 per annum. He is therefore taxed on £87 of 'unreal' profit. But it does not stop there; we can set out the figures for that fifth and subsequent years in Table 65.

Yr 5	*pool brought forward*	£2,051		
	additions	1,000		
	disposal value	(200)		
		2,851		
	allowance	713	shortfall below depr	£87
		2,138		
Yr 6	*additions*	1,000		
	disposal value	(200)		
		2,938		
	allowance	735	cumulative shortfall	£152
		2,203		
Yr 7	*additions*	1,000		
	disposal value	(200)		
		3,003		
	allowance	751	cumulative shortfall	£201
		2,252		

Table 65

Illustration of the way in which the pool builds up in size year by year as a result of each year's disposal value being less than the written down value within the pool of the asset actually sold.

The only way of rectifying this would be to allow the tailor a balancing allowance on his sales of four-and-a-bit year old sewing machines, since it is clear that the sales always realise less than the machine's written down values, and that leaving this difference within the pool, to be allowed over future years on a 25 percent reducing basis, is not enough. That is just what the short life asset legislation in s.37 CAA 1990 achieves. It provides that on a taxpayer's election, each individual asset in respect of which he makes the election is to be treated as within its own individual pool. If it is disposed of by the end of the year during which falls the fourth anniversary of its acquisition, then a balancing allowance will be given, or a balancing charge made, by reference to its disposal value. If the asset is still in use in the taxpayer's trade at the end of that year, (four-and-a-bit years after its acquisition), then the figure in its separate pool is transferred into the taxpayer's general pool; and any subsequent disposal value would merely be deducted from that general pool amount, without any balancing allowance or charge. But cars cannot be treated as short life assets, and nor can assets leased abroad, or ships.

Machinery or plant

7.07 Each of the paragraphs in this chapter so far has made repeated use of the phrase 'machinery or plant', lifted straight out of the Capital Allowances Act. Most people believe that they can recognise machinery when they see it, but what is 'plant' ? The much quoted answer, (Lindley LJ in *Yarmouth v France*, an old workmen's compensation case, CA, (1887) 19 QB 647), is

> "there is no definition of plant in the Employers' Liability Act 1880, but in its ordinary sense, it includes whatever apparatus is used by a businessman for carrying on his business − not his stock in trade, which he buys or makes for sale; but all goods and chattels, fixed or moveable, live or dead, which he keeps for permanent employment in the business."

In the case itself, a horse was held to be plant. The references to apparatus used, and to goods etc employed in the business imply a distinction between the premises 'in' which the business is carried on, and the plant 'with' which it is so carried on. This has come to be referred to as the 'functional test'. In one of the leading cases *CIR v Barclay Curle & Co Ltd*, HL [1969] 1 All ER 732, it was held that a drydock, (63 percent of the expenditure on which related to excavation and concreting, and only the remaining 37 percent was on the gates and sluices, on pumps and piping and on the ancillary machinery), nevertheless fully qualified as plant on the basis that it was not a passive receptacle for ships, but was the means for getting them out of the water and holding them secure while repair work could be performed. Many taxpayers have over the years had resort to the courts in disputes with the Inland Revenue on the definition of plant. The boundaries may be less unclear than once they were, but are still less than totally certain. We said in paragraph 2.58 that there were a number of areas in which one party to a lease agreement will frequently if not invariably seek an indemnity from the other in respect of unexpected, and to that extent excessive, tax liabilities the first may incur as a result of the lease. Many lessors have a standard clause in their lease agreements, calling on the lessee to make good by way of an increased level of rentals any damage the lessor may suffer if the Inland Revenue should deny capital allowances to the lessor on the leased asset. It has of course to be said that the lessor's profit on the lease may be destroyed not just by such a denial of allowances, but by their being delayed by some dispute over their availability – even if this is eventually resolved in the lessor's favour. This is another aspect of the matter in respect of which the lessor may wish to extend the scope of his indemnity protection. And that leads on to a further aspect of the procedures of indemnification; if it is the lessee who is financially at risk if the Inland Revenue should deny or delay allowances, and if the lessor is effectively uninterested in the outcome of such a dispute, should it be the lessee who is put in the position to decide how the case should be fought, and what level of costs should be incurred in such a fight ? All of this is normal material for debate between lessor and lessee at the time they agree the lease terms.

What is a lease and what plant is leased ?

7.08 These questions are not facetious. Consider three drums of 35 millimetre photographic film. Unexposed they have a value, but should they become the master negative of a film starring the biggest box-office names, and directed and produced by Hollywood's best, their value will be something quite different. In the context of the leasing of plant, however, we should be thinking of cost rather than value:

- Is the cost of the drums of film purely what was paid for them in an unexposed state, or has all the cash earned by the stars and film crew come to be 'capital expenditure on the provision of plant', namely the master negative with which the film production company will carry on its business ?

- That question may seem relatively straightforward until one recognises that a filmstar's contribution to the creation of a film, and even more so the director's, has much in common with an author's contribution to the creation of a book. What results is not simply a physical object, but a network of intangible 'rights', copyright and intellectual property rights being the most important. These undoubtedly increase the value of the physical drums of film, but are they as well as it 'plant' ? And if they are not, is it totally clear that the whole of that capital expenditure can be attributed to the plant, and no part of it has to be regarded as the acquisition of whatever part of the rights the film production company has obtained ?

Clear and unequivocal answers to questions of this sort can be difficult in the extreme. In fact the answer to this particular one has been a curious balance between Inland Revenue practice and law. In 1979 the Revenue authorities issued a statement of practice (SP 9/79) making clear their willingness to treat the whole cost of the production of films as capital expenditure on plant. In 1982, this was statutorily reversed in the Finance Act; the costs of production of films being from then on regarded in principle as on revenue account, but with the proviso that the 1979 treatment could still be continued for expenditure already contracted for before March 1982, and also for subsequent expenditure provided that the film concerned qualified as a substantially British-made film. The original end-date for that second class of excepted expenditure was March 1984, but that date was later postponed to March 1987. Treating the expenditure as on revenue account removed it from the capital allowances category to the profit and loss account, but did not make it fully deductible as soon as it was incurred, because it was only to be written off during the film's period of earning income at the box-office.

7.09 That may be a very small corner of history, but it is illustrative of the difficulties that can arise in trying to decide whether allowances will or will not be available on 'capital expenditure'. The second part of the question raised in the heading of paragraph 7.08 can also be illustrated by reference to the production and distribution of films. Suppose that it was a leasing company which financed the production of the film, and which leases it to a film distribution company. The 'master print' which is the subject matter of the lease comprises those drums of film, (now containing the original picture negative), together with the original soundtrack material, the 'answer print', and a letter from the film laboratory holding the original negative material acknowledging that they hold it to the leasing company's order but to honour orders of the lessee distribution company for pre-print materials, duplicate negatives and/or positive prints of the film. The copyrights and intellectual property rights are also, to a sufficient extent, the property of the leasing company, and the use by the lessee distribution company of the material leased to it must be possible without their being infringed. If we were to assume that the worldwide distribution was handled by that single film distribution company, and that it was within the scope of UK tax on the whole of its operations, then there would be no problems under the 'leasing abroad' provisions referred to in paragraph 7.04. The only lease we would be considering would be that between our leasing company and the (UK) film distribution company. Whether the latter's arrangements with cinemas abroad (and for that matter UK cinemas) might also be characterised as 'leases' would be irrelevant, because it is absolutely clear that the 'plant' made available to such cinemas would not be the 'master print'. Therefore the film distribution company is not only the lessee but also the 'end user' of that master print; there is no possible argument that it is only an intermediate lessee, the end users (or some of them) being outside the scope of UK tax; and thus bringing within the mischief of the leasing abroad rules the plant acquired by the leasing company for leasing to the film distribution company. But that is of course not how the international film production and distribution groups operate. Although there may be a main distributor, (and it is possible that this may be a company within the scope of UK taxes), it would handle the distribution abroad through a network of other local companies, most often but not invariably under common ownership with the production company and the main distributor. If we assumed for instance that one of those local distribution companies was a fellow subsidiary resident for tax and operating only in Australia, the question then becomes:

- Is 'the plant' leased (albeit through an intermediate UK lessee) to the Australian company ? in which case its leasing to that Australian company is not a 'qualifying purpose'; and that fact disqualifies our UK leasing company's expenditure from 25 percent allowances, and means that it will get only 10 percent or may obtain no allowances.

- Or alternatively, does the arrangement between the UK distribution company and its fellow subsidiary in Australia fall short of being a lease, or at least of being a lease of the plant on which our leasing company wishes to claim allowances ? In either of which cases there would be no restriction of those capital allowances.

The answers to these questions will always be dependent on the facts of the particular case. They were however considered by the High Court against the facts of the particular case of *Barclays Mercantile Industrial Finance Ltd v Melluish* [1990] STC 314. It is clear that the main factor differentiating a contractual tenancy of land from a contractual licence, (whether the occupier has a 'stake' in the building or room in it, or only a permission personally to occupy it), is whether he has exclusive possession. The judge's view was that a similar line must be drawn between leases, contracts of bailment as they are technically called, and contracts which are not leases because they fall short of giving the Australian company that exclusive possession.

Trading

7.10   That question whether the 'sub-distribution agreements' were leases,
or fell short of so being, led directly in the *Barclays Mercantile* case to a
different and very much wider question. In that case it was a rather
specialised aspect – namely were the transactions between the main
distribution company and its UK and overseas local distribution companies
a part of the 'trade' of that main distribution company ? (They had been
held, as we saw in the last paragraph, not to be leases.) The context of
this question is again the definition of qualifying purposes and non
qualifying purposes in the provisions dealing with leasing abroad. The
actual provision that was relevant was not that paraphrased in paragraph
7.04, (which reduces the rate of, or eliminates, writing down allowances
if the lessee is outside the scope of UK taxes). It was s.39(2) CAA 1990
which was originally designed to prevent the giving of 100 percent first
year allowances unless, among other things,

> 'the machinery or plant is leased to a lessee who uses it for the purposes
> of a trade other than leasing..'

That is to say, the plant had to be leased to the main distribution company
as lessee; we know that it did not lease it on, and we can therefore call
it the end user; but the plant must also be used by that main distributor
in its trade – what it did with the master print must be a part of its trade,
and not a transaction which fell outside the boundaries of that trade. That
awkward phraseology, 'what it did with the master print', serves to remind
us that the main distributor's acquisition, as well as his disposal, of the
print and the rights needed to be looked at. The Inland Revenue suggested
that if:

• first, it was unusual for that particular (UK) company to acquire the
  worldwide main distribution rights;

• second, the lease rentals it had to pay in order to do so meant that
  it in turn needed to ensure that it could obtain sufficient income from
  the other local distribution companies – but essentially no more than
  that 'sufficient' level, because the group as a whole did not want the
  UK company to make profits beyond what it would normally be
  expected to have made out of its purely UK distribution function;

• third it could readily be seen that the whole purpose of the UK company
  having been used as the worldwide main distributor was to enable UK
  tax reliefs to be obtained;

then this took the arrangements outside the scope of that UK company's
trade. On the particular facts of the *Barclays Mercantile* case, the Inland
Revenue failed in this contention. There are lessons to be learned from

the judge's analysis of those facts, and of the law against which they needed to be viewed. But this particular point is a narrow one, and it is probably more useful to turn our attention to the more usual form of the question; not 'Is the lessee trading ?' but 'Is the lessor trading ?'

7.11 Two of the vital requirements to be met by a lessor if he is to obtain allowances on the capital expenditure he incurs, as we noted in paragraph 7.01, are that:

- he must be 'a person carrying on a trade';

- and the expenditure must be 'wholly and exclusively for the purposes of the trade'.

(There is an exception to which we will come in paragraph 7.21 below, dealing specifically with certain machinery or plant let 'otherwise than in the course of a trade'; but this is a narrow point, and need not deflect us at this stage from the generality that the lessor must be engaged in a trade). There are three possible ways in which our lessor can fail the test:

- he may not yet have started to trade, or if he has started he did not do so as early as he had claimed he did;

- he may have been trading at an earlier point, but have ceased to carry on any trade;

- his activities may not constitute a trade at all.

The last shall be first, in our study of this area. A number of disputes between taxpayers and the Inland Revenue are currently reaching the courts, or are being settled out of court, stemming from transactions in the late 1970s or early 1980s. At that time, the 100 percent first year allowances available on capital expenditure undoubtedly encouraged many taxpayers and their advisers to devise ways in which the value of these tax allowances could be turned to account. Financing of films was one such area; and as we saw in paragraph 7.09 the *Barclays Mercantile Industrial Finance* case was one case in which the Inland Revenue have recently challenged what the taxpayer claimed to be the allowances due to him in respect of such film leasing. Another case, also dealing with films, but more directly relevant to the question we are now considering, was *Ensign Tankers (Leasing) Ltd v Stokes*, [1989] STC 705.

We made a brief reference in paragraph 4.32 to certain heavily tax-based leasing deals, often with unusual rental profiles, and in which the credit risks that these might otherwise have created for some of the parties were secured (in the technical sense) by cash deposits held in escrow accounts. Neither the *Barclays Mercantile* transaction, nor the *Ensign Tankers* one, contained this feature. The comment we made in paragraph 4.32 was that all businesses involve risk, as well as the hope of reward; and that if all risk is removed, the question must be asked whether what remains is still a business transaction – a trading transaction in tax terminology. That is an entirely valid way of putting the question. But the answer it invites is too metaphysical, too subjective, to be a satisfactory basis for running a tax system. We need to be more specific, more objective.

7.12   The question the judge faced in *Ensign Tankers (Leasing) Ltd v Stokes* was whether the transactions in which the taxpayer was engaged constituted trading, and whether what would otherwise have been an affirmative answer to that question could be negatived by the undoubted 'tax' motivations of some of the parties. In fact the taxpayer entity was in that case a limited partnership. It acquired two films, each of which was at the time of its acquisition uncompleted. It contracted for each to be completed. It retained ownership of each film, but licensed the distribution of each within the UK by UK distribution companies, and their distribution abroad by overseas companies. The financial arrangements for the two films were not identical, but outlining one of them will provide a sufficient picture of what were the parties' aims:

*   The partnership acquired the film from the Lorimar group company (LPI) which was in the process of making it. The price was to be equal to the film's cost to that date, but the payment of that price was to be left outstanding in accordance with the arrangements indicated below. The partnership appointed LPI to complete the film, payment for this also to be left outstanding as described below.

*   The partnership consisted of a 'general partner' which was another Lorimar group company which put no capital into the partnership but was entitled to 2 percent of its profits, and five UK companies (of whom Ensign was one) as 'limited partners', who put in $3.25m as capital, and shared the balance of the profits in proportion to their capital.

*   The partnership borrowed, on a non recourse basis, from LPI two amounts, of $9.75m and $1.96m respectively. The first was referred to as the production loan (and included the amount of the unpaid purchase price for the acquisition of the film, as well as the balance of three quarters of the film's original budgeted cost), and the second was referred to as the completion loan.

*   The aggregate of the partnership's own capital, and the two non recourse loans from LPI, were all the finance the partnership needed to acquire and complete the film, and it can be seen that the LPI had provided three quarters of its original budget plus the whole of the

excess over that budget, whereas the limited partners' contribution had been restricted to one quarter of the original budget.

- On completion, the distribution was handled by two more Lorimar companies, and it is sufficient for us to refer only to the company handling non-UK distribution (LDII) as if its financial arrangements covered also the UK distribution.

- Out of its revenues from the film's distribution, LDII first reimbursed itself its own expenses. Next it was to pay $13m to the partnership, which the latter was to use in repaying the LPI production loan and the limited partners' capital accounts, *pari passu*. Next it was to pay a sum to the partnership which the latter could use to repay the LPI completion loan, together with the accumulated but as yet unpaid interest on both the production and completion loans. Finally, if there were revenues from the film's distribution in excess of all of the above, LDII and the partnership were to share these 75 percent 25 percent – (although this was not itself to make LDII a partner in the partnership).

The way in which company partnerships, limited or otherwise, are taxed in the UK is that if the partnership itself is trading, its profits and its capital allowances are calculated (as if it were itself a separate company), but are then split between the members of the partnership in profit sharing ratio. It will therefore be seen that the scheme, if successful, would give the limited partners a first year allowance on the partnership's capital expenditure on the film; and that that expenditure would be quantified at $14.96m, despite the fact that the limited partners had only themselves contributed $3.25m. The judge commented that it was difficult not to sympathise with the view that the limited partners had participated in an outrageous tax avoidance scheme; but on his analysis of the law and the facts, those limited partners were entitled to their allowances. We need to look at the 'trading' point in the next paragraph, and will then deal with two further matters which flow directly from this case in paragraphs 7.17 and 7.23 below.

7.13 The question about trading in the *Ensign Tankers* case was, as indicated, 'was the partnership trading ?' – not was Ensign itself as a limited partner trading when it contributed its capital and thereafter did little but act as a sleeping partner. However, the way in which that question was faced, and answered, shows clearly what the principles are and how they should be applied to any case, not just to the unique facts of this particular one. Although mitigation of tax liabilities was a greater part of the leasing scene prior to 1984 than it may be today, these principles fit it into its correct context.

- 'In order to constitute a transaction in the nature of trade, the transaction must possess not only the outward badges of trade, but also a genuine commercial purpose'. The Royal Commission on Taxation in 1956 listed six badges of trade, applicable in any business situation, designed to differentiate trading from, for instance, investing, or buying and selling purely for enjoyment of the subject matter.

- 'If the transaction is of a commercial nature, and has a genuine commercial purpose, the presence of a collateral or ulterior purpose to obtain a tax advantage does not denature what is essentially a commercial transaction'.

- 'If however the sole purpose of the transaction is to obtain a fiscal advantage, it is logically impossible to postulate the existence of any commercial purpose'.

- 'Where commercial and fiscal purposes are both present . . . the question is not which purpose was predominant, but whether the transaction can fairly be described as being in the nature of trade'.

- 'The purpose or object of the transaction must not be confused with the motive of (some one particular taxpayer who may become a sleeping partner with others) in entering into it. The question is not why he was trading, but whether he was trading'.

- 'The test is an objective one'. Many of the transactions in securities which underlay the claims for recovery of tax in the old 'dividend stripping' cases were wholly artificial devices remote from trade, and had either no possibility of profit apart from the tax recovery, or had a purely nominal or artificial element of profit built in. One has to look at the arrangement itself to see what it is intended to effect.

- 'In considering the purpose of a transaction, its component parts must not be regarded separately, but the transaction must be viewed as a whole. That part of the transaction that is alleged to constitute trading must . . . be viewed in the context of all . . . relevant surrounding circumstances, that is to say those which are capable of throwing light on the true nature of the transaction..'.

- 'If the purpose or object of a transaction is to make a profit, it does not cease to be a commercial transaction merely because those who engage in it have obtained their finance from persons who are more interested in achieving a fiscal advantage from their investment..'.

The judge's final two criteria are really no more than a summary of the above:

"Fiscal considerations naturally affect the taxpayer's evaluation of the financial risks and rewards of any proposed venture, and are often the decisive factor in persuading him to enter it. First year allowances, enterprise zones, government grants and the like operate as financial inducements to businessmen to engage in commercial activities, which would be financially unattractive or unacceptably speculative without them. Such motivations, even if paramount, do not alter the character of the activities in question. But while a fiscal motive, even an overriding fiscal motive, is irrelevant in itself, it becomes highly relevant if it affects not just the shape or structure of the transaction, but its commerciality, so that... (it) is no longer that of a trading transaction"

The judge decided that the limited partnership in the *Ensign Tankers* case was trading, and not merely seeking tax advantages. At the time we go to press, news has come through that the Court of Appeal has ruled that the judgment in the High Court cannot be allowed to stand. The Commissioners, (that fact-finding tribunal), had incorrectly analysed the questions they needed to ask to determine whether the partnership was trading. As a result, there were fatal defects in both their findings of the facts, and the way in which they set out the resultant question of law, the latter being all that the High Court should have reviewed. Only if the case were sent back to the Commissioners for a satisfactory statement of what those facts had been could it be allowed to come forward from there to the courts. It has been in this area in which commerciality and fiscal advantage should be, but are not always in practice, clearly distinguishable that lessors and their advisers have most often agonised in the past, and it has to be added, where Inland Revenue suspicions may most often have been aroused by transactions which are wholly innocent of any fiscal motivation. But there is one other area, (paragraph 7.23), in which doubts may also arise about the artificiality of leasing transactions.

'The sole or main benefit'

7.14 It is appropriate to mention at this juncture a rather different point, but one which is wholly consistent with the *Ensign Tankers* principles set out above. There are a number of anti-avoidance sections in the tax statutes which set out to counter transactions whose 'sole or main benefit' is seen by the authorities as the obtaining of a fiscal advantage, or having some equivalent, but similarly objectionable, intent. Section 75(1)(c) CAA 1990 for instance, (if one omits the inoperative wording about first year allowances which effectively no longer exist), still reads as follows:

> "...where a person incurs capital expenditure on the provision by purchase of machinery or plant, and it appears...with respect to transactions of which the sale is one, that the sole or main benefit which, but for this subsection, might have been expected to accrue to the parties or any of them was the obtaining of an allowance...there shall be disregarded for the purposes of (writing down allowances) so much (if any) of the expenditure as exceeds the disposal value to be brought into account under (the balancing adjustment section) by reason of the sale..."

Although it may not be clear from that extract, it is clear from the section as a whole the 'sale' referred to in the third line is the sale by a third party which constitutes our taxpayer's 'purchase' in the first line. So if we suppose that that third party is the manufacturer of the machinery or plant concerned, he will bring in no disposal value under a balancing adjustment section on his sale; the proceeds he realises are part of his sales figure in his profit and loss account, and nothing whatever to do with his capital allowances claim. Does this mean that the purchaser must calculate his writing down allowances on a zero acquisition value ? At least must he do so if 'the sole or main benefit' of his purchase would have been the obtaining of an allowance ? And by comparing what with what do you determine whether the allowance would have been more beneficial than any other consequence of his acquisition ? Is it the bottom-line value of the allowance against the bottom-line value of the profits earned by the machinery or plant ? Or what ? The questions become more nonsensical as one proceeds, but this is a section which our legislators thoughtfully preserved when they recently consolidated the 1971 Finance Act provision into the Capital Allowances Act 1990. Fortunately the judge in the *Barclays Mercantile* case has given us guidance:

"It is not to be supposed that the draftsman set out to play cat and mouse with the taxpayer...The main object of (Barclays Mercantile) was to make a profit by acquiring and leasing the plant. It is probable that (it) would not have been able to offer a lease back to a company in the (Warner Bros) organisation at an acceptable rent unless it could obtain a capital allowance...But it does not follow that (Barclays Mercantile's) object was to obtain an allowance; (its) object and purpose was to make a profit..."

Or in other words, if the anti-avoidance provision can be seen not to be achieving, when one reads the word 'benefit' literally, any purpose which the legislature could have had in mind in enacting it, then substitute 'object and purpose'; the provision then fits into exactly the same pattern as was outlined (in the previous paragraph) as relevant for differentiating commercial transactions and fiscally motivated ones.

Commencement of trading

7.15 'Capital expenditure on the provision of machinery or plant for the purposes of a trade by a person about to carry it on shall be treated as if it had been incurred by him on the first day on which he does carry it on', (s.83(2) CAA 1990). On that first day, he will of course meet that other leg of the requirements for capital allowances, that he is 'a person carrying on a trade'. But if a leasing company does commence to trade less than a full twelve months before the date to which it draws up its accounts, then the expenditure incurred in that 'short' period will qualify only for a proportion of the normal 25 percent writing down allowance, (s.24(2)(a)(ii) CAA 1990), the proportion being the number of months of trading divided by twelve. If one assumes, as our lessor company did in the example we have worked and reworked through this book, that the optimum position is obtained by incurring expenditure on a leased asset on day 365 of year 0, (and incepting the lease either on that day or as soon as possible thereafter), then we must also enter the proviso that year 0 must be a twelve month accounting period of the leasing company, throughout the whole of which it was carrying on a trade. Starting to trade during the period will reduce the 25 percent, and so also will drawing up accounts for a period of less than a full year. The standard advice to leasing groups in which there may be a need to establish special purpose subsidiaries (for instance to deal with particular types of customer, or particular suppliers), has therefore been:

- incorporate a company or companies before you can necessarily see a need for it;

- start a trade in it with a few small leasing transactions, and claim whatever allowances are available on them;

- so that when the company starts full-scale operations it is in a position to get its full allowances, without restrictions.

That is all right as far as it goes, but it fails to mention one famous trap, namely the Companies Act rules about accounting dates. The only way to explain what is involved is by illustration:

- assume the company we are dealing with was incorporated on 1 September 1990;

- its directors envisage it having an accounting date of 31 December, that is to say in Companies Act terms its statutory accounts will be prepared and filed to an 'accounting reference date' of 31 December in each year;

- the company writes some small leases on 1 November 1990, and is in a position to say that that is its date of commencement of trading. (In fact trading can be said to start when the company is in a position to write leases. For instance it has arranged financial facilities, and is looking for business to write. There can be no argument that trading has started when it does write its first leases);

- its full-scale activity starts only in December 1991, when it incurs substantial capital expenditure, and incepts a number of significant leases, convinced that it will obtain the full 25 percent allowance for the 1991 accounting period.

Alas, the Inspector of Taxes has read his Companies Act, and knows that the accounts which the company had purported to draw up for a four month period from incorporation to 31 December 1990 are not statutory accounts, because the first accounting reference date of a company cannot be less than six months nor more than eighteen months after its incorporation. Therefore, the Inspector argues that the only statutory accounts the company can draw up will be for a sixteen month period to 31 December 1991. When those are adjusted for tax purposes under the tax rules dealing with accounts covering periods exceeding twelve months, they have to be divided into two – a period of twelve months from start of trading to 31 October 1991, and a period of two months from 1 November 1991 to 31 December 1991. There is no possibility of doing anything else. All the capital expenditure in December 1991 therefore falls into a two month accounting period and qualifies for a writing down allowance at a generous rate of just over 4 percent. There are ways of recovering the situation, based on first changing the company's accounting reference date under the Companies Act – if this is possible. One reason why it may not be possible is that there are time limits by which the necessary action has to be taken, and another is that the company has to have a reason for making the change which can be seen as valid for Companies Act purposes. But if we assume that it overcomes these problems, it could choose 2 March as its accounting reference date, so that its first account could only be for a period of six months and one day to 2 March 1991, and its December 1991 expenditure would fall into a twelve month period to 2 March 1992 (during the whole of which it would of course have been trading). Its allowances on that expenditure would thus not be restricted, but it would have to wait two months longer than it would otherwise have had to to obtain the benefit of them, because its 'tax payment date' would be moved forward two months in line with the movement of the accounting date. There is a view that the Companies Act can in fact allow that first accounting period to be shortened to a period of less than six months, despite what seems on the face of it to be clear words (known to the Inspector of Taxes) forbidding this. But this is a very fine point which would need more space to argue fully than is available here.

Cessation of trading

7.16 The cessation of a leasing company's trading for tax purposes involves not only the ending of its liability to tax on income – with its corollary that expenses cease to be deductible – but the greater degree of uncertainty arising in the capital allowance field. The company is treated (s.24(6)(c)(v) CAA 1990) as having disposed of all of its machinery or plant immediately before that cessation; therefore a 'disposal value' needs to be brought into the capital allowance claim for that final period, and:

- if it is less than the values in the pool or pools against which it is to be set, the company will receive a balancing allowance (s.24(2)(b) CAA 1990);

- if it is greater than that pool value, the excess will be charged in the company's hands as a balancing charge, that is to say as if it were income (s.24(5) CAA 1990).

If the machinery or plant is in fact sold shortly after the cessation, the sale proceeds fix the amount to be brought in as disposal value (s.26(1)(e) CAA 1990) but without such a sale (or a loss on which insurance proceeds are received) it is necessary to agree the machinery or plant's market value. It is here that the uncertainty can arise, as referred to above. It is quite clear that a company which has stopped writing new business, but still has assets out on lease and is still collecting rents for them, has not ceased trading. That hardly needs elaboration where the company has merely paused in its taking on of new business – and is in a position to restart at any point. Inland Revenue practice seems equally clear in the case of companies which have permanently stopped writing new leases, but have made it clear to their customers that existing leases will continue to be serviced to their expiry. But it is believed that if the board of directors of a leasing company:

- knowing that its owners had in contemplation its imminent sale, had transferred from it to a fellow subsidiary the leases those owners wished to retain in their own group;

- were writing new leases (which they also wished to retain in the group) in that other subsidiary;

- knew also that the purchaser was intent on stripping the company's business out of it after his purchase;

- and in the light of the above (not simply to assist in the agreement of a price for the company being sold) had determined that no further leases should be taken onto the books of the target company;

then it could be very difficult to argue that that target's trade ceased only after its sale, and not before it. All questions of cessation of trading are ones of fact; it is accordingly one of those areas in which generalisations can never be all that helpful.

'Incurs' capital expenditure

7.17 The word 'incurs', in relation to the capital expenditure qualifying for capital allowances, has given rise to a number of different worries:

- Tax legislation used to say that expenditure was incurred when it became due. That left unclear whether in the case of a simple purchase of plant, the date to be taken was really meant to be the end of the period of credit allowed by the supplier, or whether it should not be the date of the purchase itself. Taxpayers generally used the same convention as was adopted by the accountants who drew up their accounts; if the purchase had taken place, the asset should be on the balance sheet, and the company should be able to claim its allowances. The questions whether payment had been made to the supplier, and/or whether his credit period had expired were simply not seen as relevant.

- The Inland Revenue authorities only realised in 1984 that taxpayers had never interpreted 'due' in the way the Revenue had imagined they had, and it then took two attempts, in the 1985 and 1986 Finance Acts to put the law into a workable state. The general rule is now that expenditure is incurred when the obligation to pay it becomes unconditional (ie the date of purchase, the start of the credit period) but if the credit period is more than four months, then the end of that period is substituted. There are however also a number of other, special, rules in s.159 CAA 1990 to deal with particular cases.

- Perhaps more radically, the Inland Revenue argued in the *Ensign Tankers* case that the limited partnership had never incurred at all the greater part of the capital expenditure on its film. (This is one of the two matters we said in the last line of paragraph 7.12 we would deal with later). The Revenue's argument was that the partnership could have incurred nothing if it had no obligation; and it had no such obligation in the case of funds which it had borrowed on a non-recourse basis from LPI, (the production and completion loans, which the partnership could not be called on to repay). At the High Court level, the judge's answer was that this contention was hopeless. He pointed out that the capital allowances legislation was concerned with the taxpayer's liability (obligation) to expend money in the acquisition of plant, not with his liability to repay the lender.

'In consequence'...the machinery or plant 'belongs' to him

7.18 Similarly, the word 'belongs' in the capital allowance legislation has also created difficulties almost ever since it was first inserted into the legislation. (A Glasgow butcher won a case against the Inland Revenue, claiming capital allowances on expenditure he had incurred on a van despite its never having materialised because the vendor absconded with the money. Putting into the law the requirement that any future van must 'belong' to the butcher was the Revenue's way of reversing the effect of this case):

- The Inland Revenue have long since confirmed that they will ignore difficulties flowing from the tightness of the requirement that it is 'in consequence' of the expenditure that the asset must belong to the taxpayer. That manifestly is not the case where the contract calls for payments on account – for instance a shipbuilding contract usually calls for a number of payments before the ship leaves the slip, whereas it is only handed over to the purchaser following the successful completion of sea trials. Where normal patterns of payments on account are concerned, the Revenue do not worry about 'belonging' or 'consequences'.

- Similarly, it is entirely possible that in the case of the building of some major item of machinery, its purchaser may stipulate that the materials which go into its construction should become his, and cease to be the property of the contractor, as soon as they are appropriated to the project. This would be a normal way for the purchaser to try to protect his asset from other creditors of the contractor, if the latter should go into liquidation. But it is clear that it would not be 'in consequence of' any subsequent contractual payments that the machinery came to belong to that purchaser. Once again the Inland Revenue say they are not concerned.

- But much greater problems surfaced in 1983 and 1984, when the case of *Stokes v Costain Property Investments Ltd* came before the High Court, and was appealed into the Court of Appeal (CA, [1984] 1 All ER 849). The company was not the freeholder of land on which it had carried out a development; it was only entitled to be granted a lease or underlease on completion. It had however incurred approximately £500,000 expenditure on plant which, since it became 'fixed' to the land developed, became the property of the freeholder. Costain was denied any allowances; the plant did not belong to it if it had no right to dispose of it and it did not have any such right under the lease to which it was entitled.

- In parenthesis, we have mentioned the 'belonging test', and the practical ability, (or lack of it,) of the lessor to dispose of the leased asset in paragraph 4.14. We were dealing at that point with assets which the lessor had contracted to sell at the end of the lease term under 'buy-back clauses'. Our conclusion was that where such arrangements were negotiated as a commercial matter between independent parties, the Inland Revenue appeared not to be very concerned that it might be argued that the lessor might fail the test. Their attitude thus appeared generally more relaxed than that of the individual Inspector of Taxes who took Costain to the courts.

- But coming back to the *Costain* case, the law was then changed in 1985. Under the new rules, (s.52 CAA 1990), Costain, as the holder of a leasehold interest in land, is deemed to be the owner of fixed plant belonging to his freeholder, when he (the leaseholder) has incurred the expenditure on it, and in turn sublets that land to another trader. (This is one of the transactions referred to as 'letting otherwise than in the course of a trade', a phrase we will explain more fully in paragraph 7.20 below). Equally, if Costain had itself used for its own trade the plant fixed to the freeholders land, it would be entitled to allowances as a result of s.52.

- There is a second category of lessors who can also get allowances even though they have fixed their plant to someone else's land, (s.53 CAA 1990). If a lessor lets, for instance, the baggage handling plant in an airline's terminal building to the airline concerned, he would not fit within the provisions outlined above if he was not also in the 'land and buildings chain', that is to say an intermediate leaseholder between the freeholder of the terminal, and the airline as his own subtenant. But, in theory at least, the airline would be entitled to allowances under the last sentence of the previous heading as a tenant deemed to own the plant fixed to land in which he had a leasehold interest. In the circumstances that two parties are both thus qualified, but only one of them has expenditure, they are entitled to elect that the allowances should go to the lessor.

7.19 But there is another, and rather different, aspect of 'belonging' which we need to be aware of. Although the particular type of capital allowances, and the law which governs them, are not strictly relevant to the subject matter of this book, it is probably easiest to start from the case of *Sargaison v Roberts*, Ch D, [1969] 3 All ER 1072. A farmer had incurred expenditure on agricultural buildings on land of which he was the freeholder. He was entitled to allowances so long as he retained an interest in the land. Because he wanted to settle the land in trust, but to continue farming it, he conveyed the freehold to trustees, on terms that they would the next day lease it back to him. The question was whether he had thus disposed of his interest, and lost the allowances from then on. The judge (Megarry J., probably the greatest living expert on English land law) was in no doubt that, technically, the farmer had lost his interest, but decided the case in his favour on the basis that 'where the technicalities of English conveyancing and land law are brought into juxtaposition with a United Kingdom taxing statute, I am encouraged to look at the realities at the expense of the technicalities'. The Inland Revenue appear, in *Ensign Tankers*, to have argued this same line, in a converse situation. It was said that the film had never 'belonged' to the limited partnership, because as soon as that partnership acquired it, it parted with the right to distribute and exploit it in perpetuity, retaining only the 'bare' master negative. The judge decided that point in the partnership's favour on a different basis; he said that the partnership 'did not part with the right to exploit the film, but exploited it'. But before doing so, he commented (words which therefore have to be regarded as obiter) that the partnership's acquisition and disposal were only possible if carried out in that order, and that therefore in the *scintilla temporis* between the execution of those two agreements, the negative and the rights did belong to the partnership. "But in my judgment the question does not depend on conveyancing niceties..." was then the phraseology he used to introduce his own decision quoted above. If this appears to conflict with the basis on which the *Sargaison* case was decided, the author can only contribute the thought that the point is complex, and that not only are the particular facts critical, (as always), but so also is the area of law governing the agreements concerned; although both judges used the word 'conveyancing' quoted above, the manner in which land is conveyed is not the same as that in which one deals with copyrights and intellectual property rights, and rights to exploit films are different again.

Agency

7.20 Frequently, as we have indicated throughout this book, the equipment manufacturer or dealer acts as the agent of the leasing company in signing up a lease agreement with a party who is happy to make his 'acquisition' of the equipment concerned by lease rather than by outright purchase. Sometimes the lease agreement shows the name of the leasing company concerned, and although the lease itself would not show this, the lessee is aware that the manufacturer is himself selling the equipment to that leasing company immediately before the latter leases it to him. In other cases, the name of the leasing company used for these deals may give the impression that it is a member of the manufacturer's group, while the truth is that it is an independent company, or a joint venture between such a company and the manufacturer. But other methods of making these arrangements have been used. Suppose that a manufacturer:

- signs up the lease using as lessor the name of a subsidiary company of his own;

- the lessee is not aware that his counterparty is merely an agent for an undisclosed principal, (the independent leasing company), standing behind that agent.

One might think this undesirable – but the degree to which objection could be made would at least be less than it would be if the manufacturer's next step was as follows. The manufacturer claims that the company in whose name the lease has been executed is an agent for more than one undisclosed principal – for a number of competing leasing companies – and that the one who offers him the best terms for the lease can take it onto its own books. The lease itself fixes the income stream for the leasing company which takes it on, but the price offered for it obviously comprises the sum that leasing company is prepared to pay the 'agent' for the leased asset, and possibly the terms of the buy-back deal it offers to the manufacturer. The two technical questions thrown up by this course of dealing are:

- Is it possible for a company not only to be the agent for more than one undisclosed principal at the same time, but also only to decide on behalf of which of them it is acting after the event ?

- And if not, then is the purported agent in fact engaged, as principal, in an activity of writing leases and assigning them to different leasing companies ? And are not the activities of those companies as much the purchase of these leases as the writing of others ? And in this case, does 'purchasing' carry a connotation that perhaps a significant part of the leasing companies' activities are investment rather than trading? If this were to be the case, it would drastically affect not only their ability to claim capital allowances, but also their entitlement to deduct expenses related to this activity. We said, in relation to the transfers of blocks of leases from one leasing company to another, (when one needed to shrink its book, and the other was happy to expand its), that the Inland Revenue seemed happy to regard this in the hands of the acquiring lessor as the incurring of capital expenditure on leased assets, rather than as the purchase of income streams. But is this as surely the case here ?

The more commercially orientated question the leasing companies might ask is whether they think this is the most desirable way of managing their activities – of keeping control over the size of their 'books', and of the quality of their lessees ?

'Let otherwise than in the course of a trade'

7.21 This phrase appears in s.61 CAA 1990, a section permitting claims for capital allowances by lessors who are not themselves engaged in a trade. That fact would of itself appear to deny allowances, and to be meant to do so; it may not therefore be immediately obvious why section 61 has been enacted to grant the allowances in question. The answer seems to be a pure technicality. The letting of land and buildings is not a trade. It is a taxable activity, in the sense that the rental income generated is subject to tax; but it is not treated as a component of trading profits. There are rules about the expenses which can be deducted from such taxable income, but they are far from being the same as the rules governing the deduction of expenses in arriving at trading profits. Capital allowances can be claimed on machinery or plant used in the management of land which is let, (for instance mowers and rollers on playing fields, or window cleaning cradles on office buildings), but again the concepts are different from those governing the availability of allowances on plant used by a trader wholly and exclusively for the purposes of his trade. It follows from all of this that if a lessor were to incur capital expenditure on, for instance, the installation of lifts in a building he owned, and were then to let that building complete with the lifts inside it, the income stream generated would not be trading income, (the lessor would not be a trader), and he would not be entitled under the ordinary provisions (s.24 CAA 1990) to any capital allowances. What would be an obvious inequity has been put right by section 61. It deems the letting activity, purely for the purpose of entitling the lessor to capital allowances, to be a separate trade carried on by him, alongside any other activity he may be engaged in including any other trade he may have. And it deems that separate trade to cease, so that a balancing adjustment is made, when the lessor ceases letting the building concerned (and/or the plant contained within it).

Lessees' expenditure

7.22 What might be less expected is that s.61 CAA 1990 also contains parallel provisions granting capital allowances to lessees in certain circumstances. If we pursue the example given in the previous paragraph by assuming that:

- the lease granted to the lessee for the building with its lifts inside it was for 99 years, and on a full repairing basis;

- the lifts wear out after 25 years, and have to be replaced by the tenant;

- the new lifts are the property of the lessor, not that of the tenant; but that this follows not from their being regarded as 'fixed' to the building (in a *Stokes v Costain* sense, paragraph 7.18), but because the lease terms make it plain that the tenant has no right to the plant concerned;

then the tenant would appear unable to claim capital allowances, since he neither owns the plant, nor can be deemed to own it under s.52 CAA 1990. And he could be in difficulty over a claim that his expenditure was deductible in arriving at the profits of his trade, since it has all the hallmarks of being capital expenditure on the bringing into existence of an asset of lasting (25 year) value. Once again, it is s.61 CAA 1990 which appears to rectify what would otherwise have been a clear anomaly, deeming for capital allowance purposes that the lifts belong to the lessee so long as he continues to use them in the course of his own trading activities. (And perhaps even more unexpectedly, saying that if after the lease has determined, the lessor disposes of the plant, what he should bring in by way of disposal value is not to be restricted to the level of his original expenditure on the asset, which would of course have been zero, but by reference to the lessee's expenditure on it).

'The new approach'

7.23 'The new approach' is the phrase used by the House of Lords, originally in the case of *Ramsay (W.T.) Ltd v IRC*, HL, [1981] 1 All ER 865, to indicate the way in which the courts would thenceforward examine artificial schemes designed to avoid taxes. As re-explained by the courts in a series of cases leading on from *Ramsay*, and as written about by a long string of commentators, it comes down to the following (although the warning must be given that where phrases are lifted out of the judgments of different cases, one does need to go back to the precise contexts in which they were originally used, in order to make sure that one understands what they mean and do not mean. However, for the general reader, giving the words their ordinary meanings will be sufficient):

- The approach can be relevant where there is 'a preordained series of transactions' or if you like, 'a single composite transaction'.

- Within that series, or composite transaction, 'steps have been inserted which have no commercial or business purpose'. It is important to note that this is not the same as saying that the steps have no commercial or business effect; if A, instead of selling an asset to C, sells it to B, and B not only passes the asset on permanent loan to C, but borrows on permanent loan from C the proceeds which he needs to pay to A, then the business effect is not the same. C does not end up with title to the asset, and B has an outstanding indebtedness to C. But if there is absolutely no reason other than tax avoidance why the parties adopted the route they did, one could say that some at least of the steps had no commercial or business purpose.

- Thus what one needs to identify is 'a connected series of interdependent steps designed to produce a single composite overall result', and within that series one step which is both closely connected with the others and without commercial or business purpose.

If such can be identified, then the courts can look at the composite whole to see what is or are its effects, and thus what tax results should flow from them; and are not compelled to look at each individual step in the composite whole in order to determine the (separate) tax result of each. Thus, (and this is the second point referred to in the final line of paragraph 7.12), if it had been possible to argue that:

- the formation of the limited partnership in the *Ensign Tankers* case was but a step in a composite whole comprising the network of agreements entered into between the film production companies, the distribution companies, the partners, and the bankers for each of them;

• and it had also been possible to argue that the partnership's formation had no commercial or business purpose;

then one could have looked for the composite whole, without regard to the step (or steps) one was entitled to disregard, to see what and who should be taxed or given allowances. In the High Court, the judge's view was that such a quest was hopeless. If one did ignore the partnership, one was short of one quarter of the finance needed to complete the film. If one argued that a step could be ignored, and that there was, without it, a composite whole which could be taxed, one needed to be able to see what that whole could be. 'Each step' (in the series of transactions agreed when Lorimar abandoned its original intention to finance the film entirely itself, and agreed to accept finance for one quarter of it from the limited partners) 'leads to another; no part can be ignored unless the whole is ignored. Yet the whole cannot be ignored without leaving the financing arrangements incomplete, or reverting to those which, for its own commercial advantage Lorimar abandoned in favour of the arrangements with the partnership'. The author's view is that leasing arrangements in which 'the new approach' could be held to be in point must be extremely difficult to find. As the *Ensign Tankers* case illustrates, it must be very seldom that one could find steps that could be ignored without the whole composite transaction becoming impossible.

Gloucester Railway Carriage & Wagon Co Ltd v CIR

7.24   This is one of the leading cases on leasing, which reached the House of Lords in 1925, [1925] AC 469. The principal reason for which the company went to court is no longer relevant; it was claiming that if it sold assets of a 'fixed capital' nature, as opposed to those which were its circulating capital or stock in trade, the proceeds were outside the scope of tax, (not being part of its trading profits). But the decision does still have some relevance today. We said in paragraph 4.12 'as regards the marginal doubts over the availability of capital allowances to a company which is both a dealer in equipment, and a lessor of it, see the discussion in paragraph 7.24 of the *Gloucester Wagon* case'. It is that doubt that we now need to consider. The Gloucester Wagon company manufactured wagons, selling them outright and on hire purchase, or letting them on simple hire. The wagons let were capitalised in its accounts at a figure which included a manufacturing profit, and were depreciated in the accounts. That depreciation was allowed for tax purposes. The company decided to discontinue the simple hiring, and sold the wagons which had been on hire, realising considerably more for them than their depreciated value in the accounts. It was that profit that the company claimed was 'capital' and therefore not taxable. The House of Lords held that the sale gave rise to a straightforward trading receipt. They said that the wagons were not 'machinery or plant', and that their sale was in the ordinary course of the company's trade, despite the fact that they had in the meantime been used for letting on hire. The first thing to notice about this decision is that the 'machinery or plant' to which their Lordships were referring in 1925 was not a class of asset qualifying for capital allowances. On the contrary, it was one of the types of asset which was outside the scope of the company's trade, and therefore non-taxable, precisely because it was a part of the company's 'fixed capital'. We quoted Adam Smith's definition in paragraph 6.03: "what a trader makes profit of by keeping it in his own possession". The fact that the wagons were depreciated, and that this depreciation was allowed for tax, showed in 1925 that they were not fixed capital, machinery or plant, but were part of the company's 'working capital' – 'what he turns to profit by parting with them and letting them change masters' – even if that parting was not outright but by parting with each successive year's possession. Against that background, it is surprising that the company thought it had any case to present to the House of Lords.

If we leave aside for a moment the additional complexities flowing from the fact that the company itself manufactured the wagons, and that it was also selling wagons in a straightforward profit and loss account transaction, it is worth noting that what it did with its leased wagons in its tax computations in 1925 is exactly what a finance lessor would do with leased wagons in his accounts today, in compliance with SSAP 21. When that accounting standard was promulgated, the Inland Revenue said that they had no current intention of changing the tax treatment of leased assets (in the hands of either lessor or lessee) to bring these into line with SSAP 21 treatment; but that if they did believe that a review of the treatment of leased assets were necessary at some future time, the existence of SSAP 21 would be one of the factors that would be given weight in that review. The *Gloucester Wagon* decision adds a certain piquancy to that statement. However, if we come back to the decision itself, and its present significance:

• tax principles would not allow a company to capitalise an asset at more than its manufacturing cost, implying the crediting of a manufacturing profit, since it is absolutely clear that 'a taxpayer cannot make a profit out of himself';

• therefore if a trader were to claim to have appropriated to a capital purpose an asset he had manufactured, (and which he could otherwise

have sold in the course of his trade), then that appropriation could
only be at cost;

- there is no doubt that such appropriations are possible; if a trader builds
his own factory or shop, for instance, there would be no difficulty about
his treating his expenditure as qualifying for capital allowances (except
that shops do not qualify);

- but the marginal doubts arise over the frequency of the appropriations
if the manufacturer has a continuing high volume of lease transactions.

Every professional adviser would feel more comfortable with the leasing
separated into a different corporate entity, which at one stroke solves not
only the difficulty over the manufacturing profit (which from a commercial
point of view the company probably wishes to reflect), but also the doubts
over the 'capital' or 'stock in trade' character of the leased assets.

Interest which varies with the results of the trade

7.25   This was one of the aspects of non-recourse finance which we
discussed at some length in paragraphs 4.07 and 4.08. The problems are
twofold:

- If a company pays on its borrowings interest which 'is to any extent
dependent on the results of the company's business or any part of it',
and the recipient is anyone other than another company within the
charge to corporation tax, then the payment has to be regarded as a
'distribution', the effect being that the interest concerned is not
deductible in arriving at the payer's profits (s.209(2)(e)(iii) and s.212(1)
ICTA 1988).

- If a company has borrowings which are regarded as not 'normal
commercial loans' these have to be treated as if they were equity in
deciding whether the company is a member of a group for group relief
purposes, (see paragraph 7.29 below). To fall the right side of the
dividing line between normal commercial loans and others, a loan must
'not entitle the loan creditor to any amount by way of interest which
depends to any extent on the results of the company's business or any
part of it, or on the value of any of the company's assets...' (Sch
18(1)(5)(b) ICTA 1988).

The production loan and the completion loans made by Lorimar
Productions Inc. to the limited partnership in the *Ensign Tankers* case were
both non-recourse loans, in the sense not only that they were only repayable
out of the distribution revenues derived from the film and LPI had no
right of recourse against the borrower itself, but also in that the loans

carried interest only if those distribution revenues were great enough and not if they were not. The interest was therefore directly lined up with the results that the limited partnerships achieved in terms of the distribution revenues that they were also entitled to participate in. The general rule is that a partnership in which there are company partners is itself treated as if it were a separate company. If this were so, then one might expect to see a disallowance called for in the partnership's computation for non-qualifying interest paid by it. But in fact, where interest is concerned, each partner's own proportion is treated as being his own deductible, or non-deductible, expense. Therefore it would be in Ensign Tankers' own hands that one might expect to see the Inland Revenue arguing for a disallowance. The reason why one sees no such thing is simple. The film did not generate enough distribution profits for the production and completion loans to be repaid in full – so there was no excess repayment which could have been regarded as 'interest'. The silence of the Inland Revenue cannot be taken as an indication that they would not have taken this point against Ensign Tankers, along with all the other points they did take, had it been available to take. Whenever they do have what they regard as a tax avoidance case in front of the court, as we have noted, they challenge every possible weak link in the taxpayer's armour. If one is likely to be challenged in this way, one would always prefer first to be able to show that the facts of the case made the challenge unsustainable; and if one cannot show that, then to have strong and watertight legal arguments to put forward in response to the Revenue's challenge. The legal argument in this instance can perhaps be described as respectable rather than strong, as follows:

- If the loan agreement calls for interest of, say, 12 percent provided that the payer has sufficient profits to meet this; and he does have such profits, and does pay 12 percent; then what he has paid is the percentage called for in the agreement, not a percentage dependent on the results he achieved.

- If he achieved no profits, and paid no interest, one might say that he had paid a percentage which did depend on those results, and was not the percentage set in the agreement; but if he paid nothing, the disallowance is nothing, so the argument is of no significance.

- The foregoing could be called the 'positive' argument, based on the wording in s.209 and s.212 ICTA 1988. However the wording in Sch.18 ICTA 1988 is itself in the negative, and the argument in that case becomes overwhelming. If there are sufficient profits the loan creditor is entitled to 12 percent; if the profits are insufficient 'the loan does not entitle him to to any amount...which depends..', it entitles him to no amount, zero. The loan fits exactly and precisely within the statutory wording.

- Given the closeness of the wordings in s.209 and in Sch.18, and given that the legislature cannot be assumed to have intended to achieve a different answer in the two places, it is clear that the type of non-recourse lending in which interest is in effect waived in certain circumstances cannot have been the target at which either s.209 or Sch.18 was aimed.

Insurance against 'pure' risk

7.26   The tax questions raised by this were reasonably fully discussed in paragraphs 4.10 and 4.11. What we mean by 'pure' risk is the type of risk that an underwriter cannot effectively spread, in order to reduce his own exposure. If he is insuring houses against fire, or writing term life policies for fifty year olds, he can find statistics on the number of houses that do burn down in an average year, and the number of people who die between their fiftieth and their fifty first birthdays; if he writes enough policies, the risk on each individual policy is not reduced, but the risk on the entire portfolio is. Similarly, the bookmaker accepting bets from those who think the stockmarket index will go up, can reduce or balance his overall risk by attracting bets also from those who think the stockmarket will go down. We noted that a number of the types of insurance that a lessor might seek are different in kind. Insuring against a fall in asset values which could result in the lessor not obtaining his aimed at residual is one example. 'Capping' the interest rate on a floating rate borrowing is another. One question that these insurances raise is whether the premium paid by the lessor is deductible in his own tax computation. We noted in paragraph 4.11 the Inland Revenue view that a premium paid for insurance of residuals is not so deductible, being in the nature of a 'capital' expense. There is not much more that can be added in general terms; each type of insurance, and therefore each premium, needs to be analysed to see what it covers, and against what risks, in order to decide whether the premium is likely to be accepted by the Inland Revenue as deductible.

7.27   But the second problem is perhaps even more intractable. This is the tax position of the underwriter of these 'pure' risks. His position is unlike that of the fire insurer in the following respect. The fire insurer is able to assume, three quarters of the way through his accounting year, that if three quarters of a full year's expected numbers of fires have occurred, then in the remaining three months it is unlikely that much more will burn than a quarter of an expected year's number. Statistics therefore provide a reasonably reliable guide to the likely performance in the future of the policies which currently constitute his portfolio. And this gives him a sufficiently reliable guide how he can safely recognise profits on contracts which are still open at his year end – and what provisions he may need to make for unexpired risks. The underwriter of 'pure' risks does not, and cannot, have any such statistical support; the only way he can tell whether the residual value of the asset will hold up is to wait until the end of the term of his insurance. At no intermediate year end does he have any objective method of deciding whether some of his premium can be recognised as profit, or whether he needs to make an additional provision for loss. Those who sell interest rate 'caps' are in a different position only in that they operate in a market which is liquid enough for them to be able to buy and sell their outstanding obligations; objectivity is achieved by the process of 'marking to market', that is to say valuing rights and obligations for accounting purposes at what they could be sold for, or what one would have to pay another party to take them onto his shoulders.

Tax law proceeds along principles that we first started outlining in paragraph 2.56. One starts with the profits of the taxpayer as shown in his accounts – assuming that these have been prepared on 'ordinary principles of commercial accounting'. Then one makes any adjustments that are called for by the statute, that word embracing not only the laws enacted by Parliament but the interpretation of them in decided cases. So far as concerns the acceptability or otherwise of 'provisions', there are two principal decided cases. The *Sun Insurance Office v Clark*, HL, [1912] AC 443, was in fact the fire insurance case that shows that a method of providing for unexpired risks on a 'time' basis, (as indicated above), and where that method is also shown statistically to have reflected in the past the company's actual experience, must be acceptable to the Inland Revenue. But when one has neither time, nor statistics, to rely on (and if one is unable to put a value on unexpired risks by marking them to market) then one falls within the more recent House of Lords decision in *Owen v Southern Railway of Peru Ltd*, HL, [1956] 2 All ER 728. Abbreviating that decision to the point where one is in danger of misrepresenting it, the court said that there is no rule of law that prevents the deduction of a provision (whether for unexpired risk or for anything else) so long as a sufficiently accurate estimate can be made; but the company's estimate was not sufficiently accurate and it was denied a deduction. That fails to clarify one very significant factor about the way tax cases are fought and decided. The fact finding tribunal determines in the first instance what are the facts, and on that basis whether the assessed profits should be the figure contended for by the Inland Revenue, or that contended by the taxpayer. The Southern Railway was required by Peruvian law to make termination payments to its local staff when they left its employ, those payments being based on years of service. At each year end it had brought up the level of its provision to the sum it would have had to pay on the first day of the succeeding year had all its employees left on that day. One might think that that could have been modestly overdone, in that there would be some employees who would be dismissed for cause in the future and to whom no payments would therefore be due. But what the Inland Revenue contended was that, because not all the employees would leave on the first day of the succeeding year, (most would leave a considerable time later), the amount of the provision should have been 'discounted to a present value'. Once the Commissioners, the fact finding body referred to, had found as fact that there was no practical likelihood of all the employees leaving at the time the company had used in its calculations, and that therefore those calculations were to that extent unjustified, it became impossible for the courts to disturb their decision – notwithstanding that the court, or another body of commissioners might have come to a different conclusion on the same evidence. All that it was therefore possible for the Southern Railway to argue in the courts was that the Commissioners' decision had been wrong in law, an argument which the company lost.

That leaves our pure risk underwriters in a position that the Inland Revenue can argue that since there is no statistical, time, or market-based, method by which they can put a value on their unexpired risks, any figure they do use is 'not sufficiently accurate'. It can thus be argued that the underwriters must pay tax on the full premiums they receive, when they receive them, being allowed to deduct only those claims they pay when they do pay them. This is a basis of taxation which is so unfavourable that it is bound to reflect through into the cost of insuring pure risks, and the point may come where any such insurance becomes uneconomic as a result. And the underwriters' response to this line of argument must be that not only is it unreasonable in failing to reflect the realities of the business they do, but that it is possible to make acceptable estimates – if it were not there could be no basis for their continuing to operate in that line of business. Some principles negotiated with the Inland Revenue for the recognition of the underwriter's profits are what are needed.

Tax deductibility of provisions for bad and doubtful debts

7.28   This subject was fully dealt with in paragraph 2.62, and the only point that seems worth adding is the following. Section 74 ICTA 1988 is written in the negative. Subsection (j) prevents the taxpayer, in arriving at his taxable profits, from deducting:

> "any debts, except bad debts proved to be such, and doubtful debts to the extent they are respectively estimated to be bad, and in the case of the bankruptcy or insolvency of a debtor the amount which may reasonably be

expected to be received on any such debt shall be deemed to be the value thereof"

We explained in paragraph 2.62 that the Inland Revenue take this wording to be a statutory direction to them to substitute for any deduction a taxpayer may have included in his own accounts a deduction calculated under this formula. Secondly, they take the words 'estimated to be bad' as authority for saying that a provision made on a realistic basis against a specific debt regarded as doubtful, (what is always referred to as a specific provision), is acceptable; but that a percentage provision against a portfolio does not fit the phraseology. One straightforward point we could make here is that this is wholly in line with the approach, (enquiring whether it is 'sufficiently accurate'), used by the House of Lords in the *Southern Railway* case referred to in the previous paragraph; although that case dealt with a provision made in an area other than doubtful debts. But if looked at in a wider context, one can argue very strongly that applying statistically and historically generated information to debts, groups of debts, or even whole portfolios, is a wholly valid approach to the making of 'sufficiently accurate' estimates of the level of provisions necessary for the doubtful element. The statute does not use the word 'specific', and nor does it say that an individual, debt by debt, examination is mandatory in the making of any estimate. In fact, the House of Lords in the leading case of *Absalom v Talbot*, HL, [1944] 1 All ER 642, recognised many of the difficulties and impracticalities that can arise in any attempt to put a 'sufficiently accurate' value on debts on an individual, case by case, basis. In such an instance any businessman or accountant would always try to see whether an overall approach appeared likely to give a better, or at least an acceptable, answer.

Group relief

7.29   We now need to turn to a rather different area of tax law. Everything we have so far referred to in this chapter, and most of previous chapters' discussions, has related to the tax position of the individual company. Group relief is the procedure under which a loss made by a company can be 'surrendered' to another group company, so that the recipient's profits are reduced by an equivalent amount, and its tax liabilities are reduced. (There is also a complete parallel system under which losses made by companies owned by a consortium of companies can be surrendered, proportionately, among the owners of that consortium company, or the owners' losses can be surrendered to it. Also to enable losses to be surrendered between companies one of which is in the consortium regime and the other in a group, provided a sufficient degree of 'relationship' exists. For reasons of space we will not deal with 'consortium relief' but readers need to remember its existence, and the circumstances in which it can be of value). The rules for determining whether companies have a 'group' relationship are to be found in s.413(3)-(5) ICTA 1988, as expanded in s.838 ICTA 1988. Two companies are in a group if one is a 75 percent subsidiary of the other, or if both are 75 percent subsidiaries of a third. One can trace shareholdings through any number of companies, and if any of them is less than wholly owned one takes proportions of proportions (an 80 percent subsidiary of a 90 percent subsidiary is 72 percent owned by the top company). Two particular dangers need to be watched, namely that no company which is not resident for tax purposes in the UK can be taken into account in any way, and nor can a company which is a simple investment, as opposed to a long term subsidiary, of a company whose business includes buying and selling shares. The significance of this last point is that many leasing companies are owned by banks, and banks also come to own on occasion the whole share capital of companies which need to be rescued in order to safeguard the loans the bank may have made to them. These last are unlikely to be 'group' companies with the leasing subsidiaries. There are complex anti-avoidance provisions in s.413(7) and (8) and in Sch.18 ICTA 1988 which supplements the main section – all designed to prevent companies creating artificial relationships designed to enable losses to be 'sold' between companies which are not in reality in a group relationship. We have noticed, for instance, the loans which are to treated as if they were equity, because they are not 'normal commercial loans' (paragraphs 4.08 and 7.25). That is one of the provisions contained in Sch.18; anti-avoidance legislation must always be scrutinised in the light of the facts of any case to which it could have any possible relevance, but space forbids us attempting that scrutiny here. There are also provisions in s.409 dealing with the accounting periods of companies which, during the course of the period concerned, become or cease to be members of a group. The basic rule is that the profits or losses must be apportioned before and after the relevant date, and only the proportions during the 'group' period can be taken into account. But this is subject to a requirement which must never be lost sight of in s.410(1), that if in an accounting period of any company

"arrangements are in existence by virtue of which at some time during or after the expiry of that accounting period"

the company could cease to be a member of the group, then its profits or losses cannot be taken into account for that part of the accounting period in which those arrangements are in existence.

7.30 Assuming that two companies are in a group, as defined in the last paragraph, and that one of them has trading profits as calculated for tax purposes, and the other a loss again calculated under tax rules, then 'group relief' enables:

- the two companies to agree between themselves that the 'surrendering company's' loss be surrendered to the 'claimant company';

- the claimant company to submit a claim to the Inland Revenue that its assessable profits be reduced by the amount of the surrendered losses;

- the claimant company, if desired but this is entirely at the option of the companies concerned, to make a 'payment for group relief'.

There are a number of mechanical requirements on which we do not need to spend much time, such as the rules concerning the types of losses that can be surrendered, (which go wider than the simple trading losses and capital allowances of the leasing companies with which we are concerned). But it is worth pointing out:

- That group relief operates within the same period. It is not possible for the claimant company to use the loss it receives by carrying it forwards or backwards against profits of a different period, nor for the surrendering company to surrender in a period a loss which it has brought forward from an earlier period, or carried back from a later period.

- Group relief therefore operates only up to the level of the 'lower' of the profits or losses; a surrendering company with a loss of £1,000 could only surrender £800 of it if the claimant had profits of only £800. The balance of £200 loss in the surrendering company would remain in that company, where it could be carried back or forwards, depending on the availability of profits against which it could be set, (but could not be surrendered in a future or past year, as explained above).

- However it is possible for more than one claimant company to receive different parts of the loss of a single surrendering company; and for more than one surrendering company to surrender losses to the same claimant — again with the proviso that if the claimant's profits cannot absorb all the losses of all the surrenderers, some losses will remain frozen in one or more of those latter.

7.31 To understand the implications of group relief, we need to look at some illustrative figures. Let us assume that the surrendering company is the lessor whose tax computations we worked out in paragraph 2.23, (the basis now being taken to be that the single lease we had illustrated was the entire operation of that company), and that the claimant company has profits in each and every year of £10,000. What we did not say above, but is obvious from these figures (Table 66), is that group relief only operates

	Surrendering company results	Claimant company results	Tax saving for claimant
Year 0	(2,500)	10,000	875
Year 1	(232)	10,000	81
Year 2	492	10,000	–
Year 3	1,059	10,000	–
Year 4	1,559	10,000	–
Year 5	293	10,000	–

Table 66

Tax losses and taxable profits of two companies, and the value of the losses surrendered in terms of tax savings for the profitable company.

for years 0 and 1. Secondly, if our lessor simply surrenders losses for those years without being compensated for doing so, then:

- What we had earlier characterised as the Inland Revenue's interest free loan to the lessor, comprising the tax relief the lessor was then assumed to be able to obtain from these losses, would simply not be there. To that extent the lessor's cash flow and profitability would be damaged.

- The claimant company, to the extent that it was able to retain in its own business, and not to pay away to the Inland Revenue authorities, £956 of what would otherwise have been its tax liabilities, is better off to that extent – permanently.

- The damage to the lessor's cashflow and profitability does not, however, end with its failure to benefit from an interest free loan from the Revenue; the principal so borrowed was in our earlier illustrations effectively 'repaid' to the Revenue in the form of the (larger part of) the later years' tax liabilities. The above figures show that, for years 2-5 inclusive, the lessor will need to pay tax on profits totalling £3,403, that is to say tax bills of £1,192. We know that the lessor's aggregate profits, even if he had the benefit of the freedom from interest on the Revenue's loan, were only projected at £671 pre-tax, so payment of tax liabilities of the level indicated will push him into a massive loss.

All of those reasons suggest that where a leasing company has a loss available to surrender elsewhere into its group, it is essential that it receive payment from the claimant company. It seems obvious that the appropriate level of such payment should be the value, at 35 percent, of the losses surrendered, and that the time of the payment should be the 'tax payment date', that is to say the date nine months after the lessor's and the claimant's year end dates on which the latter would otherwise have paid the sums concerned to the Revenue authorities (or the lessor would have 'recovered' the tax had he had other profits to enable him to do so). This restores the lessor's cashflow and profitability to the position illustrated earlier. Since it would treat its 'group relief receipt' in its profit and loss account in exactly the same way as we illustrated it treating its tax recovery in paragraph 2.35, that is to say as a credit on the 'current tax' line, it would also ensure that the lessor's profit and loss account remained in the logical, as well as 'true and fair' form in which it was illustrated in that paragraph. And so what benefit does the claimant company obtain out of paying £875 and £81 to the lessor, instead of paying them on that same day to the Inland Revenue? Simply that those sums remain in the group, as part of its working capital earning its profits, until the later dates at which the lessor needs to 'repay the Revenue's loan'. Group relief, where as in a leasing context the surrendering company's losses stem only from the timing differences arising from capital allowances, really cannot be treated by the claimant company as if it were an outright, and permanent, reduction of its liabilities.

Is the rate of corporation tax 35 percent ?

7.32   We promised as long ago as paragraph 2.18 to come back to this question, deceptively easy as it seems at first, and ever more problematical as one thinks a bit deeper. Throughout all our examples we have illustrated the 'cost' of tax liabilities, and the 'benefit' of tax repayments – and in the last paragraph the benefit of group relief receipts – at 35 percent. The simple proof that that is right appears to be contained in that last paragraph. Not only within a single lessor company can 35 percent be seen to produce correct answers in relation to the profitability of a lease transaction, or of a portfolio of lease transactions; when one follows through the dealings between, say, a parent and its lessor subsidiary in relation to the temporary benefits available between the two companies from the acceleration of capital allowances, (and thus the delaying of tax

	Surrendering company results for tax	Claimant company results for accounts and tax	Consolidated profits in accounts (post-tax)	Dividends (net)
Year 0	(2,500)	10,000	6,500	6,480
Year 1	(232)	10,000	6,704	6,675
Year 2	492	10,000	6,628	6.600
Year 3	1,059	10,000	6,571	6,540
Year 4	1,559	10,000	6,528	6,510
Year 5	293	10,000	6,504	6,495
	671	60,000	39,435	39,300

Table 67
Tax losses and taxable profits of a parent and subsidiary company, with profits shown in the consolidated accounts, and dividends paid by the parent.

liabilities), one can only make sense of the accounting by using 35 percent both as the measure of the benefit, and as the compensation to be paid for that benefit by the 'claimant' of group relief. But let us look at the figures once again, and this time, in Table 67, make some further assumptions about the parent and its subsidiary.

The surrendering lessor has pre-tax profits through the six years totalling £671, whether one looks at his tax computation figures shown above, or the figures in his profit and loss account, paragraph 2.35. After corporation tax at 35 percent, that leaves £435; and it is that amount, together with the claimant's post-tax profits of £39,000 which are shown in the third column, this time put into the accounting years in which they are credited in the profit and loss account. We have also assumed that sufficient profits are paid up by the lessor subsidiary to its parent to enable the latter to pay the dividends shown in the final column. If we then analyse which parties are regarded as having borne the tax that the Inland Revenue has received, (and it helps our understanding to remember the order in which the tax payments have been made), the position looks like that in Table 68.

		Retained	Distributed
Pre-tax profits	£60,671		
Comprising retained portion		208	
distributed portion			60,463
Advance corporation tax at 33.3% on net distributions of 39,300 (or 25% on grossed up equivalent, 52,400) regarded as 'franking' the shareholder's basic rate tax liability on that gross			13,100
		208	47,363
Corporation tax at 35% on retentions		73	
at 13.3% on pre-tax profits distributed			8,063
Retention		135	
Distribution			39,300

Table 68

The application of advance corporation tax to the distributions, and corporation tax to the whole profits, of the two companies in Table 67, the figures shown on an aggregate basis (all years, and both companies, taken together).

That unexpected rate of 13.3 percent for the 'mainstream' tax on the distributed profits is correct − if it strikes the reader as odd, there is no alternative but that he work out the arithmetic; what rate applied to pre-tax profit, when added to 33.3 percent applied to the net distributions comes to a total tax burden on those pre-tax profits of 35 percent, and means that the net distributions can be 65 percent of those pre-tax profits ? But looking at these figures in terms of the six years' totals has another advantage; one has effectively eliminated the timing differences. The taxable profits and the accounting profits (pre-tax) are the same. And because of this, we can very easily see what the true benefit would be of reducing those pre-tax profits — by picturing such a reduction as being of a permanent nature, that is to say reducing taxable profits while leaving unchanged the accounting profits and the distributions. If we reduce taxable profits by £208, the tax saving from doing so is £73, which is 35 percent. If we reduce taxable profits by a further £200, the tax saving is £27, which is 13.3 percent. So, in that case, could it really be argued that a leasing deal which deferred the payment of tax on £408 of profits was deferring actual tax of £143? Or only of £100 ? What we said in paragraph 2.18 was that our examination of this question would justify the stance we have taken throughout this book of putting a 35 percent value on tax reliefs. Why the author still believes that this is justified is as follows:

- the leasing company's commercial decisions whether or not to undertake a leasing deal can sensibly be made, and its cashflow and profitability worked out, on the basis of 35 percent tax 'values' for the reasons given in the previous paragraph;

- but the parent company's decision how large a dividend it can pay, and what that may cost the group in terms of 'unrelieved advance corporation tax', is a quite different matter;

- the £43 of tax that the leasing company's group failed to recover a few lines back, can be seen as the penalty flowing from the group having paid more dividends than it had the 'capacity' to pay, rather than the leasing company having written too much business.

But of course the ideal situation is the one in which the leasing subsidiary knows, in sufficient time, whether the volume of leasing it proposes could possibly bring the group as a whole into a position where unrelieved ACT could be a problem.

What is the solution to 'unrelieved advance corporation tax' ?

7.33   The group of companies we were picturing in the last paragraph only managed to recover £27 of tax on the last £200 of tax reliefs available, the reason being that although those reliefs reduced taxable profits and therefore reduced 'mainstream' corporation tax, they produced no reduction in the advance corporation tax paid on the dividends. Perhaps a purist would say that advance corporation tax cannot be 'reduced' as such, what either is or is not possible depending on the level of the taxable profits, is that all of that ACT can be set against the company's corporation tax liability, thus reducing the mainstream tax; or that some of the ACT cannot be so set off. If we assumed that the group concerned obtained, from some source or other, an extra £200 of taxable income, the tax bill that would re-emerge on that income would be £27 only. But one might realistically assume that most groups of companies would not be in such a position. £200 of taxable income in their hands would be worth £130 post-tax, not £173. So a lessor company whose group was in the 'normal' position might appear able to identify a lease on which £200 of rentals were shortly to be received, and assign it to the lessor company in the 'unrelieved ACT group' we have pictured ? If it would have been worth only £130 to the assignor, and will be worth £173 to the assignee, there is room for a deal to be done. The Chancellor and the Treasury have, up to the date of writing, appeared impervious to the pleas of companies whose tax bills are unreasonably inflated by unrelieved ACT; but there are possibilities of at least some mitigation of the position through the back door – through assignments of taxable income such as rental streams.

Deferred tax provisions – the need to cover 100 percent of the timing differences

7.34 The conclusion we have reached in the last three paragraphs is that a lessor company should not only account for its tax liabilities and savings at 35 percent, but also needs to be compensated with a payment at 35 percent if it surrenders to another its potential tax savings. That all relates to the lessor's real tax position – what accountants would normally refer to (in the jargon we introduced in paragraph 2.30) as the company's 'current tax'; what it can obtain (in the form of reductions in liability) from, or must pay to, the Inland Revenue authorities. But paragraph 2.30 and 2.31 also explained the concepts of 'deferred tax'; further tax which would be payable or which could become repayable were the timing differences between the lessor's accounts and his tax computations to be eliminated. In the early years, the tax allowances for an individual lease will usually give rise to a 'repayable' on the lessor's current tax line in his profit and loss account and balance sheet. But because the levels of those allowances later in the lease term will be less, (and because over the lease term his aggregate tax liabilities will be based on the aggregate profits that the lease produces), there will be disproportionately higher current tax liabilities in those later years. The simplest way of explaining deferred tax is to say that it is designed to smooth out those differences – and thus to ensure that the profit and loss account charge (current tax and deferred tax taken together) is lined up with the pre-tax profits in that account. The figures we calculated in paragraphs 2.23 and 2.32 were as in Table 68. (It is easier here to work with the gross equivalent figures, that is to say the amounts on which tax is payable or repayable, rather than the liabilities or repayments themselves).

	1 Capital all'ces in comp'n	2 Principal repayment in accounts	3 Excess (shortfall) of 1 over 2	4 Taxable profits (losses)	5 Excess of 3 over 4 para 2.23	6 Pre-tax profits para 2.35
Yr 0+1	4,375	1,329	3,046	(2,732)	314	314
Yr 2	1,406	1,701	(295)	492	197	197
Yr 3	1,055	2,004	(949)	1,059	110	110
Yr 4	791	2,306	(1,515)	1,559	44	44
Yr 5	2,373	2,660	(287)	293	6	6
	10,000	10,000	Nil	671	671	671

Table 68
The acceleration of capital allowances in front of (the analogue to) depreciation, column 3, is the sole explanation of the difference between taxable results in column 4 and accounting results in column 5. (In practice there could have been other timing differences such as unspecific provisions against bad debts, and/or permanent differences such as non-allowable entertaining expenditure).

Column 3 shows very clearly that the timing difference fully reverses by the end of year 5. If we were, however, to assume that the company, once it had started with the lease incepted at the end of year 0, had continued

						Revised col 3
3,046						3,046
(295)	3,046					2,751
(949)	(295)	3,046				1,802
(1,515)	(949)	(295)	3,046			287
(287)	(1,515)	(949)	(295)	3,046		Nil
	(287)	(1,515)	(949)	(295)	etc	Nil
		(287)	(1,515)	(949)	etc	Nil
			(287)	(1,515)	etc	Nil
				(287)	etc	Nil
						7,886

Table 69
The timing differences for five leases, one written in each of five successive years, summarised and totalled. It can be seen that once the fifth year is reached, the aggregate timing difference for that (and for every subsequent year in which the same volume of business is written) will be zero. Therefore it can be argued that the timing differences accumulated in the first four years are unlikely ever to reverse.

to write one lease in every year thereafter, we would see that the figures in column 3 would be as in table 69.

A reversal of that £7,886 of timing differences would only occur if the company stopped writing business, and therefore the figures in the bottom triangle became 'reversing differences', not sheltered by the 'originating differences' flowing from the new business written. The first of the four fundamental accounting concepts which accountants use as the framework upon which they normally build any company's accounts is the going concern concept, SSAP 2:

> "the enterprise will continue in operational existence for the foreseeable future. This means in particular that the profit and loss account and balance sheet assume no intention or necessity to liquidate or curtail significantly the scale of the operation".

If for a lease-per-year company, £7,886 of timing differences will never reverse under these accounting principles, (or to put it another way, a reversal could only be foreseen on a particular assumption which contradicts those underlying every other figure in the accounts), then there is a persuasive argument that the company's accounts can only be prepared on the basis that level of timing differences will continue indefinitely; and therefore that it is reasonable to allow the deduction of equal amounts (equal simply because no other spread seems more logical or fairer) in each of the first five years from what would otherwise have been the figures on which deferred tax would have needed to be provided (Table 70).

	3	3a	3b	4		
					Figure on which	
	Timing		New	Profit in	tax charge	Pre-tax
	Difference	Deduct	Difference	comp'n	now based	profits
Yr 0+1	3,046	(1,577)	1,469	(2,732)	(1,263)	314
Yr 2	2,751	(1,577)	1,174	(2,240)	(1,066)	511
Yr 3	1,802	(1,577)	225	(1,181)	(956)	621
Yr 4	287	(1,577)	(1,290)	378	(912)	665
Yr 5	Nil	(1,578)	(1,578)	671	(907)	671
	7,886	(7,886)	Nil	(5,104)	(5,104)	2,782

Table 70
One possible basis for providing the level of deferred tax that is necessary, ie on the quantum of timing differences which will reverse, by treating the non-reversing amount as building up evenly through years 1 to 5.

The net tax charges which one would have assumed should have been on profits aggregating £2,782 are in fact on a 'loss' of £5,104 (which is a figure £7,886 less than the £2,782).

Group relief revisited – non co-terminous periods of claimant and surrendering companies

7.35 If we were to assume that the lease we have been looking at throughout had been incepted not on 31 December of year 0 but on 31 March of year 1, then the whole capital allowance schedule would have been shifted forward twelve months. It is easy to think that the pattern of allowances themselves might change, because the asset's disposal would fall into year 6, and therefore it is in that year rather than in year 5 that the balancing charge is made; so does that not mean that a writing down allowance then becomes available for year 5 ? The answer is yes, of course. But the writing down allowance which is in fact given in year 5 is the figure which was, on our previous assumptions, given for year 4. The pattern changes not at all on the one year forward shift. One method of reducing the disadvantage flowing from this three month delay in incepting the lease would be to have written it in a company whose accounting year end is 31 March, and whose tax payment date is 1 January. That delays the 'benefit of the allowances' only from 1 October, (relevant for a 31 December year end company), to 1 January – that is to say a three month delay corresponding to the delay in the lease inception. But that seems at first to imply that the lessor company we are now envisaging, one with a 31 March year end, must itself have other profits against which it can obtain the relief available on 1 January of years 2 and 3, (because the parent's 31 December year end and 1 October tax payment date remain fixed). There is however a provision in the group relief legislation for the grouping of the results of companies whose year ends differ. We have noted above that it is very much better for a 31 March inception to be made in a 31 March year end company than in one with a 31 December year end. We will see below that, somewhat surprisingly, it appears better still for the benefit of the allowances then to be surrendered out of that 31 March company

Subsidiary lessor – year to 31 March year 1 *loss (being writing down allowance on asset* *purchased on last day of that year)*	£2,500
Period of overlap with parent's 31 December *year 0 accounts – 9 months – (1 Apr yr 0 to* *31 Dec yr 0) proportion*	1,875
Period of overlap with parent's 31 December *year 1 accounts – 3 months – (1 Jan yr 1 to* *31 Mar yr 1) proportion*	625

Table 71
Time apportionment of the surrendering company's loss into those parts which 'fit into' separate accounting periods of the claimant company.

to its 31 December parent. The scheme of s.408 ICTA 1988 is quite straightforward. The surrendering company's loss is divided, proportionately to the parts of its own accounting period which overlap the accounting periods of the claimant company (Table 71).

Had the lessor company been in a position to óbtain a repayment of tax on £2,500 of allowances, 35 percent of that would have been £875, and it would have been receivable on 1 January of year 2. If one discounts its value back to the date of inception of the lease on 31 March of year 1, using a discount rate of 3.5 percent per quarter, its value is £789.20. The lessor's parent obtains a repayment of £656.25, that is to say 35 percent of £1,875 on 1 October of year 1; and a repayment of £218.75, 35 percent of £625, on 1 October of year 2. If one discounts each of these back to 31 March of year 1, the first comes to £612.62 and the second to £177.95, or a total of £790.57. Readers who are mathematically disposed will see that the apparent marginal benefit flowing from the use of s.408 does in fact arise from the discounting procedure; if one discounts using quarterly rests, the figures will always favour the split recovery. If one uses simple interest rather than compound, the figures are exactly equal. But the message of these figures is as follows. 31 December is clearly the optimum date for a 31 December year end lessor to incur its capital expenditure and incept its leases. That company would not be able to offer such fine rates to its customers if they asked for expenditure to be incurred and leases incepted on 31 March. But if there is in the group a 31 March year end company, then the terms it can offer for a 31 March incepted lease will be the finest possible – and that is true whether that company itself obtains its tax repayments, or whether it surrenders losses to a 31 December year end member of the group under s.408.

CHAPTER 8

Value added tax

Supplies of goods and services, including their timing and value

8.01 The following paragraphs will make it clear that there are significant differences in the ways in which value added tax applies to goods and to services. A hire vendor is treated as making a sale of goods (Sch 2(1) VATA 1983):

- The tax point, (that is to say the date of the transaction which determines the date of payment of VAT), can be 'physical' in the case of sales of goods – the time the customer takes delivery of them. But if there is an invoice issued within fourteen days of the 'physical' date, the tax point is the earlier of that invoice date and payment date: if the fourteen day limit is exceeded, it is the earliest of the physical date, invoice date, and payment. Hire vendors will seldom let their purchasers take the goods without signing the contract, (invoice production being normally an integral part of the process of contracting), and paying the first instalment; thus, all of these dates normally coincide.

- The value of the supply is the cash price of the asset – which therefore means that the excess of the contract price over cash price may be characterised as interest.

- The place of supply is the place at which delivery is taken of the asset by the hire purchaser. This is significant in determining whether an 'export' has taken place, to be entitled to zero rating in place of a standard rate charge. But since the rules are no different for goods subject to hire purchase contracts, compared to any other goods, the only aspect which merits further mention is that if the 'interest' part of the supply can also be characterised as an 'export', it can also be entitled to zero rating in place of exemption. This does not alter the hire vendor's liability, but it does change the ratio of his taxable and exempt supplies – and possibly affects the quantum of the input tax he can recover, as referred to in the next paragraph.

The main implication to be drawn out of the foregoing from the hire purchaser's point of view is that VAT becomes payable, at the time he enters into a hire purchase contract, on the full cash cost of the asset. From the hire vendor's point of view, because he may have significant levels of exempt 'interest' receipts, as well as the amounts treated as being for outright (taxable) sales for cash of the goods themselves (and as well, possibly, as 'exports of interest' taxable at the zero rate), this may put the hire vendor into a 'part exempt' position, with the consequence noted in the next paragraph that not all of the input tax he incurs on costs and expenses he incurs will be deductible from the output tax he must account for to Customs and Excise. Leasing on the other hand is treated as a series of supplies of services by the lessor to his lessee:

- Each periodic rental as it becomes due has its own tax point. The rules for services supplied 'continuously' have the effect of regarding the invoice date as generally relevant; and lessors are normally permitted to send a single 'invoice' to their lessees covering a number of future rentals, and specifying the future tax points of each.

- The value of the supply is the full amount of each rental payment; there is no splitting between a cash price element and an interest element.

- The place of supply for most services is the place the supplier 'belongs' – a far from simple concept. However, for the purpose of imports and exports of leasing, special rules apply, to which we will come in paragraphs 8.06 and 8.07 below.

The implications of leasing are therefore essentially the reverse of those for hire purchase. The lessee pays VAT on his rentals only as and when he pays those rentals. The lessor, if leasing is his only activity, will be fully taxable, able to deduct the whole of his input tax instead of only some part of it.

Fully taxable and part exempt lessors and hire vendors

8.02 The previous paragraph will have made it clear that the VAT differences between the positions of hire vendor and lessor are even greater than is their disparity under corporation tax. But it might nevertheless be helpful to set out some of the implications of this:

- The lessor is engaged in an activity which is treated as fully taxable, that is to say chargeable to VAT at either the standard or zero rates of tax. All the input tax borne on his purchases and expenses is fully and immediately deductible against the output tax which he would otherwise have to pay over to Customs and Excise.

- But this would cease to be true if that lessor were, alongside his leasing business, to be engaged in some other activity giving rise to exempt outputs, or to be a member of a group in which some other company was so engaged. Potentially, the disadvantages could be so great as to suggest that any such other activities would be better segregated. But this is an area in which generalisation is dangerous as well as difficult, and in which facts are all important; it is an outside possibility that an advantage could be obtained from some mixing of taxable and exempt activities.

The VAT status of the 'supplies' made by a hire vendor, and his own 'part exempt' status were outlined in principle in paragraph 8.01; but it is all very much more complicated than that paragraph might suggest, and some expansion of these principles is therefore unavoidable:

* First, the phrase 'part exempt' is widely misunderstood. A business is part exempt in Customs and Excise's interpretation of those words if it incurs 'exempt input tax'; and exempt input tax is "input tax which relates to an exempt supply". Starting from the end of that two stage definition, it is clear that it may be necessary to identify specific outputs with 'related' inputs, and with the input tax (if any) on such inputs. One simple example of such an identification, (although we will see below that it may not actually result in any higher VAT burden arising), is that the grant or assignment of a short lease of land or buildings is an exempt supply and the input tax on the lawyer's feenote for arranging that transaction is accordingly exempt input tax.

* However despite having incurred exempt input tax, (and accordingly being technically part exempt), a business may still be able to deduct all of that input tax (i.e. be treated in Customs and Excise phraseology as if it were fully taxable) in one of two ways; either if the only exempt input tax it incurs is related to certain defined exempt supplies it may be making. Apart from the granting etc of the short lease already referred to and the depositing of money, these are specialised services of arranging certain insurance and credit facilities. Exempt input tax will be fully deductible if the only amounts incurred are in these categories. Alternatively, exempt input tax will be fully deductible if it falls below certain *de minimis* limits; here, the exempt input tax related to the grant etc of the short lease must be counted into the limits, but the other categories of ignored exempt input tax need not.

* Assuming that the business has exempt input tax which the foregoing rules fail to make fully deductible, it becomes necessary to determine how much of it (if any) can be deducted; and that calculation is made under either 'the standard method' or some 'special method' agreed by the taxpayer with Customs and Excise.

* The basic aproach used in 'the standard method' is attribution. Input tax can be deducted where it can be related to outputs which are taxable;

it cannot be deducted if related to outputs which are exempt; and if there is a residue of input tax which cannot be related to either class, it is probable that it may need to be rateably apportioned (− but any such proposals to do this need to be discussed with Customs and Excise in advance).

- It is this context that we need to look again at the status of the supplies that a hire vendor makes. In paragraph 8.01 we said that he made a supply of goods at a value which was the total contract price (i.e. the aggregate of the cash price of the asset and the interest element built into the hire purchase contract). It is quite clear from Customs and Excise guidance on this that they identify three separate classes of transaction, each to be dealt with differently. It is where a single hire vendor becomes involved in more than one of these classes that the complications arise, and it becomes essential to agree a workable method for calculating non deductible exempt input tax.

- The first class of transaction is where the hire vendor owns the asset concerned, and disposes of it under a contract in which he discloses to the hire purchaser both the cash price of the goods, and the charge being made for credit, assumed for illustration to be £1,000 and £300 respectively. In this case, £1,000 is the value of the supply of goods, on which VAT of £150 is chargeable. The separately disclosed £300 charge for credit is exempt. The customer will therefore have to put his hand in his pocket for £1,450. Because the supply of credit is separately disclosed, the charges for it become a supply of a series of services, (not goods) each treated as occurring when paid for − but for administrative reasons it is normal for the hire vendor to request (and Customs to agree) that the timing of all these supplies be taken to be the same as that of the goods themselves.

- The second class of transaction is where the hire vendor owns the asset but does not separately disclose the credit charge. In this case the supply is treated as one of goods only. If one could assume that the hire vendor made only supplies of this type, then he would be fully taxable, not part exempt; we could therefore reasonably assume that what was non-deductible exempt input tax in the previous example, (which that hire vendor built into the price charged on to his customer) will now be deductible and therefore not passed on in the price. We therefore assume the taxable supply is £1,295 (i.e. £5 less than the aggregate of goods and credit previously). VAT on this is £194, and the hire purchaser needs to put his hand into his pocket for £1,489.

- But a fully taxable hire purchaser would rather pay £1,489 knowing that £194 of it was recoverable from Customs and Excise, than he would pay £1,450 of which only £150 was recoverable. A hire purchaser who was not registered for VAT would be in the opposite position. And one who was himself part exempt, (a bank for instance) might fall into either category.

- The third class of transaction is one which Customs and Excise describe as being one 'involving a finance company which does not become the owner of the goods'. This phrase implies that the substantive transactions are (1) a 'credit sale' by the supplier of goods; (2) a loan by the finance company to that supplier of the cash price of the goods; and (3) the diversion from the supplier to the finance company of the amounts receivable from the purchaser of the goods, in repayment of the loan at (2) above. In this case, the finance company's only supplies are the wholly exempt supplies of credit; he is not involved in any way in a supply of goods.

Fully taxable and part exempt lessees and hire purchasers

8.03 There are also significant differences in these parties' positions:

- The lessee pays input tax, rental by rental, through the lease term. And assuming he is himself a fully taxable person, he deducts it in full from his output tax quarter by quarter. Because lessors are not in the habit of allowing a period of credit for payment of rentals, the lessee will inevitably find himself having to 'finance' the VAT on the rentals for some weeks or months before he gets the benefit of the deduction.

- The fully taxable hire purchaser pays, and has to finance, the entire VAT on the cash price at the front end of his deal, as well as needing to find the cash for any initial deposit under the contract.

- If either of these parties is part exempt, then the way in which his irrecoverable VAT is calculated may or may not result in some part of this VAT (on rentals or on cash price of hire purchase goods) being in the irrecoverable category. If it is, the normal basis would involve some provisional disallowance in the VAT quarter in which the input tax had been incurred, with an adjustment made after the end of the VAT year, (on a cumulative basis for the four quarters).

- Customs and Excise introduced in April 1990 a 'capital goods scheme' under which the input tax non-deductibility for computers costing over £50,000 (and buildings over £250,000) would be recalculated not just once for the year in which purchase took place, but annually (cumulatively for all years to date) for a period of years from purchase date. This is obviously going to be an extremely complex arrangement for Customs to administer (not to mention the labour involved for taxpayers); and it must also be borne in mind that each recalculation of non-deductible input tax will also reflect through into a necessary adjustment to the future corporation tax capital allowances on the asset.

Leasing transactions which are outside the scope of VAT

8.04 Although leasing is in principle an activity which is fully within the scope of VAT, generally at the standard rate of tax, there is one particular transaction which is treated as outside VAT's scope, that is to say as not constituting a supply of either goods or services by one person to another, and as not giving rise to any charge to tax:

- When the leased asset is sold off the lease, this should normally be dealt with as a sale by the lessor to the person purchasing the asset concerned. Clearly the lessor should issue an invoice to the purchaser and collect VAT as well as the price of the goods from him; and equally clearly that VAT should be accounted for in the normal way to Customs and Excise by the lessor.

- In practice, it is often the lessor who permits, or even instructs, the lessee to find a purchaser, and to deal with the entire sale. Where that lessee is both registered for VAT and fully taxable, it is not unknown for the lessee himself to invoice the asset's purchaser. So long as the VAT on that invoice is accounted for in the normal way to Customs and Excise, they will have received the correct amount of tax, and the purchaser will have paid the correct VAT-inclusive price.

- It is obvious that the invoicing is incomplete. What should then happen is that the lessor should invoice the lessee for a supply of goods, namely the leased asset at a price of £2,500 plus VAT; and the lessee should invoice the lessor for a supply of services, namely the rebate of rentals of £2,450 plus VAT. It seems, however, that Customs and Excise took the view that there was some doubt whether the rebating of rentals by the lessor to the lessee could be treated as a service supplied by the latter to the former: or as a reduction in the value of the service earlier supplied by the lessor to the lessee.

- The result was a letter written by Customs and Excise in January 1984 to the Equipment Leasing Association, stating that the rebating of rentals by lessors to their lessees should be treated as outside the scope of VAT.

- It appears to be that instruction, (which incidentally has never been publicised so that lessees could discover its existence, despite its being

Residual values
    insurance 4.09-4.10, 7.26-7.27
Reverse charge
    for VAT 8.06
Reversing differences
    deferred tax 7.34
Risk (pure)
    introduced 4.09-4.10
    further considered 7.26-7.27
Role-playing
    introduced 4.12
Rule of 70
    introduced 3.04
Rule of 78
    introduced 2.13
    for lessor's accounting 2.45
    hire purchaser's deduction of interest element 6.09
    hire vendor's profit recognition and tax calculations 6.09
Sale and leaseback
    introduced 1.08
Sargaison v Roberts [1965] 3 All E R 1072 7.19
Security
    introduced 1.06
    deposits in escrow accounts 4.32
    in hire purchase 6.06
    lessee's covenants 2.59, 4.05, 5.24
    realisable value of asset 2.61
Ship's cat
    method of weighing 6.20
Short life assets
    capital allowances 7.06
Sole or main benefit
    capital allowances 7.14
SSAP 2 (accounting principles)
    accruals basis 2.17
    going concern 7.34
    matching 2.17, 2.30
SSAP 15 (deferred tax)
    introduced 2.30
SSAP 20 (currencies)
    introduced 2.68
SSAP 21 (leasing)
    constant rate of return 2.26, 2.43, 4.30
    definitions of finance and operating leases 3.02-3.06
    full pay-out lease described as purest form of finance lease 1.19
    lessors and lessees apply separately the finance/operating definitions 3.12
    (see also finance lessee)
    (see also finance lessor)
    (see also hire purchase)
    (see also operating lessee)